The Series on Social Emotional Learning

Teachers College Press
in partnership with the Center for Social and Emotional Education and the
Collaborative to Advance Social and Emotional Learning (CASEL)

Jonathan Cohen, *Series Editor*

CONSULTING EDITORS:
Maurice Elias, Norris M. Haynes, Roger Weissberg, and Joseph Zins

EDITORIAL ADVISORY BOARD:
J. Lawrence Aber, Diana Allensworth, Michael Ben-Avie, Robert Coles,
James P. Comer, Ann Lieberman, Pearl R. Kane, Catherine Lewis,
Karen Marschke-Tobier, John O'Neil, Nel Noddings,
Seymour B. Sarason, Thomas Sobol

Educating Minds and Hearts:
Social Emotional Learning and the Passage into Adolescence
JONATHAN COHEN, EDITOR

Caring Classrooms/Intelligent Schools:
The Social Emotional Education of Young Children
JONATHAN COHEN, EDITOR

Social emotional learning is now recognized as an essential aspect of children's
education and a necessary feature of all successful school reform efforts. The
books in this series will present perspectives and exemplary programs that foster social and emotional learning for children and adolescents in our schools,
including interdisciplinary, developmental, curricular, and instructional contributions. The three levels of service that constitute social emotional learning
programs will be critically presented: (1) curriculum-based programs directed
to all children to enhance social and emotional competencies, (2) programs and
perspectives intended for special needs children, and (3) programs and perspectives that seek to promote the social and emotional awareness and skills of educators and other school personnel.

CARING CLASSROOMS/ INTELLIGENT SCHOOLS

The Social Emotional Education of Young Children

Jonathan Cohen

EDITOR

FOREWORD BY JAMES P. COMER

Teachers College, Columbia University
New York and London

Published by Teachers College Press, 1234 Amsterdam Avenue, New York, NY 10027

Library of Congress Cataloging-in-Publication Data

Caring classrooms/intelligent schools : the social emotional education of young children
  / Jonathan Cohen, editor ; foreword by James P. Comer.
      p. cm. — (Series on social emotional learning)
    Includes bibliographical references and index.
    ISBN 0-8077-4057-8 (pbk.) — ISBN 0-8077-4058-6 (cloth)
      1. Affective education.   2. Social learning.   I. Cohen, Jonathan, 1952–   II. Series.
    LB1072 .C35 2001
    372.01′9—dc21   00-066989

ISBN 0-8077-4057-8 (paper)
ISBN 0-8077-4058-6 (cloth)

Printed on acid-free paper
Manufactured in the United States of America

08   07   06   05   04   03   02   01   8   7   6   5   4   3   2   1

To Gabriel and Zoe—my greatest teachers.
With love and appreciation.

CONTENTS

Part III Programmatic Efforts

Part IV Current Issues and Future Directions

FOREWORD

In a time when success in school has become an absolute necessity for life success, this book reassures us that adults can make a difference in the lives of our children. Specifically, it brings attention to a key fact about human learning: The fact that cognitive growth is dependent on the development of social and emotional understanding.

Left on their own, children are unable to prepare themselves for academic learning. They are born with both aggressive energy and the capacity to develop relationships. Yet they are dependent on adults for socialization. It is during the socialization process that children learn to form positive, productive relationships.

Unfortunately, many adults in our society are guided by an inaccurate notion of human learning—one that attributes academic achievement to the intelligence and will of the child. Misled by this myth, we have constructed and maintained a mechanistic model of education. This model concentrates only on students' cognitive learning through transfer of facts and figures. At the same time, it disregards children's level of readiness for such learning. As a result, we are faced with an educational predicament. Our schools prepare only a select few to be life-long learners. Those few are the students fortunate enough to have adult support in their home and community. With that support, they managed to form the building blocks for academic learning—including a strong social and emotional education—before entering school.

Children's minds are not like computers. They cannot simply take academic knowledge as input. Instead, humans grow along a number of developmental pathways—the cognitive, the physical, the language, the psychological, the social, and the ethical. Because these areas of learning are so closely connected, underdevelopment in any one area inhibits growth in others. We have continued to find that the opposite is also true. When children grow along one pathway, their potential for expanding along others is furthered.

When I entered two low-performing schools in New Haven in 1968, along with a team from the Yale Child Study Center, we witnessed a severe lack of developmental support for children. In response, we set out to help parents, teachers, and administrators change their approach. All changes were to be guided by an understanding of the importance of whole-child development. The aim of these changes was to create an environment designed to nurture such development.

Through the years, our program saw dramatic positive changes in the social climate of these schools. As the adults in the students' lives learned to work collaboratively, they themselves experienced social and emotional growth. In time, these adults changed an overwhelmingly chaotic environment into a calm, supportive learning environment. The strong, positive relationships that children formed with adults encouraged them to imitate, identify with, and internalize the adults' values. Significant gains in academic performance soon followed the improved social climate. Since then, our School Development Program has intervened in hundreds of other schools. We have continued to measure similar patterns of progress in student achievement. These positive outcomes demonstrated how attention to development of the whole child fosters cognitive development.

It is a national imperative that schools partner with families and communities to take responsibility for the development of the whole child. As they strive to achieve this goal, school communities will benefit from drawing on the social and emotional strategies discussed in this book.

—James P. Comer
Yale University Medical School

ACKNOWLEDGMENTS

This volume—like most important ventures in life—has been a collaborative endeavor. The authors in this volume have been active, ongoing learners and teachers with one another as well as the growing groups of children, educators, and parents that we work with. This work is the heart of the volume.

I am grateful to core staff, board of trustees, and professional advisory board at the Center for Social and Emotional Education (CSEE) in New York City (http://www.csee.net). Growing out of our work at the Project for Social and Emotional Learning at Teachers College, Columbia University, CSEE has become the professional home that supported this and a related series of social emotional educational and research projects with educators, parents, and children. I am grateful to our core staff members (Margaret Jo Shepherd, Jacqueline Norris, Robin Stern, Linda Bruene, and Ellie Lazarin), our board of trustees (George Igel, Richard Aslanian, Richard Bergman, Barbara Eisold, Carl Fisher, Robert Fribourg, Trev Huxley, Bruce LaMont, Lawrence Madison, Yvonne Marsh, Nancy Neff, George Papagopitos, Kenneth Schulman, Jamie Stecher, and Gerald Rothstein) and the members of our professional advisory board (Mark Alter, James Comer, Maurice Elias, Peter Fonagy, Howard Gardner, Catherine Lewis, Steven Marans, Ramon Murphy, Nel Noddings, Donald L. Rosenblitt, Peter Salovey, Stuart Twemlow, and Roger Weissberg). Their support has created the platform for this volume and a growing number of collaborative projects to promote social and emotional literacy for our children.

I am also grateful to the members of the Collaborative to Advance Social and Emotional Learning (CASEL) who cosponsored a series of conferences and Summer Institutes as well as this book series with CSEE. CASEL's support and partnership in this series has been invaluable. The National Association of Elementary School Principles cosponsored a conference that helped bring together some of the authors in this book. I am grateful for their support.

Carol Collins of Teachers College Press and Natalie H. Gilman have continued to provide invaluable editorial assistance and support. Their wise counsel has enhanced the clarity and organization of this book.

On a daily basis, George Igel and Ellie Lazarin have helped provide the platform that allows me to work. I depend on their support and wise counsel in so many ways. I am extremely grateful to them both. Margaret Jo Shepherd has been a colleague, friend, and fellow teacher-learner for over 20 years. In the last few years—at Teachers College and at CSEE—I have been honored and privileged to work with Jo in a growing number of ways. Our ongoing dialogue has enriched my work here and all that we are doing at CSEE.

As always, I am deeply grateful to my Mother—Alden Cohen—who has always nurtured my love of learning and continues to provide invaluable editorial assistance to me. Finally, Stacey, Gabriel, and Zoe provide the foundation for all that I do. There are no words to communicate my gratitude, love, and good fortune.

All of the royalties from this volume will be donated to the Social Emotional Learning Foundation.

Jonathan Cohen
Center for Social and Emotional Education
and
Teachers College, Columbia University
April 30, 2000

INTRODUCTION

Jonathan Cohen, Ph.D.

Teachers College, Columbia University and
The Center for Social and Emotional Education

When your child grows up what kind of person do you want her or him to be? As parent or teacher, virtually all of us want our children to be healthy, responsible, active, growing, caring individuals who are passionately involved with their work and relationships. We hope—in our heart of hearts—that our children will be able to learn and solve problems in ways that allow them to be all that they can and all that they want to be. Effective social and emotional education provides the foundation for these achievements. Social and emotional education refers to learning skills, understandings, and values that enhance our ability to "read" ourselves and others and then, to use this information to become flexible problem solvers and creative learners.

In our homes and schools there is a tremendous amount that we can do to promote social and emotional learning and literacy. In fact, parents and educators *always* color and shape children's developing social and emotional capacities: but our influence is not always mindful, helpful, consistent, or empathic. In recent years, we have learned a great deal about how we can most effectively promote social and emotional competencies that provide the foundation for healthy character development and academic achievement.

In this volume, we focus on the many ways that teachers of young children can promote these skills, understandings, and values. Just as there is no "one way" or "best way" to teach reading, there is no one way or best way to promote social and emotional literacy. But, just as educators and school specialists have learned about the centrality of phonemic awareness in language learning, we have learned a great deal about which social and emotional skills and understandings reduce physical and verbal violence, enhance students' cooperative and healthy problem-solving abilities, and foster academic achievement.

Historically, pre-K and elementary school teachers have been attuned to the value and importance of social and emotional development as well as linguistic, mathematical, aesthetic, motoric, and musical capacities. This volume builds on this integrative tradition. In reading the chapters that follow, I trust you will recognize the many ways that you are already involved with social and emotional education. I also trust you will discover ways to build on what you, your colleagues, and parents are already doing to foster more effective social and emotional learning.

This volume is the second in the Teachers College Press *Social Emotional Learning* Series. Books in the series present information for teachers, school specialists, and administrators about the two major, overlapping perspectives that seek to further social and emotional learning (SEL): efforts that promote social and emotional learning for all children; and mental health–school partnerships that seek to understand when and why children become developmentally "derailed" or "stuck," as well as what interventions and treatments support their learning and healthy development. This book series—and this volume—also present the range of ways that we can infuse effective social emotional learning into school life: from formal curricular-based programs that can be taught as "stand alone" courses (Kusché & Greenberg, Chapter 9) to programs that can be integrated into morning meetings or language arts or physical education (Shure & Glaser, Chapter 8). The first volume in this series focused on middle school children; this volume focuses on younger children (pre-K through elementary school). There are literally hundreds of SEL curricular-based programs available to educators today. The programs and perspectives in this volume are representative examples of the best SEL work being done today.

The foundation for any mode of literacy—be it linguistic, mathematical, musical, or social and emotional—is *decoding*: being able to recognize and understand the data that defines a given domain. Just as decoding phonemes is the foundation for language learning, being able to decode ourselves and others is the foundation for social and emotional literacy. To be able to understand or decode children we must think in a developmentally informed manner. This is the foundation for all effective social and emotional education: recognizing and understanding children's relative strengths and weaknesses as well as their progressions and regressions within a developmental context. What is normal for a 5-year-old may be seriously problematic for a 9-year-old. Initially as a teacher and then as a child analyst–teacher-learner, Anna Freud was the first to detail the complex and changing developmental experiences of children's lives over time. In more recent decades there has been a growing chorus of voices underscoring the fundamental importance of thinking in a developmentally informed manner. Development is uneven. Children are not consistently "good" or "not so able" across the board. As all teachers and parents know, children present an array of particular strengths and weaknesses, which can change—sometimes dramatically—over time.

Eisold's (Chapter 2) description of two children's lives over a short period of time—Steven and Malika—is an organizing chapter for the volume. I have asked the authors to describe how they understand these children and/or how their particular programmatic efforts might understand and seek to work with their particular sets of strengths, weaknesses, vulnerabilities, and promise. We often talk about development. It is harder to make the developmental process "come alive." Understanding and commenting on Steven and Malika's developmental experience is one of the ways that the contributors have sought to make this fundamental process a vital one here.

In this book series we also seek to maintain a balance between empirically validated instructional programs or "best practices," and points of view that may not be amenable to empirical study. Educators, parents, and policy makers all want to know more about what kinds of educational or instructional programs are most effective and reliable for children of particular ages, strengths, and weaknesses. What works? There has been a shift over the last 2 decades that has emphasized the importance of empirically valid instructional programming. Empirical study forces us to specify what we think we are doing and to assess to what extent we are reaching defined goals.

The SEL programmatic efforts presented in Part III of this volume include detailed curricular-based materials that have been studied empirically and shown to be effective. Some of these multiyear programmatic efforts emphasize one or more organizing ideas. For example, the Child Development Project's work (Chapter 6) focuses on cooperative learning, the use of literature to foster SEL, and building caring communities. The Peaceful School Program (Chapter 10) emphasizes the bully-victim-bystander cycle as a core, underlying force in the culture of a school. The I Can Problem Solve Program (Chapter 8) underscores the fundamental importance of creative and adaptive problem-solving capacities. Other programs explicitly focus on an array of social and emotional skills and related sets of understandings, like the Reach Out to Schools Program (Chapter 7) and the PATHS Program (Chapter 9). However, as I describe in Chapter 1, all of these programmatic efforts seek to enhance some overlapping core processes that provide the foundation for effective SEL efforts: creating a safe, caring and responsive school; creating long-term school-home partnerships; enhancing awareness of self and others; and using that awareness to support children's ability to solve real problems and learn creatively in a wide range of ways (e.g., to form relationships, to say "no," to regulate impulses, to become more self-motivating, and much more). Empirical study has shown that the programmatic efforts mentioned above are effective. These programs affect behavior and, often, academic functioning. We are in great debt to the educational and social science researchers who have worked with practitioners for years to study these educational efforts.

However, empirical study alone can never capture the complexity of teaching and learning. Just think about a moment between a student and a teacher: There is so much happening internally—cognitively, emotionally, and socially—and interpersonally on verbal and nonverbal levels. We will never be able to empirically study, let alone describe, the process of learning and "teachable moments" in behavioral terms alone. Fopiano and Haynes (Chapter 3) as well as Charney and Kriete (Chapter 5) focus on recognizing and using "teachable moments" and on creating the optimal platform for learning: safe, caring, and responsive classrooms and schools. Similarly, teachers often struggle to understand when a child's difficulties are a normal part of the "ups and downs" of growing up or when they signal more serious problems. Although we are developing better and better screening instruments to aid the identification of problems, these questions will never be answered by questionnaires. Mugno and Rosenblitt (Chapter 4) detail a way of thinking of development and social emotional behavior and problems that represents a profoundly helpful point of view.

Systematic study and the craft of teaching need to go hand-in-hand and inform each other. Empirical study that is not grounded in thoughtful practice becomes empty and devoid of meaning; but practice also needs to be monitored and analyzed. We are all vulnerable to becoming absorbed and too comfortable in our familiar and customary practices. Systematic study forces us to be discoverers! What is really helping? What are the key ingredients?

Effective social and emotional education programs necessarily involve more than classroom practice alone. As educators and parents, we must create a long-term partnership. Like language learning, effective social and emotional education needs to be an integral part of school. In the final two chapters, Aregaldo (Chapter 11) discusses effective long-term implementation efforts, and I (Chapter 12) describe steps that we can take to come together locally and nationally to further social and emotional literacy.

Part I

Social Emotional Education
and the Young Child

Part I of this volume provides an overview of the core principles and practices that characterize effective social and emotional educational practices (Chapter 1) as well as the developmental experience of the young child (Chapter 2). These chapters are organizing "anchors" for the volume.

Social emotional education refers to teaching and learning about skills, knowledge, and values that promote social-emotional competencies. There are hundreds of social-emotional learning (SEL) programs available to educators today. Chapter 1 presents a framework to consider the core organizing ideas or principles that characterize effective SEL programmatic efforts as well as detailing the range of ways that can translate these principles into practice.

Chapter 2 focuses on the developmental experience of the young child. Understanding child development provides the foundation for SEL and essential help that we all need to empathically tune into the child. Children are always changing; both progressing and regressing. Barbara Eisold's portraits of two children—Malika and Steven—provide a thread that runs through almost all of the chapters in this book. We will see how the various programs and perspectives that educators can use to further SEL in their schools might relate to and effect these two young children.

Chapter 1

SOCIAL AND EMOTIONAL EDUCATION: CORE CONCEPTS AND PRACTICES

Jonathan Cohen, Ph.D.

Teachers College, Columbia University and
The Center for Social and Emotional Education

There is a growing body of research and practice that underscores what parents and teachers have long known: that learning how to "read" ourselves—and the reactions of others—is as important as learning how to read words and numbers. The chapters in this volume and other recent reports (Cohen, 1999b; Elias et al., 1997) establish that social emotional literacy reduces violence, enhances adaptive capacities, and provides the foundation for learning and healthy development.

To achieve our educational goals, we need to promote social emotional literacy as well as the three Rs. The purpose of education is to enable children to be lifelong learners and effective citizens. Historically, elementary school educators have been particularly attuned to the fact that social emotional learning provides the platform for learning to learn and for the development of self-reflection, responsibility, caring, cooperation, and effective problem solving. And over the past 2 decades we have deepened our understanding of how essential these capacities are and how we can more effectively integrate them into the academic setting.

Social and emotional education refers to the process and methods we use to promote social emotional competencies. Although I suggest that the capacity to "read" ourselves and others is the foundation for social emotional learning (just as the capacity to decode phonemes is the foundation for language learning), competence and learning in this area refers to a broader set of knowledge and skills. *Social and emotional competence* measures the ability to understand, process, manage, and express the social and emotional aspects of our lives. The degree to which we are able to do so is predictive of life satisfaction and productivity, whereas grades and SAT scores by themselves are not (Goleman, 1995; Heath, 1991; Vaillant, 1977). We have also learned that schools can and should be a forum in which social emotional understanding and related skills are taught. There is a growing consensus, then, that effective social emotional education needs to become an integrated part of the curriculum, pre-K through 12th grade (O'Neil, 1997; Elias et al., 1997; Gardner, Feldman, & Krechevsky, 1998; Goleman, 1995; Lieberman, 1995; Noddings, 1992).

It is abundantly clear to those who work with young children that how children feel about themselves and others colors and shapes their ability to learn. Their social emotional capacities powerfully affect, and even determine, their ability to listen and communicate; to concentrate; to recognize, understand, and solve problems; to cooperate; to modulate their emotional states; to become self-motivating; and to resolve conflicts adaptively—in short, the ability to become a member of the group.

Social emotional learning (SEL) is a relatively new label for a process that is as old as humankind. It has been a part of schooling since the beginning of formal education 3,000 years ago in Egypt, India, and Greece in one form or another (Cohen, 1999b; Gardner, 1999b). For many centuries, only upper-class men were educated and the pedagogic content typically reflected the dominant religious teachings of the time as well as the wish to instruct students about social norms. Some ancient education (e.g., that of ancient Greece) explicitly focused on enhancing awareness of self and others as a valuable educational endeavor in and of itself. However, it is only in the last century that there has been a more explicit and ongoing appreciation that we can and should teach all schoolchildren about the social and emotional dimensions of life. We must provide them with a basic understanding of the concept of social emotional competencies, as well as with the specific skills needed to attain them.

The range of SEL practices presented in this volume have been nurtured by many overlapping traditions: the progressive education movement, in general, and elementary school education, in particular; affective education and the reflective educator movement; special education; the Civil Rights movement; the woman's movement; psychoanalytic and other school-based mental health work; and research in primary prevention and the development of social emotional competencies.

In recent years, there has been growing concern that more and more children are distressed and disturbed and are not motivated to learn. We all know that psychological and, too often, physical violence complicate and often derail educators' capacity to teach and children's capacity to learn. In

America, a child is abused or neglected every 11 seconds; a child is arrested for a violent crime every 4 minutes; a child is shot dead every 98 minutes. On a typical school day, over 135,000 students bring weapons to school (Hamburg, 1992; Mott Foundation, 1994). Twenty-five percent of 10- to 17-year-old American children suffer from school adjustment problems, problems that are predictive of later, more serious problems (Dryfoos, 1990). Recent studies show that as students move into adolescence (14- to 17-year-olds), 35% of them engage in high-risk behavior. Between 15 and 22% of our nation's youth experience social, emotional, and other problems that necessitate mental health treatment, but approximately 80% of them are not receiving needed services (Dryfoos, 1997). These and related findings about the distressed state of children both nationally and internationally have intensified our search for more effective ways by which we can help them develop into responsible, caring, and healthy individuals.

Social emotional education is a fundamental part of the solution to these problems. Over the course of the last 2 decades, educators and researchers have discovered that high-quality SEL programs improve students' academic performance, their adaptive social emotional behavior, and peer relations; they put a brake on drug problems, high-risk sexual behavior, aggression, and other forms of antisocial and maladaptive behavior (Consortium on the School-Based Promotion of Social Competence, 1994; Institute of Medicine, 1994; Weissberg & Greenberg, 1998). To the extent that we integrate social emotional learning into the life of our schools and homes, we are increasing our chances of having healthy, responsible, and caring learners. The specific social emotional skills, understanding, and values that these programs promote are a vital model for life.

There are literally hundreds of SEL programs and perspectives available to educators and school specialists today. In addition, there are scores of programs that focus on a particular facet of social or emotional functioning, such as conflict resolution, cooperative learning, and sex education programs. In this chapter, I suggest a way of conceptualizing the core concepts and related practices that characterize effective SEL programs. Before doing so, however, it will be useful to consider what is meant by social emotional competencies as well as how SEL programs vary with regard to three basic dimensions: focus and scope, audience, and modes of infusion. This will, I hope, further our ability to compare and contrast the programs and perspectives that comprise this essential domain of education.

SOCIAL EMOTIONAL COMPETENCIES OR MODES OF INTELLIGENCE

Social and emotional competence refers to the capacity to understand, process, and express the social and emotional aspects of our lives. These competencies represent modes of intelligence (Gardner, 1983; Sternberg, 1997). What does it mean to be intelligent? Gardner defines *intelligence* as "a set of skills of problem solving—enabling the individual to resolve genuine problems or difficulties that he or she encounters, and, when appropriate, to create an effective product—and must also entail the potential for finding or creating problems—thereby laying the groundwork for the acquisition of new knowledge" (p. 60).

Building on Gardner's formulation, I would add that intelligence refers to three core processes or abilities: (1) "reading," "decoding," or understanding information (in a given domain), and then (2) using this information to solve real problems, and finally (3) being a creative learner. For example, gifted linguists or poets need to be able to decode written and spoken language and then to use language to solve problems (e.g., how to make the next line rhyme in a manner that captures or extends the image of the developing poem) and finally to learn (e.g., to discover or create the next set of images in the poem). People who are musically gifted have abilities that allow them to read musical information. But more than this, gifted musicians must build on their ability to hear or read musical information in order to play or to create a continuing score.

Social emotional intelligence involves the decoding of others and ourselves. That ability provides the foundation for problem solving, as well as the means by which we are enabled to grapple with a wide variety of learning challenges: how to modulate our emotional experiences; how to communicate; how to generate creative solutions; how to form friendships and working relationships; how to cooperate and, at the same time, become self-motivating.

Whether we label these fundamental capacities competencies or modes of intelligence, it is clear that children evince normal variation as well as deviations. Just as there is a normative range of linguistic or mathematical abilities, infants and children evidence a normative range in their capacity to be self-reflective and to recognize thoughts and emotions in others (Baron-Cohen, 1995a; Brother, 1990; Izard & Harris, 1995). There are very rare instances where children present with major problems—that is, deviations—in their underlying capacity to read others (Baron-Cohen, 1995b) or their own emotional states (Sifneos, 1996). Nonetheless, except in those extreme instances, it is important to recognize the ways in which we, as parents or educators, intentionally or not, act to promote the development of these fundamental capacities: how we model, praise, and punish promotes or retards these capacities. Do we in our understanding of others stand as role models? Do the ways in which we praise or punish enhance or undermine self-understanding? Do we articulate the value we place on social emotional literacy?

By the same token, social and emotional intelligence is one of the most important strengths an educator, school specialist, or parent can have. This capacity underlies our ability to read the classroom (or the dinner table), to pay attention to but not be overwhelmed by our emotional experiences, to know when to push and when to wait—in short, to discover how we use so many moments to teach and to learn.

FOCUS AND SCOPE, MODES OF INFUSION, AND AUDIENCE

Social emotional education varies in regard to which concepts and skills the program focuses on, what audience it is intended to address, and how it seeks to infuse the particular skills and related sets of understandings. Figure 1.1 lists these three dimensions of SEL in a way that allows one to locate a given programmatic effort or point of view.

Focus and Scope

Most available SEL programs and perspectives seek to promote a wide range of social and emotional competencies. In varying degrees, they focus on skills, understanding, and values. Implicitly or explicitly, all effective

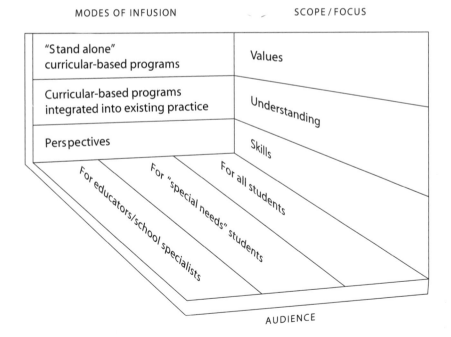

FIGURE 1.1. Social and Emotional Education: A Program Grid

SEL efforts work to enhance children's motivation to put social skills and understanding into practice.

Skills. My review of the programs now in place reveals that most seek to promote the development of the following overlapping sets of social emotional skills: awareness of self and others; emotional self-regulation; communication; self-motivation; problem solving and decision making; collaboration; and the formation of a more realistic, positive sense of self. As noted earlier, some programs focus on a specific social competence, like cooperative learning or violence prevention. In fact, cooperative learning and conflict resolution programs are the most widespread SEL programs in our nation's schools. As useful as these focused programs may be, recent educational research shows that it is more useful for schools to implement comprehensive child-school-home-community social emotional learning programs that address a wide range of social emotional competencies; they then become an integral facet of school life from kindergarten through the 12th grade (Elias et al., 1997; Weissberg, Gullotta, Hampton, Ryan, & Adams, 1997). Otherwise it is too easy for programmatic efforts to be the latest in a series of educational fads that come and go in schools. Just as I believe that all children need to become linguistically literate and foster linguistic learning throughout children's educational life, so too do I underscore the continuing importance of social and emotional literacy.

While hundreds of curriculum-based SEL efforts may seem to overlap or even duplicate each other in the skills they set out to teach, they are not equally helpful. First of all, only some of the programs actually teach socially and emotionally relevant skills in an empirically validated and effective manner. Although empirical research will never capture the full complexity of emotional and social life, it is essential that these programs (like any intervention designed to be useful) are studied: rigorous research can lead to discovery about which kinds of individual and group interventions help. There is another and very different reason why some SEL efforts are not helpful to a particular school or district: there is no one program that will meet the needs of every school. Just as different children need different sorts of help to learn to read, the same holds true for emotional and social literacy. The "Reflective Questions" sections in this chapter are meant to further educators' ability to assess the effectiveness of what they are doing now and what further social emotional learning work may be most useful to institute in their particular school districts.

Understanding. In addition to skill acquisition, SEL programs—to a greater or lesser extent—also seek to enhance understanding, socially and emotionally intelligent values, and an increased motivation to learn. As we learn more about ourselves, about others, and about the helpful (or unhelpful) ways that we solve problems, we are developing a greater understanding about what provides the foundation for the use of skills. For example, what does it mean to be "responsible," to "fail" or "make a mistake," to "not know"? Like all substantive learning, discussion and reflection are typically an integral part of successful SEL programs. There are other kinds of simple but profound understandings that these programs foster, for example, that emotional life influences and often determines behavior; that we do not always recognize what we feel; and that learning how to read emotions—our own and others'—is useful.

Values. Skills, understanding, and enhanced motivation all contribute to the development of what I call "socially and emotionally intelligent values": a way of thinking about others and ourselves that reflects particular concepts, standards, and qualities that we consider worthwhile. It colors and shapes what we perceive. While the development of such values has become an implicit part of most SEL programs, it is interesting to ask just what it means to adopt socially and emotionally intelligent values. There is no consensus here. I suggest that it means believing that it is valuable and worthwhile to be a social and emotional discoverer, to use what we learn about ourselves and others to be helpful, and to comprehend and appreciate that virtually all of the time people do their best. Other values that are explicit or implicit facets of many SEL programs include believing that we sometimes need to say "no" and that this is acceptable, and that we can and should be caring, cooperative, and helpful in respect to others.

Social emotional learning programs seek to enhance children's motivation to put social skills, understanding, and values detailed above into practice. One of the many reasons why educational researchers and practitioners are increasingly focusing on the school as a whole is that when students experience school as a community, they become more motivated to care about its values—to engage in effective problem-solving strategies, perspective taking, respectful conversation, and the use of other social and emotional skills they have acquired (Comer, Ben-Avie, Haynes, & Joyner, 1999). In fact, this is one of the core concepts of effective SEL programs that I will describe in more detail later in this chapter: school-home-community partnerships. The motivation to put social skills and understanding into practice is enhanced to the extent that schools underscore the intrinsic reasons why it is important to be responsible, collaborative, and caring—such as the good feeling these behaviors engender or the need to make the world a better place—rather than relying on adult praise or external rewards.

Formally or not, many educators and schools are involved with SEL today. When I confer with teachers, principals, and superintendents, I often ask a series of questions that I hope will lead to a collaborative process of discovery and, sometimes, program planning.

Reflective Questions to Assess Program Planning

- What do you think your school or district is focusing on in this area already? How broad or narrow is the scope of your schools' work here?
- What is the sequence and scope of specific skills—and linked sets of understandings—which are being taught?
- In what ways do you believe these efforts are helpful or not helpful?
- If you could, what one or two areas of social emotional functioning do you believe would be most useful for your school or district to focus on in the short and long term?

Modes of Infusion

Social emotional learning programs and perspectives vary with regard to how they are infused. At one end of the spectrum, some programs are quite directive and detailed, for example, a stand-alone academic course. Just as we teach language arts and social science as a standard part of the curriculum, we can teach SEL as a formal course of study. I believe that the oldest example of this is the Ethics classes that have existed within the Ethical Culture School, an independent school in New York City, since its founding by Felix Adler over a hundred years ago (Caroline, 1905; Radest, 1969). A more recent and empirically studied example can be found in New Haven, Connecticut: The Social Development Program is a K–12 curriculum-based sequence of courses, with detailed lesson plans for every class, mandated by every school in the city (Shriver, Schwab-Stone, & De-Falco, 1999). The PATHS program (see Chapter 9) is another example of a stand-alone curriculum. For some educators and schools this kind of program is what they want and need.

At another point along a spectrum of ways that we can infuse SEL into school life, there are programs that present a more or less detailed perspective about child development and SEL, with a variety of methods that can be integrated into whatever we are doing in schools. For example, the Social Problem-Solving/Decision-Making Program is a programmatic effort that can be used as a stand-alone course or as an approach integrated into whatever the teacher is doing in a morning meeting, in an academic class, or in a sports session (Elias & Bruene-Butler, 1999; Elias & Tobias, 1996). Although this program uses problem solving and decision making for organizing ideas, a range of skills and understandings are presented and taught.

The Responsive Classroom Approach (Charney, 1992) is another example of an effort to present a point of view about learning, development, and discipline that can be integrated into any and all facets of daily school life.

At the other end of the spectrum are perspectives that present a point of view about child development and social emotional competence; they provide ways of thinking about how we can promote social emotional capacities. Arts education, for example, represents a powerful point of view about how we can use analysis and imagination about musical sounds or a depicted scene as a way of learning about ourselves (e.g., Burton, Horowitz, & Ables, 1999). By the same token, a psychoanalytically informed perspective about child development and learning suggests that discovering more about our unrecognized as well as conscious thoughts and feelings profoundly furthers our ability to make sense of the world and become more effective problem solvers (Marans & Cohen, 1999).

Reflective Questions to Assess How Well SEL Is Working

- Different schools, like different people, have their own set of needs, wants and resources: What are your goals?
- In what ways are you and/or your colleagues infusing SEL into the classroom?
- What modes of infusion have the potential of building on what you are already doing in these areas?
- How do you know what is helping?
- What can you do to further clarify whether current as well as planned efforts are actually furthering your goals?

Audience

Social emotional learning can serve three overlapping audiences: (1) all children as part of the regular education process, (2) special needs students in special education programs, and (3) educators and school specialists, the adults working with our children.

Children in Regular Education Settings. Social emotional learning programs for "normal" children are designed to promote strengths. This effort represents an effective and extraordinarily important primary prevention and health enhancement effort (Weissberg & Greenberg, 1998). In recent years, we have learned that educators can teach children social emotional skills and values. Some children learn these skills and related sets of understandings without any formal instruction; they are simply an ongoing facet of home and/or school life. For many reasons, other children need and greatly benefit from more systematic instruction in schools. In any case, high-quality social emotional education is fundamentally beneficial to all children. For example, we want children to become lifelong learners; however we define that term, it is clear that social emotional competence provides the foundation for continued receptivity to learning. "What do I care about?" "What do I really want and need to learn more about now?" "What do I do when I am confused or stuck?" "What is the problem here and how can I begin to solve this problem?" "How do I motivate myself to take the next step?" Our ability—or inability—to be reflective and then to use the information to solve problems and learn from it provides the platform upon which we can and do address all kinds of questions.

Special Needs Students. SEL can also focus on special needs students. When we work with the learning disabled, for example, we recognize that there are substantive psychosocial as well as neurocognitively based vulnerabilities that need to be addressed academically, socially, and emotionally. The two major reasons why students are referred to special education in America today is for reading and behavioral problems. Social emotional educational efforts with special needs students includes not only understanding and dealing with the child's weaknesses or disabilities but also the drive to promote psychosocial strengths and build on "islands of competence" (Brooks, 1999). Historically, the training of special educators has not included substantive work in the theory and practice of social emotional development and SEL. This is curious—and unfortunate—given that virtually all special educators are acutely aware that social emotional experience so often derails instruction and learning. Training in this area will make special education more effective, in general, and will further the national trend toward increased inclusion (integrating special education students into mainstream classes).

Educators and School Specialists. Social emotional learning efforts can also serve educators and school specialists in two ways. On the one hand, educators can, and often do, informally and formally engage in SEL to further empathic and educative efforts. We must ask ourselves, for example, how can we "tune in" even more to where our students are developmentally? Or, what in the classroom makes us most angry and how does this affect our ability to learn and teach? Discovering more about "what gets to us" and the range of helpful (as well as unhelpful) ways in which we can manage these moments enhances our ability to teach. It can also be rejuvenating. Then too, SEL staff development efforts can be used to strengthen effective communication and team building between educator and educator, teacher and administrator, and educator and parent (see Cohen, Shelton, & Stern, 1999).

It is important that all members of school communities—regular and special education students, faculty, administration, staff, and parents—become involved with social emotional learning. When children learn about effective and flexible problem solving in the classroom but see their parents and administrators fighting in rigid, problematic ways, classroom-based instruction can go out the window. The fact is that the extent to which all of the adults in the child's life collaborate in SEL—from coaches to teacher aids, janitors, educators, and parents—will determine our chances of creating a community of learners and teachers who help one another, a community populated by a range of role models from whom students can learn.

Reflective Questions to Assess Audience for SEL

- Currently, who (if anyone) is the audience for SEL efforts in your school?
- Are there any plans afoot to create additional and complimentary efforts to include educators and/or parents in your work? Or, could such a plan be initiated?

CORE CONCEPTS

There are five core concepts that characterize effective social emotional learning efforts. My understanding of these intrapsychic, interpersonal, and systemically related concepts has grown out of three overlapping endeavors: the Education and Preparation Work Group of the Collaborative to Advance Social and Emotional Learning (CASEL); the Columbia University Social Emotional Learning Summer Institute faculty meetings; and my review of scores of SEL programmatic efforts. Although different programmatic efforts use somewhat different terms and focus on a range of specific skills and understandings, I believe that all effective endeavors in this realm are shaped by these same concepts. I hope and expect that others will critique this schema and that, over time, further research and practice will refine and redefine the central concepts that characterize effective efforts in this area:

1. The "first R"—reflective capacities or an enhanced awareness of ourselves and others—is the foundation for all learning and development.

2. A developing awareness of self and others needs to be used to enhance our ability to solve problems flexibly.
3. A developing awareness of self and others needs to be used to enhance our ability to learn and to be creative in a wide range of ways.
4. The creation of safe, caring, and responsive environments in which learning can take place is of essential importance.
5. Collaboration between school, home, and community needs to be a part of long-term implementation planning.

Here I have listed the concepts beginning with an internal-interpersonal focus (becoming more reflective) and ending with a much broader focus on systems (school-home-community) and long-term planning. However, I could just as easily have begun with the fundamental importance of creating a safe, caring, and responsive learning environment. Note that these concepts overlap in a variety of ways, for example, learning and creating inevitably overlap with solving problems: We hope that when we solve problems, we learn; and we often have to be creative to solve the problem! There is also a range of ways that educators translate each of these core concepts into pedagogic practice. Here I will briefly discuss some examples of the ways educators and school specialists have put these ideas into school-based practice.

The First Core Concept: Reflectiveness

Promoting reflective capacities, that is, an ability to read ourselves and others, is the first core concept of effective SEL programs. It is the foundation for all learning and, as such, the "first R" (Cohen, 1999a). Reflective capacities involve a personal and an interpersonal component that provide a person with the ability to understand and learn from social emotional experience. Just as children's capacity to decode phonemes is the foundation for language learning, so too does the ability to decode others and ourselves become the foundation for social and emotional competencies or modes of intelligence. These fundamental capacities are described in developmental research (Baron-Cohen, Tager-Flusberg, & Cohen, 1993), in cognitive psychological studies (Morton & Frith, 1995), and in clinical psychotherapeutic research (Fonagy & Target, 1996).

Reflective capacities are important for many reasons. When children's attributions of thoughts and feelings enables them to see actions as meaningful, their behavior becomes predictable. When parents have the ability to reflect on children's inner experience empathically, they foster secure attachment; core psychological structures; and, by extension, a coherent, stable sense of self (Fonagy & Target, 1997). Reflective capacities promote communication; acknowledging the point of view of others, after all, is the essential ingredient in meaningful communication, in general, and effective social problem solving and conflict resolution, in particular. It is this capacity that allows teachers to form meaningful and helpful relationships with students, so crucial to learning (O'Neil, 1997; Pianta, 1999). What's even more important to know, however, is that we, as educators and school specialists, are able to enhance these skills and related sets of understandings within our students. In fact, whether we mean to or not, we influence the ways in which reflective capacities develop.

The "first R" provides the foundation, in short, for all that is essential in schools, be it the three Rs or, as Gardner (1999a) suggests, the learning of "truth, beauty and goodness." Reflective capacities also allow educators and school specialists to take two critically helpful steps, detailed next: (1) the early detection of social emotional problems and (2) the promotion of social emotional literacy.

There is mounting evidence that suggests that reflective capacity—like children's phonetic decoding capacities—are biologically based (Baron-Cohen, 1995a, 1995b; Baron-Cohen et al., 1993). Like all neurocognitive basic building blocks of learning, children vary with regard to their reflective capacities: a normal variation. And, there are a very small percentage of children (e.g., those who suffer from an autistic disorder) who are significantly disabled in this regard: deviation. What is most important for parents, educators, and school specialists to know is that virtually all children can develop the ability to decode themselves and others, and that these adults have it within their power to help them do so.

Becoming more aware of others and ourselves involves content and knowledge, on the one hand, and a process of learning, on the other hand. These are examples of emotional knowledge: People feel. Important facets of our emotional-cognitive experience are unrecognized, but they color and shape behavior. Sometimes people project how they feel onto another. When we have powerful emotional experiences, this can complicate or interfere with our ability to think. Some of these ideas are simple and we tend to take them for granted: People feel. Yet, there are many instances when this basic truth is minimized or negated. However, being reflective is more than learning about emotional truths or knowledge. Being reflective is also a process of discovery, for example, when I seek to recognize what you are feeling and thinking now or what I am thinking and feeling now. At their best, effective SEL efforts help children to recognize that learning—be it about themselves or language or music—always involves a process of discovery.

Pedagogically, educators put this core concept into practice in a variety of ways, ranging from structured lesson plans and particular ways of organizing morning meetings to values that underscore the importance of self-discovery and learning about the experiences of others. Many social skills training programs focus on three overlapping behaviors: awareness of feelings, perspective taking, and active listening. Some programs teach children "steps" and skills to become more aware of experience. For example, some programmatic efforts teach children to "stop," "pay attention to their body and their feelings," and go through a series of cognitive-emotional steps to discover how their experience is "now." Other programs seek to integrate this concept into all that they do in an ongoing manner. In the Wisdom of the Heart Program in Tel Aviv, every kindergarten classroom has a dream corner where children can tell and enact their dreams. Educators in this innovative SEL effort recognize that dreams can signal unrecognized feelings and thoughts that color and shape behavior. Discovering unrecognized feelings and thoughts is a critical part of enhancing reflective capacities. All of the programs featured in this volume include efforts to further this fundamental concept in a wide variety of ways. Here I would like to describe briefly four examples of the importance of the "first R" as it relates to diversity, imagination, "not knowing," and joy.

Diversity. Recognizing real and imagined differences, how we feel about them, and how we manage these perceptions is profoundly important for us all to learn about. Race, religion, and gender—to name just a few categories of difference—commonly evoke reactions such as these: "You are like me . . . or different." "Because I label you in this way, I have a preconception (a prejudice) about who you are." All SEL efforts seek to enhance students' capacity to recognize who the other person is. Some efforts are particularly invested in helping us to learn about the problematic as well as extraordinarily wonderful facets of this basic dimension of life.

Imagination. Learning to listen to our imagination is another way that educators can promote the "first R." This can and does overlap with the best of arts education. Although there has been only a limited dialogue between SEL practitioners and arts educators, they share a common ground: being invested in creating opportunities for students to discover more about who they are. Promoting imagination and the process of experimenting with various artistic mediums can be a powerful way of becoming more aware of self and others.

"Not knowing." There are many factors that allow children to learn. For example, being present and paying attention as well as being open to new ideas are fundamental ingredients that allow us to learn. Being able to

tolerate "not knowing" is another profoundly important and often unrecognized element that allows people to be active learners. When we do not understand something, do we *really* let ourselves "not know" or do we, consciously or unconsciously, act as if we understand more than we do? So often, children and adults alike have such a need to know that they pretend that they understand something before they do. This can easily become a significant impediment to learning and discovery. A common linguistic example among young children are readers who too quickly "guess" how to pronounce a new word instead of letting themselves "not know": "I don't know this word; I've never seen it before; I have to struggle a bit to sound it out; I might need to ask for help here." This openness to "not knowing" the word and then struggling to sound it out for the first time allows new language learning to occur.

Learning to be more aware of ourselves—the "first R"—supports our becoming more mindful of when we are confused or unsure. Most social and emotional education teaches children to become more active listeners: to themselves and others. Sometimes when we actively pay attention to experience, we immediately know what we think and/or feel; but sometimes we are confused or initially blank or filled with a mix of seemingly confusing emotions and thoughts. Enhancing students' awareness of self and others necessarily involves giving students permission to "not know," and this is often a powerful gift that will hold them in good stead for a lifetime.

Joy. Becoming more aware of ourselves and others often leads to a precious educational experience: joy. Joy is an organizing experience for learners: it moves us and touches us deeply. Learning more about what we and others experience does not necessarily lead to joy, but it certainly enhances the likelihood that we will connect to what is most important to us, creating fertile ground for an almost ineffable but profound experience. Educators yearn to foster the joy of discovery and learning within their students, yet we rarely write or talk about this in educational circles. It is interesting to reflect upon what we do—or do not do—to foster greater awareness in our students and how this sometimes leads to a joy of learning.

Beyond pedagogic practice, how we act as educators is, as always, another powerful way to underscore the fundamental importance of being attuned to others and ourselves. Our own reflective capacities influence how we tell stories, which, in a sense, is what we do all day. Reflective capacities also shape how we interpret literary and historical texts and relate to the development of scientific reasoning and critical thinking (Astington, 1998). Educators thus set an example of appropriate behavior for students. Students learn about being related or not, being sensitive or not, being responsive or not, being open to discovery or not, being joyful in this process or not, from us. It is worth reflecting on our own reflectiveness.

Reflective Questions to Assess Reflectiveness:

- In what ways are you or are you not reflective in your own day-to-day work with students?
- How do you promote curiosity about others and yourself?
- To what extent do you encourage students to "not know," or appreciate confusion, which is so often the platform for new reflective learning?

The Second Core Concept: Problem Solving

The second core concept that characterizes effective social emotional learning programs is that they enhance our ability to become more flexible and able problem solvers. We all have problems. A *problem* is a question to be considered or solved, a person who presents difficulties, or a thorny situation. There are good problems and bad ones; some we solve automatically and some we struggle with; some make us happy and some make us very anxious or depressed. In fact, life can be seen as a series of problems. What varies is how we solve them: rigidly or flexibly, adaptively or unhelpfully, anxiously or calmly.

Much of what we do in school is to help students learn about various ways of solving problems—linguistically, artistically, kinesthetically, musically, historically, visually, mathematically, and also socially and emotionally. Although there are many definitions of intelligence, virtually all agree that the ability to solve real problems provides an essential facet of intelligence (Gardner, 1983).

Pedagogically, we can put this concept into practice in a variety of formal and informal ways. Some programs explicitly and centrally focus on problem solving and decision making (see Chapter 8); they delineate specific "readiness" skills as well as a sequence of skills needed for effective problem solving. The following capacities are often considered essential: being able to listen, to remember and follow directions, to keep calm, and to resist provocations. These skills are taught to students step-by-step so that they become automatic and available, even in stressful situations.

Although SEL programs define the route to problem solving in different ways, most include some version of the following eight steps: (1) Look for signs of different feelings that may signal a problem; (2) tell yourself what the problem is; (3) decide on a goal; (4) stop and think of as many solutions to the problem as you can; (5) for each solution, think of all the things that might happen; (6) choose what, in your opinion, is the best solution; (7) plan it out and make a final check; and (8) try it and consider its ramifications (Elias & Bruene-Butler, 1999, p. 82). Some programs advocate teaching these and other social emotional skills in isolation, before applying them. Some children clearly benefit from learning these steps, just as it is easier for them to learn the "silent *e* rule" in reading before opening a book. Other programs emphasize analysis of literature as one of many ways to enhance awareness of self and others and then to apply that knowledge to solving problems. Still other non–curriculum-based SEL perspectives implicitly and explicitly integrate an appreciation of problem solving into virtually all that we do.

Conflict resolutions programs, like the Resolving Conflicts Creatively Program (Lantieri & Patti, 1996), represent the largest and most common way that hundreds of schools have sought to teach students about one particular kind of problem. Learning to recognize when there is a conflict and how to manage it and learn from it is invaluable. These focused programs do make a difference (Aber, Jones, Brown, Chaudry, & Samples, 1998). Interestingly, more and more programs that focus on one topic, such as violence prevention, are expanding the scope of their work to include more of the concepts delineated here.

Many of the best studied SEL programs emerge from a cognitive-behavioral tradition and emphasize a social skills training perspective. Many of these programs focus on two fundamental skills: (1) being able to recognize and define our goals, and (2) decision making. The eight steps to solving problems are an example of this. Yet the best teacher and trainers who work with these explicitly cognitive models are wonderfully and importantly attuned to the subtle and necessarily complicated emotional and social processes that characterize human experience. Other SEL programs are less explicitly focused on the cognitive processes and steps involved but instead emphasize a point of view about learning and development and the fundamental importance of being able to create "teachable moments" from the ongoing "soup" of classroom life.

Reflective Questions to Assess Problem Solving Abilities

- How do you define a *problem*?
- When you have a problem, what range of responses do you have?
- What do you say to yourself?
- What do you think it means to be a flexible and able problem solver?
- To what extent do you think about the steps that are involved in effective problem solving?
- Is problem solving an explicit and/or implicit part of what you do with children?

The Third Core Concept: Creative Learning

The third core concept that characterizes effective social emotional learning programs is that they enhance our ability to learn and become more creative in a wide range of ways. Beyond problem solving, intelligence encompasses the ability to learn, to create, and to generate the kinds of questions that open the door to new learning (Gardner, 1983). Different kinds of learning that many SEL programs emphasize include collaborating with others, to managing one's own emotional life, becoming self-motivating, setting realistic goals, communicating clearly and directly, and using what we learn about ourselves and others to foster social relations and friendships.

Programs that seek to enhance students' ability to be cooperative learners are probably the longest standing and best studied formal interventions that fall under the rubric of social emotional learning. Virtually all SEL efforts include cooperative learning as an important facet of their efforts. Teaching children to cooperate is certainly something that teachers of young children have done for decades, even before the important studies of the 1970s and 1980s by the Johnsons and others (Johnson & Johnson, 1989). Teachers of young children have recognized that this and other social emotional capacities provide the foundation for traditional academic learning; historically, these teachers have been very attuned to the importance of teaching children to listen to others and to themselves, to form new relationships, to control themselves, to communicate clearly, to become more self-motivating, and to follow and to lead.

In the last 2 or 3 decades researchers have confirmed what teachers and parents of young children have known for a long time: social emotional learning is as important as linguistic and mathematical learning—if not more important; it provides the foundation for all learning. We have also learned more about which particular skills and related sets of understanding are relatively more important and more likely to reduce violence, enhance resiliency, and further healthy learning and development. To a greater or lesser extent, the focus and scope of SEL programs seek to use this research-based understanding. We have also learned more ways to teach these social emotional skills and understandings to children so that they become social emotional learners, creators, and problem solvers.

There is a wide range of ways in which this third concept is translated into pedagogic practice. Many programs teach a series of specific skills—initially in isolation—as a part of a curriculum-based program. For example, the following social skills are often explicitly taught in SEL efforts: management of feelings, social norm analysis, prosocial orientation, expressive communication, cooperation, negotiation, refusal, and help-seeking skills. Other programs, curriculum- and non–curriculum-based, may teach a single specific skill, sometimes alone and sometimes in the context of a subject-based course. And still others seek to influence the climate of the school system in such a way as to encourage caring, motivation, and responsible behavior.

Reflective Questions to Assess Creative Learning Abilities

- In addition to learning how to solve problems, what are the most important skills and linked sets of understanding that you would like your children and/or students to learn?
- What are you doing already? For example, many schools have been involved in teaching cooperative learning.
- To what extent are children learning this fundamental and profound capacity? What is contributing to this?
- What kinds of "learners" and "creators" do you most want your students to become? What are you doing now to promote these capacities?

The Fourth Core Concept: Safe, Responsive Environments

Promoting safe, caring, and responsive environments in which learning optimally takes place is the fourth core concept of effective SEL programs. How children and adults alike experience themselves and others inevitably colors and shapes their ability to learn. Thus social emotional experience is the foundation for learning, be it linguistic, mathematical, aesthetic, athletic, visual, or psychosocial. For example, how do you feel right now as you read these words? To the extent that you are feeling anxious, depressed, or distracted, you will have more trouble concentrating on the words and whatever associations they generate. On the other hand, the extent to which you are feeling safe, "present," focused, calm, and receptive to the idea of "not knowing," you will be more able to process, to reflect upon, to disagree or agree, to understand, and then to assess the value and meaning of the ideas you are reading about. This is even truer of children who are still in the midst of developing the capacity to modulate emotional life.

We all remember the best and the worst moments of our own elementary school experience. For virtually all of us, the best moments are the ones when we felt recognized, understood, cared for, and supported. Those moments were profound. Conversely, our worst memories of elementary school were when we felt misunderstood, shamed, anxious, or alone. These were the moments that cast complicating and undermining shadows over the learning process. In both cases, relationships provided the context for learning. Just as we know that relationships provide the foundation for security and the experience of attachment in infancy and childhood, so too are they the foundation for a sense of well-being and healthy relationships (Cassidy & Shaver, 1999; Silverstein & Auerbach, 1999). That feeling of well-being, instilled in students by caring educators, is what promotes learning and development (Noddings, 1992; Pianta, 1999).

There is a range of practices that can be integrated into classrooms and schools to promote safe, caring, and responsive centers of learning. Creating such places reflects the kind of relationships we engender in our classrooms, hallways, and playgrounds, as well as in our faculty rooms and parent-teacher encounters. The extent to which we create classrooms and learning communities in which children feel comfortable, safe, and protected determines how successful they will be in identifying with and forming secure relationships with adults. In fact, this is an explicit facet of the Comer School Development Program and the Responsive Classroom Approach (Charney, Crawford, & Wood, 1999). In some important respects, in fact, this is the heart of the Comer School Development Program, an SEL program that has had a transformative effect on hundreds of schools across America: creating an active collaboration between school and home in order to foster a climate where children feel safe and helpfully responded to. It is difficult to internalize a sense of well-being, positive self-regard, and a passion for achievement, not to mention simple concentration, when schools or households are chaotic, abusive, or characterized by low expectations for students (Comer et al., 1999; O'Neil, 1997).

Reflective Questions to Assess Safety, Caring, and Responsiveness

- What do you do to promote a sense of safety, caring, and responsiveness in your work with children?
- What things do you do or what kinds of moments interfere with your being able to foster such a climate?
- What are two or three actions you would like to set in motion to further promote a caring, responsive, and safe classroom and school?

The Fifth Core Concept: School-Home-Community Collaboration

The final core concept that characterizes effective SEL programs is that they include thoughtful and collaborative long-term planning between school, home, and community. This concept combines interpersonal with systemic processes: how we work together as individuals and also how the larger systems in the community operate together or inadvertently in opposition.

Children learn at home as well as at school. Educational practitioners and policy makers alike recognize that no single institution can create all of the conditions that students need in order to learn and develop in healthy, responsible, and caring ways (Dryfoos, 1998). Educators, parents, and members of the community need to be effective and collaborative partners. It is simply common sense that when both parents and teachers value literacy (be it learning to read a book or learning to read ourselves and others) children are more likely to appreciate this mode of learning as well. By the same token, SEL is undermined when parents and teachers cannot resolve conflicts creatively and peacefully among themselves, but at the same time conflict-resolution and related values and skills are taught in the classroom.

Active and involved parents, neighborhood leaders, religious leaders, community-based organizations, local government, and the media all have an important role to play in supporting the school's mission. By the same token, schools need to understand what parents value, want, and need. Creating a partnership between school and the community is an organizing facet of many, if not most, effective school reform efforts. As educators and policy makers have recognized this, there has been a dramatic increase in the number of school-community partnerships in the last decade (Melaville, 1999). Effective school-community partnerships do make a difference in improving educational quality, academic outcomes, and effective reform efforts. For example, most high-performing schools serving disadvantaged children include innovative ways to create educator–parent–private sector partnerships (National Association of State Coordinators of Compensatory Education, 1996). Creating a genuine, active partnership between the school and parents is the foundation of the Comer School Development Program (Comer et al., 1999). And, it is a guiding concept for effective social emotional learning programs (Elias et al., 1997).

There are many ways that reform efforts can further partnerships between the school and the community. Most often, educators initiate reform efforts and parents and members of the community are involved in genuine and vital ways. School-community partnerships contribute to school improvement by fostering positive, healthy relationships, focusing on and building upon strengths, and enhancing the adults' ability to identify issues, mobilize resources, and promote social emotional as well as economic well-being for families, neighborhoods, and the school itself (see Melaville, 1999, for a recent review of these issues).

School-community partnerships in general and social emotional learning in particular need to be an ongoing facet of children's lives to be most helpful and effective. A year is not enough for the acquisition of social emotional competence. Instead, SEL should be a long-term programmatic effort from preschool through grade 12. Parents, educators, and society value language abilities and do not expect that students will learn to read or write within a year or two or three; the same needs to be true for social emotional learning.

There are some SEL leaders and trainers who only agree to learn and teach in a given school or district that has made a 3-year commitment. They have found that it is unrealistic to expect that substantive change will occur when the educational system creates a shorter term plan. There are certainly many schools and districts that value short-term awareness presentations or minicourses about any number of new and potentially useful educational ideas. However, virtually all agree that substantive SEL is a long-term and ongoing process.

Reflective Questions to Assess Collaborative Plans

- In what ways do parents and educators in your school or district create partnerships to find solutions to problems and/or to define the values and goals for your class and school?
- What are the concerns (if any) that exist about creating a school-community partnership? How realistic are these concerns and what are realistic options that exist to address these concerns?
- How do people in your school or community manage a conflict between school and home?
- What kind of reflection, learning, and problem solving does your community most need to recognize the stumbling blocks that exist?
- To the extent that your school and community are considering the implementation of SEL programs, what kind of short- and long-term planning are you considering?

CONCLUSION

Social emotional education refers to the process of learning to read ourselves and others and then using this growing awareness to solve problems flexibly, to learn, and to be creative. To a greater or lesser extent, educators have sought to foster this kind of learning for decades, if not centuries. In recent years, researchers and practitioners have affirmed how fundamentally important these modes of learning are. We have also learned a great deal about how to effectively integrate SEL into school life, although there is no one best way to promote it. There are literally hundreds of educational efforts that fall under the rubric of social emotional learning.

This chapter presents a number of dimensions that we can use to understand, compare, and contrast these efforts. First, social emotional education varies with regard to which concepts and skills the program focuses on, what audience it is intended to address, and how it seeks to infuse particular skills and related sets of understandings. Focus, audience, and modes of infusion, then, are three dimensions that schools can consider when they are reviewing what has already been done in this field and which SEL program and/or perspectives may be most useful for the needs of their system. In addition, this chapter describes five core concepts that characterize effective SEL efforts as well as some examples of the many ways that we can translate these concepts into pedagogic practice.

The rest of this volume will present a range of ways that we can promote social and emotional learning with the young children we teach and learn with in schools today. To a greater or lesser extent, all of the chapters in this volume underscore the fundamental importance of recognizing what our children are feeling and thinking as well as where they are developmentally. Several focus on how we can create safe, caring, and responsive learning situations. Finally, most present a range of ways in which we can further development and learning in this fundamental and profound dimension of life: social and emotional.

Some Final Reflective Questions

- How would you describe what you are already doing to enhance social and emotional capacities in your school?
- What is clear and not so clear about additional goals (understandings and/or specific skills) that you believe you and your colleagues can and should focus on?
- What do you need to learn and/or to do that will further the creation of a realistic plan to accomplish these goals? Consider creating a small-group or schoolwide process of actually writing statements about your commitment to this work and specific actions plans that will be used to collaboratively further planning and implementation.
- How can we help each other to further learning about and implementing effective SEL programs and perspectives in our schools today?
- What can organizations like the Center for Social and Emotional Education (CSEE) and the Collaborative for the Advancement of Social Emotional Learning (CASEL) do to further support your efforts?

Acknowledgments. I am grateful to Tom Berner for reminding me of this core experience: joy. I am also grateful—and pleased—to thank the members of the CASEL Education and Preparation Working Groups Group and CSEE's Social Emotional Learning Summer Institute faculty who helped shape my understanding of the core concepts and related practice. I am also grateful to Roger Weissberg for his helpful suggestions and support.

REFERENCES

Aber, L. J., Jones, S. M., Brown, J. L., Chaudry, N., & Samples, F. (1998). Resolving conflict creatively: Evaluating the developmental effects of a school-based violence prevention program in neighborhood and classroom context. *Development and Psychopathology, 10,* 187–213.

Astington, J. W. (1998). Theory of mind goes to school. *Educational Leadership, 56*(3), 46–48.

Baron-Cohen, S. (1995a). *Mindblindness: An essay on autism and theory of mind.* Cambridge, MA: MIT Press.

Baron-Cohen, S. (1995b). Theory of mind and face processing: How do they interact development and psychopathology? In D. Cicchetti & D. J. Cohen (Eds.), *Developmental psychopathology: Vol. 1. Theory and methods* (pp. 343–356). New York: Wiley.

Baron-Cohen, S., Tager-Flusberg, H., & Cohen, D. J. (1993). *Understanding other minds: Perspectives from autism.* Oxford: Oxford University Press.

Brooks, R. (1999). Creating a positive school climate: Strategies for fostering self-esteem and motivation. In J. Cohen (Ed.), *Educating minds and hearts: Social emotional learning and the passage into adolescence* (pp. 61–73). New York: Teachers College Press.

Brother, L. (1990). The social brain: A project for integrating primate behavior and neurophysiology in a new domain. *Concepts in Neuroscience, 1,* 27–51.

Burton, J., Horowitz, R., & Ables, H. (1999, April). *Learning in and through the arts: The issue of transfer.* Paper presented at the AERA national conference, Montreal, Canada.

Caroline, T. H. (1905, December 12). *The ethical culture school—Its past.* Unpublished manuscript, Fieldston School, Riverdale, NY.

Cassidy, J., & Shaver, P. R. (1999). *Handbook of attachment: Theory, research, and clinical applications.* New York: Guilford Press.

Charney, R. S. (1992). *Teaching children to care: Management in the responsive classroom.* Greenfield, MA: Northeast Foundation for Children.

Charney, R. S., Crawford, L., & Wood, C. (1999). The development of responsibility in early adolescence: Approaches to social and emotional learning in the middle school. In J. Cohen (Ed.), *Educating minds and hearts: Social emotional learning and the passage into adolescence* (pp. 95–111). New York: Teachers College Press.

Cohen, J. (1999a). The first "R": Reflective capacities. *Educational Leadership, 57*(1), 70–75.

Cohen, J. (1999b). Social emotional learning past and present: A psychoeducational dialogue. In J. Cohen (Ed.), *Educating minds and hearts: Social emotional learning and the passage into adolescence* (pp. 3–23). New York: Teachers College Press.

Cohen, J., Shelton, C., & Stern, F. (1999). Why social and emotional learning for educators? *Journal of the New York State Association for Supervision and Curriculum Development, 14*(1), 23–27.

Comer, J. P., Ben-Avie, M., Haynes, N., & Joyner, E. T. (1999). *Child by child: The Comer process for change in education.* New York: Teachers College Press.

Consortium on the School-Based Promotion of Social Competence. (1994). The school-based promotion of social competence: Theory, practice, and policy. In R. J. Haggerty, L. R. Sherrod, N. Garnezy, & M. Rutter (Eds.), *Stress, risk, and resilience in children and adolescents: Processes, mechanisms, and interventions* (pp. 268–316). New York: Cambridge University Press.

Dryfoos, J. G. (1990). *Adolescents at risk: Prevalence and prevention.* New York: Oxford University Press.

Dryfoos, J. G. (1997). The prevalence of problem behaviors: Implications for programs. In R. P. Weissberg, T. P. Gullotta, R. L. Hampton, B. A. Ryan, & G. R. Adams (Eds.), *Healthy children 2010: Enhancing children's wellness* (pp. 17–46). Thousand Oaks, CA: Sage.

Dryfoos, J. G. (1998). *Safe passage: Making it through adolescence in a risky society.* New York: Oxford University Press.

Elias, M. J., & Tobias, S. E. (1996). *Social problem solving: Interventions in the schools.* New York: Guilford Press.

Elias, M. J., & Bruene-Butler, L. (1999). Social decision making and problem solving: Essential skills for interpersonal and academic success. In J. Cohen (Ed.), *Educating minds and hearts: Social emotional learning and the passage into adolescence* (pp. 74–94). New York: Teachers College Press.

Elias, M., Zins, J. E., Weissberg, R. P., Frey, K. S., Greenberg, M. T., Haynes, N. M., Kessler, R., Schwab-Stone, M. E., & Shriver, T. P. (1997). *Promoting social and emotional learning: Guidelines for educators.* Alexandria, VA: Association for Supervision and Curriculum Development.

Fonagy, P., & Target, M. (1996). A contemporary psychoanalytical perspective: Psychodynamic developmental therapy. In E. D. Hibbs & P. S. Jenson (Eds.), *Psychosocial treatments for child and adolescent disorders: Empirically based strategies for clinical practice* (pp. 619–638). Washington, DC: American Psychological Association Press.

Fonagy, P., & Target, M. (1997). Attachment and reflective function: Their role in self-organization. *Development and Psychopathology, 9,* 697–700.

Gardner, H. (1983). *Frames of mind: The theory of multiple intelligences.* New York: Basic Books.

Gardner, H. (1999a). *The disciplined mind: What all students should understand.* New York: Simon & Schuster.

Gardner, H. (1999b). Foreword. In J. Cohen (Ed.), *Educating minds and hearts: Social emotional learning and the passage into adolescence* (pp. ix–xi). New York: Teachers College Press.

Gardner, H., Feldman, D. H., & Krechevsky, M. (Eds.). (1998). *Building on chil-*

dren's strengths: The experience of project spectrum. New York: Teachers College Press.

Goleman, D. (1995). *Emotional intelligence.* New York: Bantam Books.

Hamburg, D. A. (1992). *Today's children: Creating a future for a generation in crisis.* New York: Times Books.

Heath, D. H. (1991). *Fulfilling lives: Paths to maturity and success.* San Francisco: Jossey-Bass.

Institute of Medicine (u.s.). Committee on Prevention of Mental Disorders. (1994). *Reducing risks for mental disorders: Frontiers for preventive intervention research.* Washington, DC: National Academy Press.

Izard, C. E., & Harris, P. (1995). Emotional development and developmental psychopathology. In D. Cicchetti & D. J. Cohen (Eds.), *Developmental psychopathology: Vol. 1. Theory and methods* (pp. 467–503). New York: Wiley.

Johnson, D. W., & Johnson, R. (1989). *Cooperation and competition: Theory and research.* Edina, MN: Interaction Book.

Lantieri, L., & Patti, J. (1996). *Waging peace in our schools.* Boston: Beacon Press.

Lieberman, A. (Ed.). (1995). *The work of restructuring schools: Building from the group up.* New York: Teachers College Press.

Marans, S., & Cohen, J. (1999). Social emotional learning: A psychoanalytically informed perspective. In J. Cohen (Ed.), *Educating minds and hearts: Social emotional learning and the passage into adolescence* (pp. 112–125). New York: Teachers College Press.

Melaville, A. (1999). *Learning together: The developing field of school-community initiative.* Flint, MI: Mott Foundation.

Morton, J., & Frith, U. (1995). Causal modeling: A structural approach to developmental psychology. In D. Cicchetti & D. J. Cohen (Eds.), *Developmental psychopathology: Vol. 1. Theory and methods* (pp. 357–390). New York: Wiley.

Mott Foundation. (1994). *A fine line: Losing American youth to violence—A special report.* Flint, MI: Author.

National Association of State Coordinators of Compensatory Education. (1996). *Distinguished schools report: A description of 56 school-wide Title I projects.* Washington, DC: Author.

Noddings, N. (1992). *The challenge to care in schools: An alternative approach to education.* New York: Teachers College Press.

O'Neil, J. (1997). Building schools as communities: A conversation with James Comer. *Educational Leadership, 54*(8), 6–10.

Pianta, R. C. (1999). *Enhancing relationships between children and teachers.* Washington, DC: American Psychological Association.

Radest, H. (1969). *Toward common ground.* New York: FrederickUnger.

Shriver, T. P., Schwab-Stone, M., & DeFalco, K. (1999). Why SEL is the better way: The New Haven Social Development Program. In J. Cohen (Ed.), *Educating minds and hearts: Social emotional learning and the passage into adolescence* (pp. 43–60). New York: Teachers College Press.

Sifneos, P. E. (1996). Alexithymia: Past and present. *American Journal of Psychiatry, 153*(7), 137–142.

Silverstein, L. B., & Auerbach, C. R. (1999). Deconstructing the essential father. *American Psychologist, 54*(6), 397–407.

Sternberg, R. J. (1997). The concept of intelligence and its role in lifelong learning and success. *American Psychologist, 52*(10), 1030–1037.

Vaillant, G. E. (1977). *Adaptation to life.* Boston: Little, Brown.

Weissberg, R. P., & Greenberg, M. (1998). School and community competence-enhancement and prevention programs. In W. Damon (Series Ed.) & I. E. Sigel & K. A. Renninger (Vol. Eds.), *Handbook of child psychology: Vol. 4. Child psychology in practice* (5th ed., pp. 877–954). New York: Wiley.

Weissberg, R. P., Gullotta, T. P., Hampton, R. L., Ryan, B. A., & Adams, G. R. (Eds.). (1997). Healthy children 2010: *Enhancing children's wellness.* Thousand Oaks, CA: Sage.

Chapter 2

DEVELOPMENT IN CONTEXT: IMAGINING THE CHILD AT HAND

Barbara K. Eisold, Ph.D.

The "I Have a Dream" Foundation and
New York University

Development itself is extraordinary. It has a biologically based, forward-moving thrust, which carries along with it change of all kinds. But change, even physical change, is enormously affected by the complex interaction of biology with environmental factors. As an example of this, consider Itard's (1807/1962) description of the Wild Boy of Aveyron, a child approximately 10 years old, captured naked in 1799, after years at large in the forest outside of Paris:

> [A]ll his habits bore the marks of a wandering and solitary life. He had an insurmountable aversion to society . . . to our clothing . . . our living in houses and to the preparation of our food. . . . His locomotion was extraordinary . . . because of his constant tendency to trot and gallop. He had an obstinate habit of smelling at anything . . . his mastication was equally astonishing, executed as it was solely by the sudden action of the incisors. . . .
>
> If . . . a stormy wind chanced to blow, if the sun behind the clouds showed itself suddenly illuminating the atmosphere . . . there were loud bursts of laughter, an almost convulsive joy, during which all his movements . . . resembled a kind of leap he would like to take . . . into the garden. Sometimes instead . . . there was a kind of frantic rage, he writhed his arms . . . gnashed his teeth audibly and became dangerous to those who were near him. . . .
>
> Several times during the course of winter I have seen him crossing the garden . . . squatting half naked upon the wet ground, remaining thus exposed

for hours on end to a cold and wet wind. . . . When he was near the fire and the glowing embers came rolling out of the hearth it was a daily occurrence for him to seize them with his fingers and replace them without any particular haste upon the flaming fire. He had been discovered more than once in the kitchen picking out in the same way potatoes that were cooking in boiling water. (pp. 8–15)

In order to acclimate him to temperature and to initiate the use of clothing, Itard says,

every day I gave him, and at a very high temperature, a bath lasting two or three hours. . . . After some time our young savage showed himself sensitive to the action of cold . . . [and] he soon began to appreciate the utility of clothes which until then he had only endured with much impatience. (p. 16)

This child's biology, his unique set of inherited possibilities, had interacted so deeply with the extreme restrictions of his particular environment, the forest outside Paris, and with the animals living there that these had become most meaningful to him, most useful to the adaptations he perceived as necessary for him to survive. As a consequence, he had learned to perambulate like some animals, to eat like others (presumably vegetarian others), and, perhaps most remarkable of all, to be immune to changes in temperature that are generally devastating to human beings. His affective life, far from having been destroyed, took place without words (from whom could he have learned them?) in response to the "beings" in his universe—the sun, the clouds, the snow, the open fields.

Despite the fact that he had no language, this child's intense wish to survive had bent and shaped him, body and soul alike, in order to achieve necessary and therefore meaningful adaptations. Thus his development was a process of growth and change over time that required the ongoing integration of his biology with environmental factors in a manner that assured the most useful adaptation that he could organize considering his unique set of needs. Development, I believe, is always guided by the givens of an individual's biology in interaction with an environment within which the best adaptive meaning must be made. Perhaps it is most fully realized when the individual in question feels safe enough to take reasonable risks without fear of the loss of integrity. Anxiety on this last account can badly curtail the entire developmental process, which at best has no definitive end. Unfortunately, Itard's account does not tell us anything about how or what the wild child thought about himself; in part because of this, we do not know how much of a reasonable risk taker he was. That he was a social animal despite his isolated origin, however, is clear from the account, which chronicles, among other things, the ways in which the child became intensely attached to Itard.[1]

In our very different world, full of other human beings, important among the changes that development can bring are changes in the beliefs that children hold, both about themselves and about the rules that determine the place they occupy in their social world. Together these beliefs will have an untold effect on their willingness to be open, to take risks, and to learn. A child who can recognize her own strengths and weaknesses, who can reflect on these and accept help, will be more securely engaged in the world and thus able to risk new experiences than will a child who tries endlessly, on her own, to do what she cannot. Similarly, a thoughtful, considerate child who understands that social rules are often flexible and who also has friends with whom she can cooperate on an equal footing to create play scenarios or other projects that are satisfying will have far more opportunity to learn than one who plays in isolation, unable to think with others.

PORTRAITS OF TWO CHILDREN

The best developmental outcome in regard to these beliefs cannot unfold in a vacuum; much will depend on opportunities that are provided by parents, teachers, and peers. For the sake of a discussion of contrasts in regard to these opportunities, I will describe broadly some aspects of development in the elementary school years, and I will focus briefly on the growth of self-reflective capacities and knowledge of social rules, looking especially at the ways these can or cannot be enhanced by the specificity of a child's milieu. To illustrate, I will describe two children, each one very able, each one somewhat troubled, but one with much greater opportunity than the other to grow in every way, just by virtue of the accident of birth. I begin with Steven, the younger, more advantaged child.

Steven

The elder of two siblings, Steven has just turned 7 and is the youngest boy in his class; he is about to finish first grade in a small private religious school in a big city. There are 25 children in his class with 2 teachers. Attractive and well-coordinated, he is quite good at gym, although he does not seem much interested in athletics. Despite his solid intelligence (apparent in frequent and thoughtful comments), his capacity to concentrate, especially on schoolwork, is notably short; and aside from the few words he recognizes by sight, he has not yet learned to read. His arithmetic skills, in contrast, seem robust, and much to the relief of his teacher, he manages to get these assignments done, even though he frequently drops pencil and paper on the floor during the process.

He is particularly frustrating to his small-group reading teacher because he accomplishes absolutely nothing with her and *sub voce* angrily calls her "mean." Moreover, he says he "hates reading," and insists it is for "older kids." In the past he has complained at some length about having to grow up. Otherwise, when he can take in directions (about half of the time), he is generally quite cooperative in school. During group projects he either is bossily telling other kids to behave or is completely, but quietly, inattentive himself. Although he is not unruly, his mind often seems to wander. This seems to be the way in which he handles anxiety: he checks out of what is going on in the world at large into his own preoccupations.

Outside of the classroom, while the kids are waiting to be picked up after school, Steven's behavior toward his 4-year-old sister (who attends the same school) is unusually loving and responsible. He keeps an attentive eye on her whereabouts and intervenes if she strays too far away. In addition, he seems to have friends and to seek out the company of a range of different boys in his class. However, during free time he seems to have difficulty following the more complex game rules set down by other kids; he would much rather do things his own way. In fact, much of the time he seems to have all kinds of fantasy games going on inside his head. Many of these revolve around toy guns and swords, some of which he brings with him to school to show boastfully to other kids. He is passionately interested in these. Last year this behavior may have won him attention, but these days other kids are frequently unimpressed, both with Steven's toy weapons and with him. They have more complex things on their minds and little patience for what they regard as baby stuff.

At home, his parents—both of whom are professionals and have odd work schedules—are angry at each other all the time; they are slugging out the structure of a contentious divorce, and his father especially is yelling a great deal. Religion, his father's special love, is one of the subjects they are fighting about. Far more important to Steven, however, is the fact that his mother has a new man in her life, a person Steven already knows. This man often comes to school with his mother to pick up Steven and his sister. Without much affect, Steven refers to him as "the man my mother is in love with." Meanwhile, his father, who comes to school for Steven on other days, is a shadow of his former self, thin, disheveled, and unshaven. Steven is obviously worried about his father and talks about him all the time; he has told his teacher that his father will be "moving to a new apartment," which is now "a mess," but when it is cleaned up "there will be a room for me."

Where is Steven, in terms of the promise that development itself would seem to offer? How much can he reflect about himself now? How does this help or hinder his capacity to take risks and to learn? How much outside help can he accept? How does he understand social rules and, as a result, how well does he manage with his friends? Considering his status in regard to all this, what does his particular future promise, given the ways in which his development is likely to unfold and the help he is likely to get with it from his particular milieu?

Steven, at age 7, is almost at the beginning of elementary school. Biologically determined changes have taken place in his brain at ages 4, 5, and 6, which have altered his potential in many ways and which are behind the forward thrust his development is taking. His brain size at birth was 10% of what it will become by the time his adolescence is complete. By the age of 5 or so his brain was 90% of the size it will be when he is an adult. The remaining 10% will grow slowly over the next nine years (Brooks-Gunn & Reiter, 1990; Schechter & Combrinck-Graham, 1991).

If, among other things, his relationships at home have been and continue to be relatively stable and growth takes place in a relatively unchaotic atmosphere (Lyons-Ruth, 1996), changes in his brain—myelization of neurons and enlargement of the frontal lobe, as well as the capacity to coordinate input from both sides of the brain (Shore, 1996)—will bring in their wake not only better physical coordination (the capacity to skip, ride a bike, throw and catch a ball, and so forth) but also increased ability to use concepts, to think self-reflectively (Fonagy, 1995; Fonagy & Target, 1996), and to socialize. Practice during the elementary school years, which children frequently seem to do compulsively, of their own accord (in endless hours of one activity or another), will be the bedrock upon which Steven's skills and abilities will become established. All this, the forward thrust of development, so to speak, can be derailed at almost any point by any number of circumstances that make necessary less than optimal modes of adaptation; primary among these are exceptionality in the child himself, impoverished early opportunity, and excessive internal conflict.

Steven is lucky. He is not disabled and has had a rich, relatively well protected, early life. He attends a small parochial school in a relatively safe neighborhood; it serves a fairly homogeneous group of children. Because classes are small and order is kept, because he has teachers who have the energy to focus on learning in the classroom, his school promises greater progress, academically at least, than would be promised by the unexceptional, somewhat chaotic public school in his neighborhood. This promise of private school will be particularly important as Steven ages.[2]

In addition, Steven's parents are not poverty stricken. The basics of his life are cared for and do not cause him anxiety. Moreover, there are people in his life who want to encourage his thoughtfulness. Although his parents are presently preoccupied with other things, the uncertainty of their situation is likely to be resolved in the next few years. Short of some unforeseen accident, both of his parents will probably continue in his life and will be moderately available to him. When and if they cannot help him themselves, they will get outside help for him and will do so in cooperation with the staff at his school. They are highly motivated to have his development unfold in the best way possible, and they have the resources to help him substantially in this regard.

Steven himself takes his time putting thoughts together and defends his right to do this by putting off those who expect him to learn fast. But he does not assess his own abilities out loud, and it is thus difficult to tell what he thinks about them. However, he can already think quite objectively about the people around him; for example, he can think about "the man my mother is in love with" as a distinct entity in his life, separate from himself. He understands that he is not the center of the world and that he must learn to get along with others in it and to obey the rules, although these may sometimes seem very restricting. As for the slow pace at which he reads, the reasons for this have not yet been diagnosed. He may have conflicts that have derailed him here or some kind of exceptionality. However, if reading does not soon come of its own accord, his parents (who take pride in education) will see to it that he learns by getting him whatever help he needs.

In time he will learn to do other things as well, things that he now puts off, describing them as designed "for older kids." In time, with support from his surround, it is likely that he will come to feel more certain of himself in many ways and will thus be better able to take reasonable risks, especially those implicit in reflecting more openly about himself and accepting help. At first, the changes he will make may not look much like change at all; he may continue to say that he "knows" all there is to know about a subject, or that the subject is "for older kids," but at the same time, it will become apparent that he is listening attentively, taking in all that another person can tell him on a given subject. Perhaps eventually he will become more willing to acknowledge lack of knowledge (often the biggest threat to a sense of self and therefore the most difficult to acknowledge). Some call willing acknowledgment of this kind the foundation of emotional intelligence and therefore an essential component of emotional learning

(Cohen, 1999; Gardner, 1983). It implies a certain wisdom, an understanding that one's self is big enough to survive, even if one does not know something at the moment. Therefore, the more Steven can be open to what he does not know,[3] to more his capacity to learn and to reflect about himself and others will grow.

Steven will also become better able to contend with rules as he ages. In the beginning, at ages 6, 7, and 8, the new cognitive capacities described earlier are often accompanied by changes in a child's sense of the seriousness of rules. Rigidity about doing things "right" may seem to take over at first or may be externalized and appear in the belief, as indeed Steven has about his reading teacher, that a perfectly kind and decent authority figure is "mean" (Furman, 1991). With growth and encouragement, Steven's rigid standards will soften, especially as his experience with and confidence in his capacity to control his impulses takes root and grows. He will begin to see that rules can be flexible, that at times they can even be changed using legitimate means.

Finally, with changes in his perception of the rules and with an expanded interest in taking in new things, Steven will have a greater capacity for friendship. Since Steven is already quite caring (witness his behavior with his sister), his friendships will probably become more and more caring and cooperative. Good social skills, the capacity to join a twosome or a group and to resolve conflict, are evident in the very fact of having and keeping friends. Not all friendships are equivalent, however. There are differences in the degree to which friendships are close, symmetrical, and constructive (Hartup, 1996). Friendships in which those involved spend little time together, in which one child is submissive and the other has all the power, or in which the friends engage in undoing things or in humiliating others are obviously less conducive to growth; these types of friendships are therefore less beneficial to both parties than are friendships in which there is greater symmetry and the activities engaged in are constructive.

Although Steven already has friends and can play imaginary games with them, his difficulty in understanding complex rule structure and/or his wish to avoid rules by doing things his way tend at times to limit the depths to which his friendships can develop. The capacity to use fantasy is definitely a plus.[4] But learning to share it in imaginary play, to develop it with another (supportive) person, needs time and the opportunity to practice. In this area parents who encourage socialization and a classroom teacher who does the same can be extremely instrumental. Given that Steven's school is small and that some of his teachers are probably inclined to develop projects designed to enhance cooperation and other socialization skills, and given also that there is not an overwhelming amount of stress in

Steven's environment, it is likely that his social skills will develop (Mc-Guire, 1998). Moreover, as he develops the capacity to contain his own impulses, his friendships will deepen.

Thus, although Steven has some qualities that are quite problematic, his prognosis is very good, given the natural unfolding of his development in conjunction with an encouraging environment. In contrast, consider Malika and her very different opportunities for growth.

Malika

Just completing fifth grade, Malika attends an unsafe, inner-city school outside of her own neighborhood. One of a handful of African American children in a school in which Asian American children predominate, Malika is in a class of 35 extremely diverse children with one teacher. An energetic, dynamic 11-year-old (the oldest girl in her grade), Malika looks 9 or 10: there are no apparent signs of puberty about her. Short, sturdy, and very dark-skinned, she has an unusually compelling gaze. Like all the members of her family, she is a Muslim; as such, she has been told that she is not supposed to like White people. Her teacher (a White woman whom Malika talks to a lot) knows that Malika's family is large: there are two older sisters who live at home, one with a baby, and an older brother who is in reform school upstate. Her mother, for whom Malika is named, is legally blind and (presumably) receives disability payments as a result. Her father is in jail. Malika is always hungry and comes regularly for the breakfast provided in school; there is not enough food at home.

However, despite all this, Malika's intelligence shines out. She reads well, understands math, and despite poor grades (she almost never completes an assignment) has consistently done well on city-wide achievement tests in the years when she has shown up to take them. Above all, she loves to talk and talks very well; she participates in every class discussion, contributing commentary and questions that demonstrate an unusual degree of comprehension; she is often inclined to argue. She is particularly lively and astute when it comes to the subject of women, whose subjugation to male power she bears witness to every day in the project where she lives; this angers her intensely. At the same time, she seems confused about how women can protect themselves or even about what "smart" women should do. In private, Malika (who does not take suggestions very well) cautiously acknowledges that she thinks her mother may not have been so "smart," that she may have made wrong decisions about many of the things that led to her present plight.

Unlike many of her classmates, Malika can live with her confusion from day to day and thinks about it, or so it seems. Malika also writes a lot, poetry especially. Much of this is not shared at school. Once, the teacher assigned the writing of an autobiography to the entire class. Malika's was the longest and technically the best. In it, however, there was no mention at all of her family. Instead, it was all about three brothers who had just moved into her neighborhood, what they looked like, how they dressed, what they did. There was also no mention of any feeling or relationship in her account anywhere. When asked about this, Malika irritably insisted that she liked it this way.

Outside of the classroom, Malika is always with the few other African American girls in school, talking up a storm. Often she and these girls cut school and hang out somewhere (her teacher does not know where). Malika seems to spend a great deal of energy in the company of these girls, talking, laughing, whispering, and carrying on. Often, however, she seems to be "telling" on one girl to another, or alternately having her own feelings hurt because they leave her out. In contrast to others in this group who have special friends, no one seems to be especially a friend of hers. The other girls seem to enjoy her energy and verve, but individually she seems to put them off.

Malika is also always pushing the teaching staff to have her "rights" respected. Intermittently, she calls them "racist" and makes a lot of herself. She is often noisy and outspoken when she stands with her group. However, if asked to do anything on her own, to stand up in front of the class and do a math problem, for example, or give any kind of report, Malika cringes, covering her face with her hands. She literally cannot stand up by herself and look directly at others in the room. Despite encouragement, she has made no progress with this all year.

She is also unwilling to have a regularly scheduled appointment with the guidance counselor at school, something her teacher has advised. Malika says it makes her feel too uncomfortable to be with this woman alone.

In contrast to Steven, where is Malika in terms of the capacity to maximize her potential as her development proceeds? How much is she able to reflect about herself? How does this help or hinder her capacity to learn? How much outside help can she accept? How does she understand social rules and how well does she manage with her friends? Considering her status in regard to these questions, what does her particular future promise, given the ways in which her development is likely to unfold and the help she is likely to get with it from her particular milieu?

Unlike Steven, Malika often has to worry even about getting enough to eat. For her, school attendance has meant, perhaps above all, that she will get breakfast and lunch. Needless to say, this is a very different motivational set from Steven's. One important consequence is that she has been far less focused than he on the necessity of doing well academically. In addition, she is older than Steven and her time in elementary school is almost over: Behind her lie the years of practicing basic skills that this period in life implies; before her lie the middle and high school years, as well as her own adolescence. For her, each of these phases will carry its own brand of chaos, in part because she will have to negotiate it on her own. Her mother, nearly blind and overwhelmed as she is, is unlikely to visit school to consult with teachers; nor will she do the considerable work that will be required to find Malika the help and the good schooling she needs.

There is an outside agency that might assist Malika in her search, for she is a member of a local "I Have A Dream" Foundation project.[5] However, she has only been able to avail herself erratically of the services provided there. In part this is because of her mother's provisos against them (her mother is suspicious of the Whiteness of the staff); but there are also Malika's own reluctances. Individual counseling, for example, is one of the services this program offers. When she was younger, Malika was able to let herself see a counselor for one year because at that point there was little separation between what was called "counseling" and another aspect of the program called "tutoring" in which all of her friends were involved. During that year the extra attention provided by the counselor seemed to calm her down, and except for periodic outbursts, she has been able to maintain much of that calmness. But since counseling has been clearly separated from tutoring and located in a different place, Malika has refused individual counseling because it calls too much attention to herself. Occasionally, however, she participates in a girls' counseling group, which was originally a sex ed group. She also sporadically drops by the counseling center to maintain some small contact with its director, whom she likes. But none of these contacts is regular.

In addition, as she ages, Malika is being pressured more and more by her mother to assume the stance of a docile Muslim woman, one who spurns sex entirely until she is married and avoids deep personal contact with people outside of her religion as well, especially people who might help her to succeed in the world at large. In fact, Malika's mother has highly ambivalent feelings about the meaning of success in what convention tells her is the White world. Unlike Steven, therefore, Malika's mother and the other adults in her life are not even remotely of the same mind about how her future ought to unfold. As a result, Malika, who has not fully sided with either camp and feels the conflict between them, is becoming more and more isolated as she tries to contend with the increasing pressures of day-to-day adolescent life, in school and out.

Compounding the effects of Malika's isolation is the fact that during the elementary years her attendance at school was poor and the grades she received were therefore also poor. This fact alone is likely to lessen her opportunity for entrance to one of the better high schools in her city, even if she does give herself permission to compete with others for this honor. Although she is bright and can also think reflectively (she can take an idea and turn it around in her head while she holds contradictions in mind), her thinking is seriously curtailed because she is ambivalent, first of all, about what she wants and, at a closer personal level, about taking center stage, even in her own imagination, even as a competitor with a chance of success at high honor and achievement. Although recent research seems to indicate that a growing reticence is characteristic of many girls in high school (Brown & Gilligan, 1990; Orenstein, 1994), Malika's social milieu adds additional emphasis to the more ordinary pressures that may be at work among the general group of her peers All in all, Malika's wisdom about her own emotions, her capacity to decode and use them creatively for her own growth (Cohen, 1999), indeed her ability to deal with them at all, seems cripplingly forestalled.

Finally, and perhaps in keeping with the limited capacities discussed, Malika's relationships with peers are very strained. Although she likes to feel included and works hard to keep this up, she does not seem to understand the most basic aspects of relationship rules. Indeed, Malika has no sense of reciprocal trust at all. Nor does she understand the parameters of confidentiality. As much as she seems to want to be a confidante of some, she seems equally happy to be telling tales on them to others. Her anxiety in regard to the issue of acceptance leads her on to this betrayal almost inadvertently. Without some help, her ability to care for others and to have friends are not likely to deepen.

Perhaps Malika cannot accept much help because she herself has been betrayed in relationships too many times. In contrast to Steven, it is probably unlikely that there will be changes in her ability to trust the world and, accordingly, she is unlikely to be able to accept help. To do so would mean risking too much; it would mean giving in or giving up more than she can afford to give up because she trusts no one to "hold" her present sense of herself while she explores other ways of being. In other words, she cannot be sure that anyone will be there for her except herself as she presently knows herself to be. What will happen to her is difficult to know, given the restrictions of her milieu, her wish to be included by her peers, her lack of trust, and her grand unwillingness to reflect about herself. In all likelihood, she will have a difficult time; as adolescence approaches, the pressure (both biological and social) to become sexual will pit her extreme reluctance about getting close to others against her equally powerful wish to be liked by others. Her future is likely to be seriously curtailed unless she can learn to think about herself without embarrassment.

CONCLUSION

In this chapter I have defined development as a process of change over time. It requires the ongoing integration of biological and environmental factors in a manner that assures the best, most meaningful adaptation that a given individual can organize considering his or her unique set of needs. It is perhaps most fully realized when the individual in question feels safe enough to take reasonable risks, including the risks implicit in reflecting on the self and acknowledging lack of knowledge.

With this definition loosely in mind, I have tried to assess two intelligent children by observing them closely (as a teacher might) in order to better understand how open they are to the forward thrust of their own development. In doing this, I have briefly considered each child's school history, the givens of his or her home environment and the kind of school each child attends. In addition, I have considered the ways in which these children interact with others, especially in regard to their understanding of the rules that guide peer interaction and their capacity to care for others. Finally, I have tried to assess the ways in which these children think about their own strengths and weaknesses in assessing their own needs and in accepting help with these.

Of the two children presented here, Malika, probably the more intelligent one, has the bleaker future, despite a range of well-developed academic skills. Her history has left her almost entirely unable to center her thoughts on herself and unable to tolerate the anxiety she experiences when others pay attention to her. Her social relationships are also limited because she does not understand the nature of trust, implicit in all good friendship. Her difficulties are not academic; they are entirely in the social emotional sphere. Unless she can establish some ongoing, consistent, tolerable relationship with someone, in which she is eventually required to examine herself, she will be lost, especially to any more education. Because she gets by academically, her needs in the social emotional sphere have been and will probably continue to be overlooked in school. This is unfortunate, perhaps even tragic, for it is in this sphere that her greatest pitfalls lie.

Steven, in contrast, is less intelligent, more disruptive in school, and seems to have some academic problems. In spite of these difficulties, his overall environment is far less threatening than is Malika's and it has allowed him to develop, in the social emotional sphere, in ways that Malika has been denied. He is already quite caring of others and, although he is just beginning to understand social "rules," he does understand trust and the need for confidentiality. Moreover, without demanding it, he also has no trouble at all being the center of attention. Although not especially self-reflective at the present time, his potential for openness in this way is considerable, given his thoughtfulness and his capacity to care. Finally, the elementary years are still ahead of him; he has lots of time left to practice before adolescence and sexuality are upon him. Soon he will learn to read. He will have a way, then, independently to feed his interests and to bond, through them, with other kids. He also does not feel alone nor is he alone; there are others upon whom he can rely for help. Despite his difficulties in learning (whatever they turn out to be), Steven will most probably do well.

Neither of these children attends a school in which any ongoing attention is paid in the classroom to social emotional learning. Each one has a teacher or teachers who considers that subject matter beyond her sphere, out of the range of her responsibilities. Needless to say, each child, but especially Malika, could benefit from a well-designed program in which a sense of responsibility for oneself and cooperation with others are both encouraged in a reflective manner. Perhaps in the future more attention will be paid in school to these crucial aspects of development.

NOTES

1. Francois Truffaut has made a movie based on Itard's text, called *The Wild Child*, in which he stars as Itard. It is wonderful and available on video cassette.

2. Our nation provides good public schooling in some communities. There are also the newer charter schools and schools that parents have initiated, schools that are safe, caring, and responsive, as some chapters in this volume describe. But inner-city schooling is often very poor. Especially for children who come from chaotic homes (which is not the case for Steven), a well-organized school that provides relatively small classes (in which children are likely to feel safer and more cared for than in larger ones), available faculty, and some real academic challenge can make an enormous difference in the life of a child.

3. In a very interesting essay called "Knowingness and Abandonment: An Oedipus for Our Time," the philosopher-psychoanalyst Jonathan Lear describes Oedipus as a man tyrannized by his belief in his own capacity to use logic, without

consideration of the fact that there are also deeper layers of meaning (1998, p. 48). In this regard, Oedipus is like a 7-year-old boy who cannot tolerate thinking about what he does not know. Luckily, most 7-year-olds do gradually develop greater capacity to tolerate not knowing.

4. There are cultures in some parts of the world in which fantasy ("symbolic play") is not encouraged and therefore not learned (Tizard & Harvey, 1977). In Western culture as well, not all children are capable of fantasy. Sarnoff (1976, pp.185–194), for example, describes a 7-year-old child, Josie, who, in part because she did not "dare," was not self-sufficient in this regard, had never learned to use stories or family dolls or other symbols to represent events in play. He describes the ways in which he, as therapist, structured situations (set up play scenarios and stories) to help her begin to use symbols (family dolls) in play. Adults can be very useful to children in this regard, even to those who can already use symbols (Fonagy & Target, 1996).

5. The "I Have A Dream" Foundation was founded in 1982 by Eugene Lang. It is organized around the "adoption" of a class of children by a sponsor or sponsors in a particular neighborhood; funds donated by these sponsors are set aside each year to provide a college education if and when the children graduate and to provide ongoing after-school services, presumably to bolster the possibility of graduation.

REFERENCES

Brooks-Gunn, J., & Reiter, E. O. (1990). The role of pubertal process. In S. S. Feldman & G. R. Elliott (Eds.), *At the threshold: The developing adolescent* (pp. 16–53). Cambridge, MA: Harvard University Press.

Brown, L. M., & Gilligan, C. (1990). *Meeting at the crossroads: Women's psychology and girls' development.* Cambridge, MA: Harvard University Press.

Cohen, J. (1999). Social emotional learning past and present: A psychoeducational dialogue. In J. Cohen (Ed.), *Educating minds and hearts: Social emotional learning and the passage into adolescence* (pp. 3–23). New York: Teachers College Press.

Fonagy, P. (1995). Playing with reality: The development of psychic reality and its malfunction in borderline patients. *International Journal of Psychoanalysis, 76,* 39–44.

Fonagy, P., & Target, M. (1996). Playing with reality I: Theory of mind and the normal development of psychic reality. *International Journal of Psychoanalysis, 77,* 217–233.

Furman, E. (1991). Early latency: Normal and pathological aspects. In S. I. Greenspan & G. H. Pollock (Eds.), *The course of life: Vol. 3. Middle and late childhood* (pp. 161–204). Madison, CT: International University Press.

Furstenberg, F. F. (1990). Coming of age in a changing family system. In S. S. Feldman & G. R. Elliott (Eds.), *At the threshold: The developing adolescent* (pp. 147–170). Cambridge, MA: Harvard University Press.

Gardner, H. (1983). *Frames of mind: The theory of multiple intelligences.* New York: Basic Books.

Hartup, W. W. (1996). The company they keep: Friendships and their developmental significance. *Child Development, 67,* 1–13.

Itard, J. (1962). *The wild boy of Aveyron* (G. & M. Humphrey, Trans.). New York: Appleton-Century-Crofts. (Original work published 1807)

Lear, J. (1998). *Open-minded: Working out the logic of the soul.* Cambridge, MA: Harvard University Press.

Lyons-Ruth, K. (1996). Attachment relationships among children with aggressive behavior problems: The role of disorganized early attachment patterns. *Journal of Consulting and Clinical Psychology, 64*(1), 64–73.

McGuire, P. (1998, October). School-based prevention: One size does not fit all. *APA Monitor,* p. 17.

Orenstein, P. (1994). *School girls.* New York: Doubleday.

Pine, F. (1991). On phase-characteristic pathology of the school-age child: Disturbances of personality development and organization (borderline conditions) of learning, and of behavior. In S. I. Greenspan & G. H. Pollock (Eds.), *The course of life: Vol. 3. Middle and late childhood* (pp. 393–446). Madison, CT: International University Press.

Sarnoff, C. (1976). *Latency.* New York: Jason Aronson.

Schechter, M. D., & Combrinck-Graham, L. (1991). The normal development of the seven- to ten-year-old child. In S. I. Greenspan & G. H. Pollock (Eds.), *The course of life: Vol. 3. Middle and late childhood* (pp. 285–318). Madison, CT: International University Press.

Shore, A. N. (1996).The experience dependent maturation of a regulatory system in the orbital prefrontal cortex and the origin of developmental pathology. *Development and Psychopathology, 8,* 59–87.

Tizard, B., & Harvey, D. (1977). *Biology of play.* Philadelphia: Lippincott.

Part II

CREATING SAFE, CARING, AND RESPONSIVE SCHOOLS

Part II of this volume focuses on the fundamental importance of creating safe, caring, and responsive classrooms and schools. This is the optimal foundation for all learning and development. Effective SEL efforts always include concrete strategies for fostering such a nurturing climate.

Chapter 3 presents an overview about how we can effect a school's climate in ways that foster safe, caring, and responsive schools. This work is importantly based on "lessons learned" from the Comer School Development Program. This is one of the oldest and most successful SEL programmatic efforts; it has focused effectively on building partnerships between educators and parents to affect the culture and climate of schools. Chapter 5 presents a wonderful and moving example of how we can and need to recognize and then utilize teachable moments in the life of the classroom to foster a sense of safety and caring. Teachers of young children know that virtually all classes include some children who are particularly vulnerable socially and/or emotionally. Chapter 4 focuses on how we can understand and help these children. Lessons learned from this chapter are important and applicable to our work with all children.

Chapter 3

SCHOOL CLIMATE AND SOCIAL AND EMOTIONAL DEVELOPMENT IN THE YOUNG CHILD

Joy E. Fopiano, Ed.D. and *Norris M. Haynes,* Ph.D.

Southern Connecticut State University

Social and emotional learning is a critical and vital aspect of the overall development of the elementary-school-age child. While the foundation for later development is established long before a child enters school, the early school years constitute a period in the child's life during which there is phenomenal physical, cognitive, and emotional growth (Tudge, 1990). The early school experiences to which a child is exposed contribute significantly to the individuality and perceptions that determine how this individual may view and respond to the world.

School, for many, is the first formal arena in which the children engage with adults and other children who are not members of the primary family system. To be successful in this new arena, more is demanded of a child than academic achievement. A child must also acquire the ability to interact in socially acceptable and effective ways with others. Howard Gardner (1983, 1993) refers to this as "interpersonal intelligence." Further, children must learn to monitor and regulate their emotions and behaviors. This requires the development of what Gardner calls "intrapersonal intelligence." School success, then, involves not only developing cognitive skills, but also forming friendships, developing interactive skills with groups, and understanding oneself and one's behaviors. Each skill set is equally vital and significant.

These social and emotional abilities are more readily acquired and mastered in a supportive school context where adults model healthy behaviors and strategies. To address children's social and emotional needs directly, however, structured activities designed by educators can be used to facilitate social and emotional goal attainment. Therefore, the responsibility to foster social and emotional skills must also be considered when designing curricula for growing children.

Educators and developmental psychologists have long been aware that much significant teaching in schools takes place outside of the formal academic curriculum. This teaching has been referred to as the "hidden curriculum" and often is aimed at improving intrapersonal and interpersonal skills essential to school success. The hidden curriculum typically incorporates the nonacademic psychosocial climate that supports effective teaching and learning in schools. Certainly, the social and emotional experiences of children in the elementary school years are an essential determinant of their successful transitions in the later school years. We suggest acknowledging and validating the hidden curriculum by formalizing the necessary and significant intrapersonal and interpersonal skills within the basic goals and philosophy of elementary education.

In the school, classroom, neighborhood, and family (and later on as adults in the workplace), children rely on their understanding of Self and their knowledge of how to work in cooperative groups, to solve problems, and to communicate effectively in order to be successful. Beyond academics, these are the necessary skills of life. The context in which these life skills are taught and practiced is as important as the skills themselves, hence the importance of school climate. A school must be able to provide learning opportunities to build and strengthen children's affective and cognitive skills simultaneously. Schools must also consider that children of average intellectual abilities but with superior social and emotional skills may be found to be more successful both in and outside of school than children of superior intellectual abilities who are less socially and emotionally skilled. Since the goal of schooling is to prepare children to succeed, it is paramount for students of all cognitive skill levels to have increased school exposure to expanded education in the social and emotional realm.

THE IMPORTANCE OF SCHOOL CLIMATE

It is widely acknowledged that children develop differently and at different rates. Their early life experiences, including home and school environments, influence how they grow and achieve developmental milestones, such as their abilities to effectively respond to daily challenges. The experiences of Malika and Steven, the children introduced in Chapter 2, provide us with the opportunity to reflect on how a consistently supportive and responsive school climate, facilitated by sensitive adults, may foster a sense of belonging and promote resiliency while mitigating possible negative circumstances of the home environment. This may occur with Steven and Malika even as their learning needs are addressed in the classroom environment. Indeed, social and emotional needs are congruent with learning needs and not at cross purposes with the overall goal of school success.

As with every student, these two youngsters have unique circumstances at home that may trigger social, emotional, and behavioral responses that may be expected to impact learning and academic progress. Thus it is reasonable to address those needs in the classroom context to facilitate learning and growth. The negative circumstances that children face at home may take many forms such as conflict, violence, a struggle to have basic needs met, uninvolved and uninformed parents, overcrowding, and belief systems different from those supported in the schools. These circumstances, and how they are processed by the child, will influence the child's perception and thus the child's responses to learning objectives presented in the school environment. The child is a whole individual. To be wholly successful learners, children need to learn more than the academic skills in isolation.

Steven and Malika experience different events and face developmental issues that affect their lives in varying ways; their home circumstances and the challenges they face are very different. Yet both of them can be equally helped by a school experience in which their social and emotional development as well as their cognitive development is supported and cultivated. A school climate that is sufficiently responsive to their developmental and learning needs would provide them with many of the protective factors needed for each of them to be successful. They can be expected to actualize their achievement potential in a school climate that nurtures, supports, and challenges them. School failure does not have to be inevitable, even when a child is significantly challenged socially, emotionally, or academically. Instead, school can provide a consistently safe and supportive environment in which new cognitive and social skills may be effectively taught, learned, and practiced. The cases of Steven and Malika are clear examples of how multiple needs can be addressed through the enhancement of school climate.

Steven

Although Steven's parents have the financial ability to provide him with professional help outside of school, such clinical support alone does not necessarily assure that his social, emotional, and academic needs will be fully met and addressed. His immediate needs, including learning, reading, and following directions, as well as divorce-related issues, may be effectively addressed in a school context where he consistently receives support and guidance.

In Steven's case a consistently supportive climate will deepen his sense of belonging and motivation to achieve. While he does have challenges and issues with which he must contend, the age of this child—youngest in his grade—must be taken into consideration when weighing his immediate developmental needs: He has just completed the first grade! A more inclusive and accepting environment may stimulate higher levels of learning and allow him to take the necessary emotional risks that will propel him toward greater academic growth and development. A climate in which Steven can showcase his strengths and feel safe to risk facing challenge while bolstering his weaknesses is ideal for strengthening academic self-esteem.

Steven's abilities may not be evenly developed, especially considering his younger age. Further, although he may be somewhat disconcerted by changes that are taking place outside of school, his reaction may be considered well within normal limits as he seeks to learn how his needs will be met. Divorce is a new idea to him; he is not yet aware of how he may be impacted by these changes, which may not have been discussed with him either at home or at school. A sense of connectedness to classmates and the larger school community can serve to bolster his sense of continuity, security, and self-worth. It will be important to foster a sense of belonging and consistency, and this can be done through helping him feel good about himself in a nonthreatening school climate. As changes occur within the home, the consistency and structure that school provides through a caring climate takes on increased significance and can even serve to strengthen Self. In such a supportive climate, showcasing Steven's math strengths and helping him see that it is not unusual to have areas in which he does not excel (such as reading) are helpful. His learning needs may be addressed concurrent to his emotional needs where the culture of the school accepts the whole child.

Malika

Malika offers a striking contrast to Steven. While this student is older and exhibits strengths in her cognitive skills, her personal and social skills are in need of support. Bright, talented, hungry, and angry, Malika may be expected to struggle on her own to develop the sense of inclusion and belonging that every youngster seeks. Although she may be able to perform at her present grade level without additional support, when increased independent academic demands are made of her in higher grades, she is likely to falter in an arena where she previously has enjoyed success. In a climate in which she is more socially connected to the school and feels ownership of her learning within the school environment, she may be more likely to continue to strengthen and grow. Presently, without evidence of such school support, she has difficulty with social relationships, especially with others who are not members of her racial-ethnic group. In higher grades and in the larger world, she will need good social skills to succeed in many facets of life even if she continues to progress academically.

Unless the school reaches out to embrace her now, Malika may attempt to seek support and a sense of belonging outside of school on her own. This may result in her alienation from school peers and adults who could serve as successful models for her. She may be at risk for seeking affiliation and bonding with peer groups whose values may further undermine desirable positive social and academic development. The linkage between Malika's interpersonal and intrapersonal skills and her potential for academic development is particularly significant. She may be less likely to continue to progress steadily and achieve her academic potential in school if she continues to experience a sense of detachment from her school and her family. Uncomfortable with the role of females in her family's religious orientation, she experiences conflict which further exacerbates her own internal struggle to express and develop herself.

Malika can benefit significantly from a nurturing and responsive school climate where the guidance that she receives at home is supported and augmented in school. Her difficulty in establishing meaningful and positive social relationships may be expanded if she is exposed to healthy examples of positive interactions with children and adults from different cultural backgrounds. Of course, it would also help significantly if her mother's relationship with the school could become more inclusive and positive.

SOME ESSENTIAL SCHOOL CLIMATE FACTORS

There are several important school climate factors that support and sustain the healthy social, emotional, and academic development of elementary-school-age children. These include adult nurturing, good peer relationships, and sensitive and responsive support services.

Adult Nurturing

At the elementary school level, the relationships that children establish with adults and other children form the basis for the developmental transitions that they must make later on in school and outside of school. Studies on school climate (Haynes & Emmons, 1997) indicate that elementary-school-age children are particularly influenced by the relationships that they establish with the significant adults in their schools, especially their classroom teachers. The research shows that relationship with teachers is significantly correlated with students' learning, achievement, and behavior. Further, the goodness-of-fit between teaching style and learning style as part of the climate that prevails may be considered significant in successfully addressing both learning and emotional needs. This should not be overlooked by educators in planning, as different teaching and learning styles are more or less effective and successful for different students. Items on the School Climate Questionnaire developed by Haynes and colleagues (1997) that measure student-teacher relationships ask about the nurturing and support that teachers provide. The nurturing school climate includes the following features:

- Access to supportive and caring adults
- Opportunities to interact socially with adults outside of the classroom
- Opportunities to share concerns and problems with adults who respond in a helpful way
- Adults who are willing to provide one-to-one guidance and mentoring on academic issues
- Adults who maintain consistent and proactive contacts with the home
- A feeling of mutual trust and respect between school and home and between adults and children in the school

In considering Steven and Malika's situations, the extent to which these nurturing elements exist is unclear. In Malika's case, there is clearly a lack of trust between her mother and her teacher. This no doubt has impaired the student-teacher relationship and jeopardizes Malika's education. Trust is basic to the existence of productive and helpful relationships, particularly for the education of the elementary-school-age child.

Good Peer Relationships

The relationships that children have with their peers in school contribute significantly to their sense of belonging, social importance, self-esteem, and connectedness to the learning environment. There is considerable evidence of the significance of social relationships among peers for elementary-school-age children. Our own research (Haynes & Emmons, 1997) and research conducted by others (Garmezy, 1989; Gottfredson, Gottfredson, & Hybl, 1993) find a significant relationship between children's peer group relationships and their assessments of their social competence and self-esteem. Teachers also rate children's social skills based on their abilities to establish and maintain cooperative working relationships with other children and often judge their growth in maturity based on these ratings.

Conscious and deliberate efforts to help children develop strong interpersonal skills through planned activities are an essential aspect of a socially and emotionally sensitive school climate. Cooperative learning strategies have been shown to be effective in promoting social competence and prosocial values while reducing antisocial and behavioral problems among elementary-school-age children. The New Haven Social Development Program begun by Roger Weissberg and colleagues serves as a national model on how schools can use curricula and staff support to teach social and interpersonal skills to elementary school children (Weissberg, Caplan, Bennetto, & Jackson, 1990).

Planned interactions of a cross-cultural nature, as an integral aspect of the school's hidden curriculum, may help Malika deal with her learned inability to trust persons of other racial and ethnic groups. Her view of her teacher as racist is a reflection of her mother's influence and may have significant implications for her own social development. How she perceives and receives others will impact her ability to study, work, and collaborate with others who are different. Her ability to accept others must begin with her ability to see herself as an important and valuable person, worthy of acceptance by others.

A school climate that is characterized by good peer relationships includes the following features:

- Planned and structured social activities that bring students together
- Group cooperative learning experiences in the classroom
- Caring and respect among students for one another
- Acceptance and respect for cultural, ethnic, racial, gender, and physical differences
- Sharing of resources
- Absence of teasing and acts of violence

Sensitive and Responsive Support Services

There are many who express the view that schools are being asked to do too much for children, and there are those who feel that schools are not doing enough. Regardless of the position that one takes on this issue, there is little doubt that children and families need the support of schools and the wider community to meet the daily challenges of living. Children's academic development and achievement in school is linked to social and emotional well-being. Many children and families need psychological services in the form of individual assessments, counseling and guidance, mentoring, after-school programs, referral services, parent training workshops, and family therapy. While schools may not be in a position to provide all of these services, they can support children and families in identifying and accessing these services. Some of these services should be provided by schools themselves. Consider the value in regulating services by offering them through the schools: This would provide children and families with superior quality services disseminated by professionally trained staff with consistency and under supervised conditions.

There are many schools that have recognized the value of addressing the multifaceted needs that children have while in elementary school. They have developed teams of mental health providers who meet on a regular basis to discuss individual cases and make recommendations for addressing the concerns and problems that many children face. These teams often work with families under stress to help alleviate social conditions that affect children's school performance and their social and emotional development. The composition of these teams vary from school district to school district and sometimes between schools in the same district. However, the teams are usually staffed by the following professionals: school counselor, school psychologist, social worker, school nurse, special education teacher, resource teacher, speech and language therapist, and any other mental health or pupil personnel staff member who is available to that school (Haynes, 1998).

Such teams begin to work on a case when a referral is made by a parent, teacher, or another staff member. The referral gets included on the agenda for the next team meeting. Each member on the team contributes his or her perspective to the discussion of the case. At the end of the discussion, recommendations are given for action. Sometimes a team member may be assigned to gather more information from a parent, agency, or teacher to complete the picture before final actions are decided. When action is decided, there is a clearly articulated process for following through, following up, and reporting back to the team on progress and final outcome before closure is brought to the case.

This proactive team approach differs from other approaches in that it is truly interdisciplinary, it involves parents and families in the process as much as possible, and it has a clearly defined operational procedure that leads to action, follow-up, and closure. It is also unique in that it not only addresses individual student and family concerns but also considers global school climate issues as well. For example, the team may consider whether or not Steven's deficient academic performance or Malika's difficult social skills interactions, including her perceptions of her teacher as racist, may be in part a function of larger school climate issues that may need close attention and remediation. This global, systemic perspective distributes the responsibility for students' psychosocial and academic development among key stakeholders in children's development.

This approach, combining proactive, preventive, and early interventions with systematic global improvements, has reduced the numbers of students who are misidentified as socially and emotionally maladjusted, reduced disciplinary referrals in schools, and promoted learning and achievement among students who would otherwise fail and drop out of school (Comer, 1998; Comer, Haynes, Joyner, & Ben-Avie, 1996; Haynes, 1998).

A school climate that provides supportive services to children and families with needs is characterized by the following features:

- The presence and availability of knowledgeable, competent, and well-trained mental health professionals in the school
- A clear, coordinated strategy for integrating the work of trained professional staff to maximize their positive impact on children's mental health
- A systematic process for students, teachers, other staff, and parents to seek and receive support from trained personnel
- An emphasis on promoting a global school context that is consistently in tune with the social and emotional needs of all students
- Positive relationships between the school and service providers in the larger community

To better illustrate the way in which a supportive school climate can be attained, it might be useful to briefly outline some guidelines that are implemented by the Comer School Development Program (Comer et al., 1996):

1. *Involve parents in significant ways in the life of the school.* In the Comer School Development Program (SDP) there are three levels of parent involvement: At Level I, there is broad-based parental support for the school's social and academic agenda. At Level II, parents volunteer their time to serve in the school in needed capacities such as classroom aides, lunchroom monitors, and after-school facilitators. At Level III, parents are involved in collaborative decision making with staff on the school's Planning and Management Team, which has responsibility for coordinating and managing the social and academic plan for the school.

2. *Establish an interdisciplinary team of mental health professionals who meet on a regular basis to address the social and emotional needs of students and who also address the overall psychosocial and academic climate of the school.* In the Comer SDP the Student Staff Services Team meets on a weekly basis to consider individual and global school issues. This team is composed of the school psychologist, counselor, social worker, special education teacher, school nurse, resource teacher, and other professionals with mental health and child development knowledge. The evidence suggests that such a team can help reduce social and emotional problems and significantly improve the school climate.

3. *Use cooperative learning strategies.* The evidence on cooperative learning approaches suggests that they promote healthy prosocial attitudes and behaviors and also enhance problem-solving skills. In many Comer SDP schools, cooperative learning strategies are successfully used to enhance students' academic performance and social skills.

CONCLUSION

Academic and social emotional learning are implacably intertwined. Learning for all children is in large part as much a social and emotional experience as it is a cognitive experience. Academic learning takes place in home and school environments where emotional and social experiences serve as the background or foreground for this learning. We cannot and do not turn off children's emotions when trying to teach them to read, or write, or solve math problems. If anything, many academic learning experiences heighten the need for children to be socially and emotionally skilled in order to be successful in school and in life generally. Increasing academic challenges require that children become more self-confident and display higher levels of self-control.

In an effort to achieve a climate that includes the three basic factors discussed above—adult nurturing, good peer relationships, and responsive support services—school administrators and staff will do well to follow the following suggestions:

- Explore deficits in basic skills and other learning difficulties to discern how best to plan for students' learning needs and implement the plan.
- Include summer and after-school services to bolster skills.
- Provide and integrate supportive academic and social services in school to help bring academic and social interactive skills to acceptable levels.

- Implement curriculum that accommodates a variety of learning styles and offers hands-on learning opportunities that are consistent with best practices for developmentally appropriate programming for young children.
- Design opportunities in which students can showcase their strengths daily in the classroom setting, even as they are challenged to improve weaker areas and master new concepts.
- Encourage parent involvement in the academic and social life of the school by inviting families into both the school community and the classroom environment and showing them how they may participate and engage cooperatively.
- Involve counselors and school psychologists both in schoolwide curriculum as well as in individual planning to best meet students' psychosocial and academic needs.
- Offer counseling services (individual and small-group) to ease students' anxieties and discomfort during transitions from one grade level to another or from one social situation to another (such as Steven faced during his parents' divorce).
- Create group cooperative learning experiences with peers.
- Model a safe place (classroom) where risk taking is encouraged and promoted in learning and where children's mistakes are accepted as opportunities for personal growth and development.

To successfully incorporate these strategies when building a supportive and responsive school climate, schools will have to implement various kinds of adult education beginning with continuous *staff training* (or development) and ongoing support for faculty and administration including the central office staff.

The next essential piece in fostering a positive school climate are ongoing *parent training* workshops, which should be held in the schools (with baby-sitters provided). These would be offered by faculty and administrators to support issues and problems that are of concern to parents and to strengthen the home-school connection. Further, a direct structuring of a regular interface of parents in the classroom allows for their increased understanding of the curriculum to promote at-home continuity and support. Welcoming parental involvement in schools acknowledges their pivotal role as partners in education.

Finally, *community education* and involvement, including private child care providers (licensed family day care providers), private preschools, community agencies, pediatricians, and other private care providers for children and families, serves again to strengthen their link to schools. This component enhances the spirit of positive school climate by modeling to the community a design of cooperation, inclusion, support, strength, and quality.

REFERENCES

Comer, J. P. (1998). *Waiting for a miracle: Schools cannot solve all of our problems but we can.* New York: Free Press.

Comer, J. P., Haynes, N. M., Joyner, E. T., & Ben-Avie, M. (1996). *Rallying the whole village: The Comer process for reforming education.* New York: Teachers College Press.

Gardner, H. (1983). *Frames of mind: The theory of multiple intelligences.* New York: Basic Books.

Gardner, H. (1993). *The multiple intelligences: The theory in practice.* New York: Basic Books.

Garmezy, N. (1989). *Report on climate as a variable implicated in student achievement.* Chicago: MacArthur Foundation Research Program on Successful Adolescence.

Gottfredson, D. C., Gottfredson, G. D., & Hybl, L. G. (1993). Managing adolescent behavior: A multi-year, multi-school study. *American Educational Research Journal, 30,* 179–215.

Haynes, N. M. (1998). Overview of the Comer school development program. *Journal of Education for Students Placed At Risk, 3*(1), 3–9.

Haynes, N. M., & Emmons, C. (1997). *The School Climate Scales: Students, parents and staff versions.* New Haven: Yale Child Study Center.

Tudge, J. (1990). Vygotsky, the zone of proximal development, and peer collaboration: Implications for classroom practice. In L. C. Moll (Ed.), *Vygotsky and education: Instructional implications and applications of sociohistorical psychology* (pp. 152–172). New York: Cambridge University Press.

Weissberg, R. P., Barton, H. A., & Shriver, T. P. (1997). The social competence promotion program for young adolescents. In G. W. Albee & T. P. Gullotta (Eds.), *Primary prevention works: The Leila Awards* (pp. 45–77). Newbury Park, CA: Sage.

Weissberg, R. P., Caplan, M., Bennetto, L., & Jackson, A. S. (1990). *The New Haven Social Development Program: Sixth grade social problem solving module.* Chicago: University of Illinois Press.

Chapter 4

HELPING EMOTIONALLY VULNERABLE CHILDREN: MOVING TOWARD AN EMPATHIC ORIENTATION IN THE CLASSROOM

Deborah Mugno, M.S. and
Donald Rosenblitt, M.D.

Lucy Daniels Center

It is well known that the foundations for social and emotional development along with cognitive and physical development are well established in the first 6 years of life (Furman, 1995; Hyson, 1994; Mayer & Salovey, 1997). A child's mastery or nonmastery of emotional tasks during this time period may have lifelong implications (Dunn & Brown, 1991; Weider & Greenspan, 1993). Numerous studies show that at least one in five children under 6 years of age have already developed emotional problems (Lavigne et al., 1996). Biological and environmental factors are intricately entwined in emotional understanding and responsiveness (Casey, 1996; Lyman & Hembree-Kigin, 1994; Wittmer, Doll, & Strain, 1996). In addition to genetic complications, which may have neurological and social emotional implications, such issues as attachment, illness, abandonment, abuse, bereavement, divorce, and interpersonal relationships significantly impact emotional development.

Children whose emotional and social development is not progressing favorably manifest internalizing and externalizing disorders which exhibit specific patterns and set these children apart. Children may regress, have difficulty controlling impulses, exhibit increased anxiety, or become depressed, requiring assistance with the modulation of affect and behavior

(Barrett & Nelson-Goens, 1997; Dodge, 1991; Dodge & Garber, 1991; Furman, 1993; Weider & Greenspan, 1993). Emerging epidemiological studies are confirming the intuitive belief that early manifestations of social and emotional difficulties are strongly associated with continuing problems through childhood (Mattison & Spitznagel, 1999). These at-risk children tend to have more than their share of negative experiences in school, and are deprived of the self-esteem that accrues from successful mastery of learning and relationships. Rather, they become embroiled in negative spirals of failure, deepening emotional challenges, and continued failure. Although well-known special education techniques can provide some assistance to certain of these at-risk children during their primary school years, we have a particular opportunity to help these children during their kindergarten or, to a lesser extent, first-grade years. How can this be done?

A school-based approach to effecting internal change within a child should have two major components. The first component is the teacher's consistent expectations, support, and encouragement, often supplemented and formalized in behavior contingency programs. The disturbed child is often seen as potentially disruptive, and the classroom is usually highly structured to minimize stimulation and emotional situations. Success may be enhanced when the child can learn from the experience of rewards, effect internal change within herself or himself, and no longer be merely dependent upon the continued supply of rewards to maintain the desired behavior. Thus, behavior programs, which function through external structuring and response, potentially have more lasting benefits when they effect change within the child.

Whether the child will internalize the basic values inherent in the behavioral approach is dependent upon a variety of internal factors which require attention in their own right. Therefore, the second component of an approach that optimally effects change within the child involves the direct attention to the internal world of the child, including his or her capacities, attitudes, and ideals. In this chapter, we will focus upon this component of effecting change, as the behavioral approach and strategies are usually familiar to those who work in the educational field. The attention to internal capacities is grounded in the assumptions that during the preschool years, as children develop an awareness of emotion, they will begin to understand and describe their own emotions and they will learn to recognize, describe, and empathize with the emotions of others (Eisenberg, Fabes, & Losoya, 1997; Furman, 1995; Harter & Whitesell, 1989). Although this chapter will focus on the at-risk child, all of the principles and approaches apply equally to children who are following a more favorable developmental trajectory. While we worry less about them, their capacity to succeed in school, in the workplace, and in relationships will be directly related to the extent to which they have developed their social and emotional competencies. In their case, sometimes the good is the enemy of the best!

PRINCIPLES OF INTERNAL DEVELOPMENT

The direct attention to the internal world of the at-risk child is based on the following principles; although they pertain to all children, it is particularly important for us to be aware of them in our efforts to assist the at-risk child.

1. *Principle of subjective perspectives.* Children attribute meaning to their internal and interpersonal experience: just like adults, children have their own personal "take" on any particular experience. No two people see the same movie!

2. *Principle of meaningfulness of behavior.* Children's behavior always has reasons and motivation, and is a form of communication. It is important to question why a behavior manifests at a particular point in time (Neven, 1996). What lies behind aggressive or destructive acts? The child may be fully, partly, or totally unaware of these reasons, motivations, and communications.

3. *Principle of adaptation.* All children are doing the best they can to be successful in their world. The choices children make are influenced by a number of factors, including their efforts to meet their needs, to grow in their capacities, to be moral, to respond to and to deal with the particular people and events in their world, and to use the internal capacities and ways of understanding and experiencing the world with which they are born and which unfold within them.

4. *Principle of relationships.* A child's emotional growth occurs in the context of deep, sustained relationships. The acquisition of any capacity, attitude, or ideal of a child is a shared accomplishment between the child and a beloved caregiver. The evolution of this relationship is from the mother's first doing "for" the child, then doing "with" the child, then being "alongside" the child as he does for himself, and finally being "pridefully at a distance" as the child does for himself (Furman, 1992).

5. *Principle of fluidity.* Childhood proceeds with regressions and progressions. A regression can involve the loss or change in any capacity, attitude, or ideal. During a time of regression, capacities are truly unavailable to a child, and the child's need for help is greater.

6. *Principle of delay and deviation.* Children's capacities to function may be less than would be expectable because the capacity is delayed in its

development or is developing in a deviational way. When a child is experiencing a delay in development, the child is behaving in a way that would be expectable for a younger child. Perhaps the child has difficulty expressing his or her needs in words, or separating from his or her mother, or relating with peers. When a capacity is not just immature, but has developed in a direction that is not characteristic of normal development, we speak of deviation rather than delay. Severely impulsive children or children whose thought processes are idiosyncratic are illustrations of children who may be experiencing deviational development.

7. *Principle of conflict.* Sometimes a child's capacity to function is interfered with because of the active workings of the child's own mind. This kind of interference involves emotional conflict. Emotional conflict, often difficult to distinguish from delays or deviations, involves the development of protections against unpleasant emotions. When a child has an excessive amount of unpleasantness to protect against, the child adapts with protections, also known as defenses, which may become so extreme that a child has difficulty being successful in the world. Sometimes a child is aware of these protections to some extent, but more often they become so automatic that they are essentially outside the child's awareness and control, and we speak of them as "unconscious."

Steven and Malika

Steven and Malika, the two children described by Barbara Eisold in Chapter 2, help illustrate how the process of understanding the internal world of children provides us valuable insight into their developmental trajectory, be it favorable or off track. Steven is seen as a somewhat anxious child with variable difficulties in school, but one who has had supportive—though somewhat disruptive—parenting. Malika, on the other hand, lives in a world that is more chaotic, less supportive, and often unpredictable. The descriptions of both children are rich with caveats that reflect their inner lives.

It is useful to think about Steven and Malika in the context of the seven Principles of Internal Development. The principle of subjectivity is evident in that both children attribute their own meaning to their lives and relationships, which is very different from that of their parents and teachers. They are faced with grown-up issues, that is, divorce, jail, and prejudice, which they do not comprehend in the same cognitive and emotional terms as do the adults who created them. Steven does not have the animosity toward his father that his mother exhibits. Malika is confused about the prejudice that her family supports, particularly in the context of her positive relationship with the white female teacher.

In respect to the principle of behavioral meaning, Steven and Malika exhibit a range of behaviors that convey very specific messages and meanings. Steven can be bossy with classmates, he tends to get angry with his teacher when he is having difficulty in school, and he tunes out or withdraws both in class and on the playground. These behaviors give us insight into the way he handles his anxiety about school, his worries about his dad, and his fear that he will not appear competent in his schoolwork or in the complex games that his friends have developed at recess.

Malika chooses to write a lot, has difficulty doing things on her own even though she is quite competent, and pushes the teaching staff to respect her rights. She is communicating through her writing; the very fact that it is often void of emotion is very telling. Malika has little confidence in her ability to perform alone, which is a clue to the anxiety and other painful emotions that are submerged beneath her emotional void. She is confused about the role that culture and race should play in establishing relationships, and those issues provide complicating layers to the more basic anger about not getting what she feels she has deserved in her family culture.

Both Steven and Malika are doing what they can to adapt to their feelings and perceptions about themselves and the world they live, as the principle of adaptation asserts. Some of these adaptive attempts fall into the category of defenses. For example, Steven's tuning out and fantasy play may help him avoid appearing inferior to his peers, and Malika's aggressive treatment of the teaching staff may help her to feel in control of herself; she is defending against her low self-esteem and poorly developed self-image. Both Steven and Malika will experience regressions and progressions as they attempt to negotiate the challenges that their lives present to them.

Deep sustained relationships will likely be more difficult for Malika than for Steven. Malika has not had the nurturing parenting that Steven has experienced in spite of his parents' divorce. Steven has a safe and organized environment even though it is sometimes irregular. His parents both continue to support him and ensure that his basic needs are met. He in turn demonstrates affection and protective instincts toward his sister and is also able to form relationships with peers. Malika's story is very different. There is little stability and consistency in the care that she has received (she even has to worry about getting enough to eat), and Malika seems to have jumped to the stage of "doing for herself" without the progression that a healthy relationship with her mother would have provided. Consequently, her doing for herself is based on unsteady underpinnings; she has difficulty trusting peers and making friends and is afraid to be alone even with the guidance counselor. Steven indeed appears to have the more favorable trajectory for emotional development: his internal world is more organized, he has begun to develop healthier means of adaptation, and he is fortunate to have deeper, more sustained relationships with his caregivers.

A SCHOOL-BASED APPROACH FOR AT-RISK CHILDREN

Based on the Principles of Internal Development, a responsible school-based approach to assisting the young, emotionally at-risk child will incorporate the following three areas of focus: environment, relationships, and communication.

Environment

Children must feel safe in their environments in order to be able to grow emotionally and socially. It is imperative that we provide a safe physical environment for children and equally important that we pay special attention to the emotional environment. As a paradigmatic example, a child's entry into preschool or kindergarten is a difficult emotional task. For many children it is the first instance that they will spend a substantial amount of time away from their primary caregiver. They are often anxious and fearful. They are sad about leaving mom and other family members at home, and they are exposed to a variety of stressors inherent in any group situation, for example, "Will somebody be there to take care of *me*?" or "Will the teacher I have know what *I* need?" Even for the child who has already been to school, starting a new year with a new teacher in a new classroom is not easy. It is difficult for us as adults to judge how a child feels in this situation based on our own adult experience. There are many other classroom situations that call for us to address the child's experience of emotional safety. Only when we can see that classroom through the eyes of children do we begin to understand what they are feeling and coping with.

What kinds of things can we as teachers do to ensure emotional safety and comfort in the classroom? A gradual, thoughtfully planned "phase-in" period, when children and parents spend time in school together at the beginning of the year, assists with the transition process and eases anxiety for parents as well as children. Predictability, clear expectations, and well-established routines all contribute to the "feel" of a safe classroom. Any change in this structure or routine requires careful preparation. Teachers should talk to children about forthcoming visitors and introduce them when they enter the classroom. Vacations and time away from school may necessitate that we help children make simple charts or calendars so that they can keep track of how many more "sleep nights" until it's time to return to school. Perhaps Mom or Dad travel; teachers can help children with their sadness and "missing Mommy or Daddy feelings" by writing them notes, drawing pictures, or charting the days until they return.

Transitional objects help bridge the gap between home and school. A transitional object is a meaningful possession that represents the connection between parent and child. A favorite stuffed animal, a picture of family members, a bracelet of Mom's, or a baseball cap that belongs to Dad all help children maintain a closeness with those whom they miss.

Familiarizing children with the nooks and crannies of the school building (closets, hallways, offices, and so forth) and with all staff members diminishes thoughts of scary places and strange faces. Children should be provided with safe places to store their art work and belongings, either in cubbies or on "saving trays." Psychological as well as physical boundaries should be defined, respecting the tolerance level of each child. Children differ in their wishes to be touched or to be in close proximity to others. Their sensitivity to varying amounts of noise and stimulation may vary greatly from child to child or day to day. A classroom is an emotionally charged environment and children's adaptive and coping abilities are a function of their emotional state as well as their developmental age.

Relationships

The depth of the teacher-child relationship is the single most important factor that will contribute to the teacher's ability to help any child, and particularly the at-risk child, develop emotionally and socially. It is vital that teachers not assume that a deep relationship must be a mostly positive relationship. Most children who are at risk emotionally are not capable of a mostly positive relationship. As long as we are able to consistently reach out in a caring and empathic way to a child, we will create a deep relationship even if the child acts in a rejecting, provoking, ambivalent, or distancing way. We can sustain ourselves by remembering that the child is acting according to the principle of adaptation. We may know only some, or perhaps few, of the reasons that the child is not responding to us for who we really are: perhaps the child is worried that he or she will be rejected; perhaps she does not want to "feel" too much because the good-bye will someday be too painful; perhaps the child worries that being overtly attached to a teacher will mean that he is disloyal to his parent.

Teachers can establish an in-depth relationship with a child through an empathy with two aspects of the child. First, we should have an empathic understanding with the world as the child sees it. Second, we should have an empathic understanding of the level of the child's need for us, including the fluctuations of this need on the basis of regressions and progressions. The empathy with these two aspects of the child deserves further discussion.

Empathic Orientation: The World as the Child Sees It. First, consider what it means to have empathy with the world as the child sees it. Such an orientation is based on the principles of subjectivity, meaning, and adaptation. These three principles together imply a fundamental attitude that teachers must always maintain with children at risk emotionally: that children are doing the very best that they can to manage in the world *as they understand it* and that any "negative behaviors" are, in children's minds, in the service of emotional survival.

This approach does not mean that we must accept problematic behavior just because it occurs for understandable reasons. We may hope to figure out why one child kicks or bites another and help the child make some connection between thoughts and actions, but such aggressive behavior should not be tolerated. Our very efforts must be to the contrary: to help a child to question, to understand more fully, and to change. Empathy involves our ability as a helper to understand the way that the child experiences the world, offering our ideas and suggestions in a dosed, noncoercive manner. When we can approach children in this way, they are much more likely to join us in the questioning of their behavior.

Empathic Orientation: The Child's Need for a Teacher. The second component of teachers' empathy with children at risk emotionally is empathy with the level of a child's need for a teacher. Such an empathic orientation is based on the principles of relationships and fluidity. With regard to the principle of relationships, we should approach children at risk with the understanding that their development will be more uneven than that of typical children. Because they may have substantial potential in certain areas or at certain times, these children often fool us into expecting more from them than they can produce. One can easily assume that they are not trying or that they are just trying to get us to do for them. However, unlike other children, these at-risk children may not be able to generalize what they are able to do in one particular setting into another setting. For example, they may be able to contain their impulses in the classroom but not on the playground. Or, they may be able to contain their impulses with one child but not with another. It may not make sense that they can sit at a circle in kindergarten if the teacher is reading but not if it is sharing time.

Therefore, we must be extremely flexible with regard to whether and when we do "for," "with," "alongside," and "from a distance" for a child. We may approvingly watch from a distance as a child contains his or her impulses in the classroom, but we may choose to be close to such a child on the playground, ready to join in and help if he or she starts to get rowdy. We will learn which children he gets along well with, not involve ourselves when he is playing well with one of these children, and may determine that we should smile pridefully at the child when he is playing successfully with a child with whom he often has difficulty. We might put the child next to us at circle, and talk with her during the difficult parts of circle, feeling that her level of difficulty requires us to "do with."

Children at risk not only have problems generalizing from one setting to another, but also a capacity that has been present may suddenly disappear. For example, a child who has been able to eat lunch without making a mess may suddenly have difficulty eating without spilling or may even throw food. Or, one day a child might finish his work on time and another day just daydream. Although we should always challenge a child to rise to his highest level, we should be sensitive to the possibility that he cannot perform the task without greater help on this occasion.

With such children, teachers should never worry about "reinforcing negative behavior." When we start from the assumption that a child who is not using a capacity that we "know she has" is nevertheless doing her best, even though she might be daydreaming, whining, or just playing around, we will be right about the child more often than if we start from the assumption that she is trying to get away with something. With such empathy, and with a teacher's ability to provide the kind of help a child needs, the relationship between teacher and parent will deepen and the child is most likely to internalize the good efforts of the teacher. She is most likely to take into herself the "way that the teacher does it," leading to the independence and stability of function that is the hallmark of social and emotional competencies.

Communication

Children at risk for the development of emotional difficulties can be supported through effective communication strategies. The intricacies and subtleties of effective communication are often underdeveloped and underutilized. Communication is the means by which we make our feelings, needs, attitudes, and ideals known to others, and it is both verbal and nonverbal. Behavior is an important form of communication, and its messages should be interpreted as such.

Receptive and expressive language acquisition in the first 6 years has a most significant effect on children's ability to control and influence their emotions (Dunn & Brown, 1991). Children can often verbally express their feelings before they have names for the emotions themselves (Bloom &

Beckwith, 1989). When children can tell about their emotions, they have acquired a powerful tool. They can enlist others for aid and comfort; they can express, ask for, and receive affection; they can achieve or avoid another affective state; and they can reflect on their own thoughts and actions. Competent communication yields effective social cognition. Positive verbal affect from caretakers is emotionally contagious and elicits changes in the information processing systems and in the behavior of young children (Bugental, Cortez, & Blue, 1992).

The principles of subjectivity and meaning guide our understandings of communication. These principles orient us toward the individual perspective of the child and help us understand that the meanings of communication are both known and unknown (unconscious) to the one who originates it. The first goal of effective communication is for the listener to be as attuned as possible. However, this is just a catalyst for the true goal: to help the child as communicator to be as attuned as possible to his or her own emotions and needs.

Verbalization

The capacity of being attuned to one's own emotions and needs is fundamental to effective emotional and social functioning. We call this capacity *verbalization*, and it manifests in a child's ability to express his or her emotions and needs in the form of words. Words provide a frame and container for needs and impulses that otherwise can proceed directly into action. By putting emotions and needs into words, children can bring their emotions and needs into coordination with a variety of other capacities including their knowledge, their judgment, their ideals, their other needs, and the needs of others. It enables them to integrate a given emotion or need into a broader picture rather than be dominated by a single impulse in a splintered way. The container provided by verbalization affords children time to organize and plan. Verbalization does not need to be "out loud." It does not need to be a communication to another person; as long as the child can "speak to himself," then he has the capacity to verbalize. There are many occasions when it is in the child's best interest to verbalize "out loud." For example, it generally is helpful for the child to express his needs and wishes to the teacher or to a playmate.

An understanding of the child's capacity to verbalize is based on the principles of delay and conflict. The capacity to verbalize involves a number of subsidiary capacities. Most of these capacities involve children's ability to make sense of their emotional life. The first capacity, the recognition capacity, involves being able to recognize the presence of an emotion. The second capacity, the container capacity, involves being able to construct some kind of organizing container around the emotion so that it processed: this is usually a visceral, bodily phenomenon. When kin ners are delayed in developing this capacity, they often will hold their body rigid and shake, literally creating a bodily container. The third capacity, the gross discrimination capacity, involves being able to determine whether the emotion feels bad or good. The fourth capacity, the fine discrimination capacity, involves being able to discriminate and label different emotions, for example, to differentiate between sadness and anger. This capacity has many levels of subtlety, such as a capacity to discriminate jealousy from anger, or shame from guilt. Since children develop unevenly, however, a child might have no difficulty discriminating among positive emotions, but might not be able to even recognize the presence of negative emotions!

Teachers need to develop a sense of the child's internal world in order to know how to intervene most effectively. With children at risk in their emotional development, a teacher needs to move beyond the request of "please use your words," because the child may not have the words or may have delays or deviations that interfere with the ability to verbally express a need or an affect. A child may need the teacher's help even to recognize that there *is* an emotion, may need a teacher to provide a physical container through proximity (or holding, if this is acceptable), or may need help with discrimination. If a child is delayed in the capacity to discriminate and label emotions, we will need to provide our guidance by interpreting and providing the words. The ability to verbalize internally or externally is the pivotal issue in a child's ability to establish and maintain meaningful relationships.

Teacher Language. In the classroom, teacher language falls roughly into two categories: restrictive language, which is direct, controlling, impersonal, and indifferent; or responsive language, which conveys respect for and acceptance of an individual's feelings and ideas, encourages give and take, implies choices, and provides elaboration. For example, if a child comes to school looking sad because his mom is away, the restrictive reaction might be, "Let's find something to do so that you won't think such sad thoughts," whereas the responsive reaction would be, "I know how hard it is for you when your mommy goes away on trips. You must miss her very much."

Responsive teacher language in the classroom encourages more independence, increases motivation and creativity, helps raise self-esteem and self-awareness, and can decrease anxiety as well as physical aggression. A responsive teacher is an attentive listener who addresses children by name, asks open-ended and reflective questions, does not interrupt, and encourages children to elaborate on their own ideas and thoughts.

Some examples of the types of phrasing teachers use to talk responsively with children are listed below. These "sentence starters" may be helpful in illustrating the insight and the attitude which teachers should try to convey to a child:

I've noticed that . . .
When a boy [girl] is scared he [she] sometimes . . .
How scary it must be to . . .
How confusing it must be to . . .
I know that you must be feeling . . .
How much fun it must be to . . .
It must be . . . when you are thinking about . . .
A boy [girl] must get angry when . . .
Look at my face. My face is telling you that . . .
You must not like it when . . . You have a frown [sad or angry look] on your face.
You are showing me by your face that you are feeling . . .
You are showing me by your actions that you are feeling . . .
Did you hear your friend's message? He is telling you that . . .
Did you hear my message? I'm telling you . . .
I heard your message. You are telling me that . . .
Your voice is telling me that . . .
When you say [do] . . . it makes him feel . . .
I think you are feeling . . . That's why you . . .
It seems to me that it is hard for you when it is time to . . .
I understand how sad it is for a little girl [boy] when . . .
When a guy changes his behavior, something must have happened to upset him.
I know that when you hit someone, something must be bothering you.
How badly you must feel when you do things that make you worry whether I will be angry with you.
You are worried that . . .
No wonder you are showing me one of those faces. You feel . . .

CASE EXAMPLES

The following examples are taken from real classroom experiences and the children discussed are actual cases.

Burt: Showing Off to Friends

Children at risk may show off to friends on a repetitive basis. They will act in ways that get a reaction from their friends. Perhaps they will act silly or use off-color words. Although it may seem like they are just misbehaving or being provocative, often children will act this way because they want to have their classmates respond in a way that feels good to them!

Burt, a 5-year-old kindergartner, would repeat rhyming words in a very silly voice, in what appeared to be a way to get a reaction from the other children. His teacher would say, "Burt, I think you are wanting your friends to like you. When they laugh at your silly voice, that must make you feel that they like you."

Burt's teacher communicated effectively and strengthened his relationship with Burt. He responded to Burt's behavior from an understanding of his standpoint: this was Burt's effort to deal with his uncomfortable feelings of loneliness and to achieve his goal of feeling that he had a friend. He did not retreat to clichés, such as "negative attention," which objectify children through abstract concepts and lose sight of the complex reasons why a child might be behaving in a particular way. He also recognized that Burt's friend's reactions were powerful reinforcers: being silly works! He avoided the reiteration of the adult viewpoint, that Burt is not "really" making friends in that way, or even that there are other ways to make friends. Burt has heard that many times, and it carries the implied message, "Don't you know that, dummy?"

It is important for teachers to convey to children that we understand why they are behaving in a particular way, and that we view this behavior as a very reasonable way to deal with their affects and goals. Only when children feel understood in a nonjudgmental way will they be able to use teachers' suggestions about alternative ways to make friends, because only then will they know that we are truly giving them help so that they can achieve their goals rather than ours!

Diane and Karen: Exposed to Anxiety

Children often transmit their anxiety by exposing another child to their anxious thoughts or behaviors. Children at risk emotionally are more likely to expose others to their anxiety and to react strongly to the anxieties of others. Perhaps children overhear some frightening tale, true or fantastical. Perhaps they overhear the anxious worries of another child. Perhaps they are exposed to the frightening play or actions of another child. Frequently, the exposed child will react to this anxiety, sometimes in a delayed fashion.

Knowing the origin of the behavior of the exposed child helps the teacher to make sense of the behavior to herself and to the child.

Diane, a 5-year-old kindergartner, spontaneously brought up the Columbine school killings, talking about high school children going into their school and killing other children. All the children in the kindergarten heard this discussion. The teachers told the class that although this was a very scary thing to think about, their teachers would never let anything like that happen at their school. They had a very safe school. The teachers did not notice any reaction from the children until playground time an hour later.

All of the children became involved in scary, killing play. Robert became Godzilla, stomping on things and killing them. Although this was not unusual play for Robert, Karen, who usually did not enter Robert's play, joined him as a full-fledged Godzilla who pretended to kill things. Karen's teacher asked her if she "was needing to play this scary game because of the scary feelings she must be having about what Diane had said. Would you like to talk about it so you don't have to play this scary game?" Karen told her teacher to eat Godzilla poop for being so mean and raced away from her teacher (but also away from the Godzilla play).

Diane's teacher understood the need to reinstate the classroom as a safe environment. Although he could not really absolutely guarantee safety, this is one of those situations in which a slight exaggeration is justified because it is entirely within the child's best interest. In addition to establishing the environment as safe for all children, Karen's teacher was able to deepen their relationship and help Karen with her own internal world through effective communication. Karen had been able to contain her anxiety within herself until she became drawn into Robert's play. As a frightened child at risk in her emotional development, she was usually afraid to even pretend to be a monster. On this occasion, her usual fear of being a monster was overshadowed by her need to adapt to her anxiety and turn the potential experience of being a victim of a monster-killer into an experience of being the monster-killer. How much safer it is to feel strong rather than weak, the one who can control killing rather than the one who is potentially controlled by a killer! The teacher helped Karen understand that she was acting scary because she was afraid herself and suggested the alternative solution of verbalization.

As is so often the case when such help is offered, Karen felt "thrown back" into the very emotions that she was running from. Her response to her teacher was characteristic of a scared child: she repeated for one time the very behavior that was being discussed. Karen acted like a Godzilla, telling the teacher to eat Godzilla poop. However, she then left the scene and the play, showing some ability to use the teacher's help to at least contain herself. She was now able to adapt in a different way. Her teacher understood that there was nothing to be gained by admonishing Karen about telling her teacher to eat Godzilla poop, as it was an instinctive, protective statement from a child who was respectful when she was not overwhelmed. The intervention of the teacher was extremely successful, although one could be misled by Karen's initial verbal response and her running away.

Jack: Expressing Anger

As previously discussed, some children don't express emotion verbally for a variety of reasons. These children often have difficulty expressing emotion through words, at least through words that are not used as "clubs." When a child has been able to grow internally to the point where he makes a first attempt at conveying his emotions, it is important to convey support.

While out on the playground, Jack, a kindergartner, was able to verbalize his feelings about being teased by Barry first to a teacher and then to Barry. Jack said, "You are making me angry. You are making me so mad. I am just so mad!" Jack's teacher told Jack that she was glad that he was able to let Barry know how he was feeling, that it was okay for him to be angry, and that she would help him talk to Barry about it. Barry stepped back, a little surprised, and Jack was able to calm himself down.

Because this was one of the first times that Jack was able to use words to express anger and to use the words to communicate and not to hurt, it was very important for the teacher to reinforce his action with her approval and also to offer her help. She understood that Jack had now ventured into new territory and would need her to do "with" him. She was aware that just because Jack "used his words," he would not necessarily have the continued capacity to keep his response in words and not resort to action. Therefore, the teacher added that she would help Jack talk to Barry about it, that is, she might even need to do "for" him. Because of the pride that the teacher showed in his accomplishment and her continued availability, Jack did not feel that he had taken a step that left him without her support and help, and he was able to calm down. If Jack's capacity to express his anger in words had been a more secure and stabilized capacity, this teacher's support would have been too much, and would have undermined Jack's capacity for autonomous function.

THE CURRENT STATE OF RESEARCH

Social emotional growth is often difficult to measure and regression and pathology make predictability and generalization tentative. But there is a growing body of qualitative research in the field of early intervention that provides systematic and rigorous data on issues of efficacy related to social interaction and social development (Bakeman & Gottman, 1997; Graue & Walsh, 1995; McGee-Brown, 1995).

Longitudinal studies can provide valuable information on the long-term effects of an approach that focuses on the internal world of the child. Emotionally at-risk children who are identified at a very early age and receive therapeutic intervention can be compared with their nonidentified peers on measures of behavior, social adaptation, and success in school over time. Researchers would hope to find that intervention for these at-risk children has had a significant impact in their social and emotional development and that their scores on selected measures tend to move into the normal range.

CONCLUSION

As professionals who work with young children, we must look beyond behavior—beyond the symptoms of internal turmoil and unrest. By exploring the internal components of a child's life, we are able to thoughtfully provide methods of intervention that are at an emotionally appropriate level. This is not necessarily the same as an intervention that might be introduced at an age-appropriate level and might very well set the stage for continued failure. When we truly take a sensitive view of the world through the eyes of a child, we are able to evoke an empathy in ourselves that will direct our intervention as well as shape its success.

REFERENCES

Bakeman, R., & Gottman, J. M. (1997). *An introduction to sequential analysis* (2nd ed.). Cambridge: Cambridge University Press.

Barrett, K. C., & Nelson-Goens, G. C. (1997). Emotion communication and the development of social emotions. In K. C. Barrett (Ed.), *The communication of emotion: Current research from diverse perspectives: Vol. 77. New directions for child development* (pp. 69–88). San Francisco: Jossey-Bass.

Bloom, L., & Beckwith, R. (1989). Talking with feeling: Integrating affective and linguistic expression in early language development. *Cognition and emotion, 3*(4), 313–342.

Bugental, D. B., Cortez, V., & Blue, J. (1992). Children's affective responses to the expressive cues of others. In N. Eisenberg & R. A. Fabes (Eds.), *Emotion and its regulation in early development: Vol. 55. New directions for child development* (pp. 75–89). San Francisco: Jossey Bass.

Casey, R. J. (1996). Emotional competence in children with externalizing and internalizing disorders. In M. Lewis & M. W. Sullivan (Eds.), *Emotional development in atypical children* (pp. 161–183). Mahwah, NJ: Erlbaum.

Dodge, K. A. (1991). Emotion and social information processing. In J. Garber & K. A. Dodge (Eds.), *The development of emotional regulation and dysregulation* (pp. 159–181). New York: Cambridge University Press.

Dodge, K. A., & Garber, J. (1991). Domains of emotion regulation. In J. Garber & K. A. Dodge (Eds.), *The development of emotional regulation and dysregulation* (pp. 3–11). New York: Cambridge University Press.

Dunn, J., & Brown, J. (1991). Relationships, talk about feelings, and the development of affect regulation in early childhood. In J. Garber & K. A. Dodge, (Eds.), *The development of emotional regulation and dysregulation* (pp. 89–108). New York: Cambridge University Press.

Eisenberg, N., Fabes, R. A., & Losoya, S. (1997). Emotional responding: Regulation, social correlates, and socialization. In P. Salovey & D. J. Sluyter (Eds.), *Emotional development and emotional intelligence: Educational implications* (pp. 129–163). New York: Basic Books.

Furman, E. (1992). *Toddlers and their mothers: A study in personality development*. Madison, WI: International Universities Press.

Furman, E. (1993). *Toddlers and their mothers: Abridged version for parents and educators*. Madison, WI: International Universities Press.

Furman, R. A., Ed. (1995). *Preschoolers: questions and answers: Psychoanalytic consultation with parents, teachers, and caregivers*. Madison, WI: International Press.

Gay, L. R. (1987). *Educational research*. New York: Merrill.

Goodwin, W. L., & Goodwin, L. D. (1993). Young children and measurement: Standardized and nonstandardized instruments in early childhood education. In B. Spodek (Ed.), *Handbook of research on the education of young children* (pp. 441–463). New York: Macmillan.

Graue, M. E., & Walsh, D. J. (1995). Children in context: Interpreting the here and now of children's lives. In J. A. Hatch (Ed.), *Qualitative research in early childhood settings* (pp. 93–126). Westport, CT: Praeger.

Harter, S., & Whitesell, N. R. (1989). Developmental changes in children's understanding of single, multiple, and blended emotion concepts. In C. Saarni & P. Harris (Eds.), *Childhood understanding of emotions* (pp. 81–116). New York: Cambridge University Press.

Hyson, M. C. (1994). *The emotional development of young children: Building an emotion-centered curriculum*. New York: Teachers College Press.

Keenan, K., Shaw, D., Walsh, B., DelliQuadri, E., & Giovannelli, J. (1997). DSM-III-R disorders in preschool children from low-income families. *Journal of the American Academy of Child and Adolescent Psychiatry, 36*(5), 620–636.

Kostelnik, M. J., Stein, L. C., Whiren, A. P., Soderman, A. K., & Soderman, A. K. (1998). *Guiding children's social development* (3rd ed.). Albany, NY: Delmar.

Lazarus, R. S. (1969). *Patterns of adjustment and human effectiveness* (pp. 97–159). New York: McGraw-Hill.

Lavigne, J. V., Gibbons, R. D., Christoffel, K. K., Arend, R., Rosenbaum, D., Binns, H., Dawson, N., Sobel, H., & Issacs, C. (1996). Prevalence rates and correlates of psychiatric disorders among preschool children. *Journal of the American Academy of Child and Adolescent Psychiatry, 35*(2), 204–214.

Lyman, R. D., & Hembree-Kigin, T. L. (1994). *Mental health interventions with preschool children.* New York: Plenum Press.

Mattison, R. E., & Spitznagel, E. L. (1999). Long-term stability of child behavior checklist profile types in a child psychiatric clinic population. *Journal of the American Academy of Child and Adolescent Psychiatry, 38*(6), 700–707.

Mayer, J. D. (1997). What is emotional intelligence? In P. Salovey & D. J. Sluyter (Eds.), *Emotional development and emotional intelligence: Educational implications* (pp. 3–31). New York: Basic Books.

Mayer, J. D., & Salovey, P. (1997). What is emotional intelligence? In P. Salovey & D. J. Sluyter (Eds.), *Emotional development and emotional intelligence: Educational implications* (pp. 3–31). New York: Basic Books.

McGee-Brown, M. J. (1995). Multiple voices, contexts, and methods: Making choices in qualitative evaluation in early childhood education settings. In J. A. Hatch (Ed.), *Qualitative research in early childhood settings* (pp. 191–211). Westport, CT: Praeger.

Neven, R. S. (1996). *Emotional milestones from birth to adulthood: A psychodynamic approach.* London: Jessica Kingsley.

Weider, S., & Greenspan, S. I. (1993). The emotional basis of learning. In B. Spodek (Ed.), *Handbook of research on the education of young children* (pp. 77–87). New York: Macmillan.

Wittmer, D., Doll, B., & Strain, P. (1996). Social and emotional development in early childhood: The identification of competencies and disabilities. *Journal of Early Intervention, 20*(4), 299–318.

Chapter 5

Creating a Classroom Community Where Social Emotional Learning Thrives: The Case of the "Cool Girls" List

Ruth Charney, M.S., M.Ed. and *Roxann Kriete*

Northeast Foundation For Children

Can we teach children to be kind, to solve conflicts without violence, to reach out to new or different classmates, to want to do their most beautiful work? We know we can teach them to read. Can we also help them take better care of themselves, each other, and their environment?

THE SOCIAL CURRICULUM

At Greenfield Center School, founded in 1981 as a laboratory school for Northeast Foundation for Children, we believe that the answer is "Yes." We are convinced that how children learn social skills and develop emotional and ethical literacy is similar to how they learn to read. They learn by doing, by practicing, and by talking about the experiences that result from the doing and the practicing. This learning is enhanced by supportive relationships with teachers in classrooms where the students feel safe.

If we believe that social learning matters, then we must give it time in our day and in our curriculum. In the 17 years since our school's founding, we have collected, borrowed, invented, refined, tried out, and sometimes discarded strategies that give students the chance to practice social skills. Our approach to teaching and learning, The Responsive Classroom, integrates the teaching of social and academic skills throughout the school day. For example, in a structure called Morning Meeting, students start the day in a circle, with greetings and sharing of important news, with a playful and mind-tickling activity.

A social curriculum is important, not just for certain children, like Malika and Steven in Barbara Eisold's discussion in Chapter 2, but for all children. Strong social skills nourish academic and personal growth because they foster confidence, competence, and curiosity. The good news is that teachers and schools can provide all this while teaching academic skills. In fact, social and academic skills are interwoven and synergistic.

Practicing Social Skills

A social curriculum, like any good educational curriculum, includes intentional methods, developmentally appropriate practices, and instruction based on what we know about how children learn best. Social and ethical literacy, like reading literacy, flourish when students are provided a mix of direct instruction, coaching, and opportunities to practice and when they are surrounded by models who value and practice the skills. Just as we want our students to see us enjoying the act of reading, so too do we want them to see us greeting each other cordially in the morning and expressing our differing opinions directly and courteously.

Caring, assertion, responsibility, empathy, and self-control are part of our routines and our expectations all through the day, every day—through reading and math groups, lunch, dismissal, and recess times.

"How's your grandma feeling today?" I hear a teacher ask a third grader. Better yet, one second grader approaches another second grader who sits alone to ask, "Want to join our game?"

"Find another way to ask me for help," the teacher tells a third grader who whines and fusses during math group. When a first grader comes running over with a problem, her teacher encourages her to try out her own conflict mediation skills: "Do you have some words you can use to tell Charles he is bothering you?"

Opportunistic Teaching

The best teaching is opportunistic as well as planned. Not only does it use direct instruction, modeling, and structures for practice, but it also capitalizes on the opportunities that spring up spontaneously all around us.

My third grade reading group and I were on a field trip to see a matinee version of the book we had just finished. Jonathan came to me after going through the box office line, clutching a handful of coins and some wadded-up bills. "I gave him a 10-dollar bill. Is this enough back?" he wondered. It was a wonderful real-life opportunity to practice the very skills we had been working on in math group. Did I ignore the question or hand him the answer because it wasn't math group time? Of course not. With 15 minutes left before the movie was due to start, we circled up, calculated together the difference between $2.75 and $10, and counted and compared Jonathan's handful of money. With 6 minutes to spare the group realized that, in fact, Jonathan had gotten back one dollar too many. Jonathan and a friend trotted back to the box office, delighted both by the chance to demonstrate their virtue and by the knowledge that even grown-ups who handle money in their jobs can make mistakes in this tricky business.

Opportunities for situational learning abound in the social realm too, and I believe that we must seize them, if we are serious about social learning. I think that sometimes we avoid dealing with social issues because we ourselves are not so sure of the right answers. While there is not a lot of ambiguity involved in subtracting $2.75 from $10, the questions raised by social issues often have multiple answers and implications: Is talking about other people always bad? Is teasing ever okay? How do you stop being bullied on the bus? We must not let our fear of not having the right answers or our knowledge that some situations do not have right answers keep us from addressing them. The very process of problem solving with our students about real behaviors and conflicts has import with its recognition and naming of problems and the ensuing dialogue. It gives weight and purpose to both social and intellectual growth.

Recently I heard a story illustrating my worry that, even in classrooms with a strong social curriculum, we sometimes avoid real social issues when they occur, thus passing up key moments for teaching and learning. Along with the real story, I will outline what might have happened and how some tools of intervention might have been brought to bear productively.

THE "COOL GIRLS" LIST: LEARNING FROM MISTAKES

A number of sixth-grade boys had prepared a list rating all the sixth-grade girls according to a criterion of "cool girl-ness." Somehow, and not surprisingly, the list had circulated quickly around the classroom so that almost everyone—girls and boys—read it before it mysteriously made its way to the teacher's desk. When the teacher came back from lunch and found it on his desk, he read it, tossed it in the trash, and said nothing. For the time being, the problem went away. Or did it?

The problem is not a single list, nor even the tendency of children of this age to sort, sift, and rate one another. They are moving into the stage where peers are of central concern and many are already consumed with the business of attractions, social appeal, and power. As they enter this stage and learn to deal with new issues that accompany it, they are going to make mistakes. The impact of these mistakes can be harsh and lasting and can affect academic performance. It does not work to ignore the gaggles of girls rushing to exchange gossip in the bathrooms, the snickering of the boys, the teasing and tormenting asides in the corners of our playgrounds or classrooms.

Whether or not we intervene, children will learn from their mistakes. What they learn and how they learn it, however, are greatly influenced by responsible adult leadership.

In this case, without adult response, the children who wield the sixth-grade power, who write up the lists, are learning negative uses of power. Many of the children at the bottom are learning to defend themselves through silence and passivity. All are receiving a message of adult endorsement of, or impotence in the face of, a social game whose rules reinforce a tyranny of popularity and social hierarchies. These rules permit children to act with cruelty, exclusion, and indifference toward one another.

Rather than tossing the list—or the children who wrote it—in the trash, I suggest that the tools of The Responsive Classroom be brought to bear on the problem. Our best intervention is the way we work together to think about hard questions. I do not suggest that we invite children to make up their own rules or that we necessarily impose our own, but that we lead a dialogue that stretches and pushes for empathy and ethical growth. Our work will seldom provide tidy solutions or magical transformations, but it will produce visions of new alternatives and the seeds of understandings.

The Best Tools to Create a Positive Community

The tools I refer to are helpful both proactively to create a community where positive social behaviors thrive and reactively to address negative behaviors when they occur. These tools are as follows:

- The creation of a classroom community in which everyone knows each other—their names, their interests, their favorite subjects
- Strong relationships between teachers and students built over months of lessons, morning meetings, reading and math groups, and trips
- An expectation of and procedures for group problem solving practiced in problems like setting up rules, deciding how to do cleanup, and figuring out how to make recess more fun and safe

- Techniques of class meetings in which procedures for conflict resolution such as expressing different opinions, active listening, and compromise have been practiced.

A climate created and tended by these tools not only makes for less cruel behavior, but also makes it easier to address when it does happen. The teacher must determine whether an incident should be dealt with as a class incident or on an individual basis. The "cool girls" list involved those who made it, circulated it, read it, and were on it, and it impacted everyone's sense of the classroom as a place of safety, friendliness, and respect. Although a few children did not even know about it and only a few really instigated the list, it affected all and it was a concrete and practical opportunity put to some use in order to help everyone gain empathy. Also, simply blaming the instigators would close down the learning. It was definitely a class incident.

Steps in Leading Learning Conversations

Working with a group to help them learn from mistakes is never prescriptive or easy. Teachers need time to think about the situation and not just react. They need to reflect in order to find words that open up discussion rather than accusations, to ask good questions, and to assert their own convictions with care. I suggest the following steps:

1. *After there is time to think, set up a time for a meeting.* Sometimes, before a whole-class meeting, it is helpful to speak with some individuals involved. In this case, I would speak with the initial list makers first and then with the whole class. I hope to help some of the more dominant students use their "say" appropriately and those with too little power dare to speak out. Premeeting conversations provide a rehearsal that can help the quality of the larger discussion. I have heard a student try out a statement in the safety of a conversation with me as the only listener and decide it isn't really what she meant, or that it sounds too aggressive or blameful. Had she made it in a group, she might have had a hard time retracting it, risking losing face in front of peers. I have seen a tearful, victimized boy get past his tears in the privacy of an audience with me, enabling him to say to the group how people's "joking" comments have made him feel. Also these rehearsals, with their window into how some of the children most intensely involved feel, help me prepare for my role as leader of the larger conversation.

2. *Set up the ground rules for the discussion.* Describe the concern in ways that avoid blame and accusation. Specific descriptions and "I-voice

statements" are helpful. I might begin, "I was upset by a list I discovered circulating in our classroom."

3. *Point out the general theme or topic.* "This is not about a few people," I continue, "but about how we all make up lists—best friend lists, in-out lists, most popular lists. Or maybe we just think about whom we like most. This is something we all do at some times, in some ways, don't we? Sometimes it's okay. Sometimes it can be very hurtful. I worry that this is one of those times when it becomes hurtful." The first part of this framing enlarges the topic, connects it to something I believe to be a universal human trait with which all can identify. The second part names why it is a problem.

4. *Start with questions that, while closely related, are more general than questions about the particular situation at hand.* For example, "What's the difference between our private, in-our-head lists and public lists? When are public lists okay? When do they become hurtful?" It is much easier for the students to consider a situation one step removed, or abstracted, than one that involves the person sitting next to them or even the students themselves.

5. *Continue the discussion, making sure that conflicting viewpoints are respectfully expressed.* If a few students persist in treating the topic with a sneer or shrugging it off, I must emphasize that I see it as significant and must insist that they at least listen respectfully to a different point of view. There may at first be posturing, acting like it is just a joke. "I don't care if I'm on someone's list," someone says. "Words can't hurt me," adds another. But then one quiet voice adds, "It's embarrassing and makes people feel bad."

6. *Often in these discussions, the lone or less popular position must be protected by the teacher.* "I agree," I say. "When I was younger, I used to pretend that what people said didn't hurt me, but it did." With this I reinforce that they are able to hurt each other as well as help each other, that their actions are powerful.

7. *Spend time trying to help children gain perspective.* "What are some reasons people circulate lists?" I might pose. Over and over, I am impressed with how readily children recognize and articulate such motivations as the desire for power or fear of being scapegoated. Often I ask questions that require them to switch positions: "If you were at the bottom of such a list, what would you feel?"

8. *Generate alternative behaviors.* "If a list gets passed to us, instead of circulating it, what can we do? Do we have to read it, pass it on?" And just as I often begin with general questions, I often move a discussion back to that plane. It is so important to remind students (and ourselves) of the significance of what can seem like trivial acts. "Can you stop things that

you don't think are fair?" I also try to honor the need for fun that is often at least one motivator of mischief. There is often a real quest for humor intertwined with the hurt in teasing, for example. In this case I ask, "Instead of making up hurtful lists, what are some fun surveys we might create?"

9. *Role reversals and new strategies lend themselves to the technique of role-play.* In this case, I generate an on-the-spot list in the notebook on my lap, tear out the sheet, and fold it over. "Hey, you wanna see my list of who are the really good kids in this class?" I ask in my best 12-year-old conspiratorial whisper. I invite the class to stop me. Hopefully they will.

A Case Study Approach

Students, as well as their teachers, can benefit from a case study approach, from the opportunity to examine a real-life situation not from their own real life. I actually brought this problem, the case of the "cool girls" list, to my own seventh- and eighth-grade class. Their first reactions were predictable. The initial people to raise their hands said that the list was nothing, didn't matter, no big deal.

"So what?" one of the eighth grade boys asked.

Then a few girls chose to speak. "If I were on that list, I'd be embarrassed," said the first.

"It would depend on who wrote it," commented the next.

"I don't think so," someone else retorted. "I'd feel bad anyway, especially if I were at the bottom."

I asked who thought the list did matter and quite a number raised their hands, first cautiously, not too high, and then more assertively. Later, when discussing in literature group the journey Maya Angelou makes towards self-acceptance, we talked about a valentine card she got.

"How did that help her feel better about herself?" I asked. And these eighth graders, versed in the doubts and mirror images of popularity, reflected on the power of feeling liked. "So back to the 'cool girls' list," I say. "Is it harmless to feel not liked?"

CONCLUSION

In a social curriculum, we pay attention to how children play, make or sustain friendships, ask and answer questions, take risks, and reach out to enjoy what is hard or new or scary. Our attention reveals the importance of the social context in which so much is actually learned, where critical teaching must occur, and where our hardest decisions must be made. Often, it also reveals the complexity and confusion of social life in the class-room.

In this realm of much uncertainty, at least one thing I know for sure. Children, even if they appear resistant, listen and care. They want to know that what they do matters. They want to know that adults will recognize their efforts to be kind and just, and that those same adults will see them and care about them, even when the adults don't always approve.

"What do you want in a high school?" I ask Kevin, an eighth grader about to graduate.

"I want teachers who know me," he says.

"Know you how?" I ask.

"Well, like help me and not be so mad if I get in trouble. I don't know . . . whatever . . . " he adds as frustration spills out of a space words can't fill.

"Do you mean that teachers will know you are smart, that you some-times do stupid things, and they will still like you?"

His crooked grin expressed affirmation. "Yeah," he nods. "That they'll help me and not get so angry."

REFERENCES

Berman, S. (1997). *Children's social consciousness and the development of social responsibility*. Albany: State University of New York Press.

Charney, R. S. (1992). *Teaching children to care: Management in the Responsive Classroom*. Greenfield, MA: Northeast Foundation for Children.

Clayton, M. K. (1995). *Places to start: Implementing the developmental classroom* [Videotape]. Greenfield, MA: Northeast Foundation for Children.

Kriete, R. (1999). *The morning meeting book*. Greenfield, MA: Northeast Foundation for Children.

Noddings, N. (1992). *The challenge to care in schools: An alternative approach to education*. New York: Teachers College Press.

Paley, V. G. (1992). *You can't say you can't play*. Cambridge, MA: Harvard University Press.

Wood, C. (1997). *Yardsticks: Children in the classroom, ages 4–14*. Greenfield, MA: Northeast Foundation for Children.

Part III

PROGRAMMATIC EFFORTS

Part III of this volume provides a representative range of programmatic efforts that educators can use with young children. The programmatic efforts presented in this section include detailed, curricular-based materials that have been studied empirically and proven effective over time.

All of these translate the core principles described in Chapter 1 in their own way. Some emphasize cooperative learning, literature and building caring communities (Chapter 6); others focus on an array of social and emotional skills and related sets of understandings (Chapter 7); others underscore the fundamental importance of creative and adaptive problem-solving capacities (Chapter 8); some have been used with special education populations as well as regular education; and some focus on the bully-victim-bystander cycle as a simple but very powerful way of influencing the culture and climate of the school, as well as skill building (Chapter 10).

Chapter 6

FOSTERING EMOTIONAL INTELLIGENCE IN THE CLASSROOM AND SCHOOL: STRATEGIES FROM THE CHILD DEVELOPMENT PROJECT

Stefan Dasho, Ph.D., *Catherine Lewis*, Ph.D., and *Marilyn Watson*, Ph.D.

Developmental Studies Center

The Child Development Project (CDP) is a comprehensive elementary school reform program designed to promote children's fullest social, emotional, intellectual, and ethical development. It seeks to help schools use the umbrella concept of A Caring Community for Learning to focus on four key goals or principles:

- Building supportive relationships
- Teaching humane values
- Fostering children's intrinsic motivation
- Teaching for understanding

HISTORY OF THE PROJECT

Initially our work at the Developmental Studies Center in Oakland, California, focused on conducting longitudinal research on the effects of emphasizing prosocial development during the elementary school years. A cohort of students entering kindergarten in six schools was followed through sixth grade, with half the schools participating in the CDP staff development. (Results of the research are described later.) The Child Development Project provided staff development to help teachers address the social and ethical domain in their teaching. Over the course of 20 years of collaborating with schools, our work changed in two major ways. First, we began to realize that the kind of teaching and school environment we were seeking to create could not be simply "put in place" in classrooms. We needed to affect teachers' and administrators' attitudes and learning philosophy as well as the culture of the schools. Therefore, we began to address systemic school reform (Watson, Kendzior, Dasho, Rutherford, & Solomon, 1998). In our subsequent projects we have worked with entire schools to include the faculty, administrators, paraprofessionals, and support staff, for 3 to 4 years in order to fully implement CDP. Second, to help teachers learn to integrate the social and ethical domains and to provide models of constructivist teaching, we also developed K–8 curriculum.

SCHOOLING: THE LONG-TERM VIEW

Educators must keep *all* goals of schooling in mind if we are to avoid pendulum swings between the social and academic goals of education (Lewis, Schaps, & Watson, 1995). Social and emotional learning can be pursued in ways that promote academic development (Lewis, 1995; Solomon, Battistich, Watson, Schaps, & Lewis, 2000), but can also be pursued in ways that undermine academic development, for example, when teachers try to create a supportive environment for students by lowering their academic standards. Since social, emotional, ethical, and intellectual learning occur within the same child and influence each other, the Child Development Project seeks educational practices that will foster all these areas simultaneously. What kind of classroom and schoolwide practices simultaneously promote children's social, emotional, ethical, and intellectual development? Theory, basic research, and our findings from the Child Development Project (see final section of this chapter) suggest that a "caring community of learners" is most likely to foster students' full development (Battistich, Solomon, Watson, & Schaps, 1997). Our first principle, building supportive relationships, comes from the research on attachment, which suggests the primacy of the need for secure bonding as the basis for psychological health (Baumrind, 1967; Sroufe, 1983).

   In a caring community of learners, all children feel like valued members of the school and classroom community, and in turn, they value the community and want to maintain their attachment to it. Embedded in the second and fourth principles—teaching humane values and teaching for understanding—are assumptions about learning and development. First, following the work of structural developmentalists (e.g., Kohlberg, Turiel, Nucci, & Berkowitz), we take the position that children's social and moral development involves constructive meaning making. Students need to experience opportunities to think and act on their understanding and to evaluate their actions in order to push their development. Second, we believe that it is the adult role to serve as a moral model and guide. As Figure 6.1 highlights, social emotional learning (SEL) entails three domains: development of cognitive understanding (thinking), development of skills (action), and development of will (motivation).

The development of will underlies the third principle, fostering intrinsic motivation. CDP conceives of a *caring community* as one in which students' basic psychological needs are being met. These needs include belonging (attachment), competence (mastery motivation), and autonomy (individuation) (Brophy, 1999; Deci & Ryan, 1985). Students' attachment to the school and classroom community is important because social and emotional intelligence is a matter of *will* as well as *skill*. Our premise is that

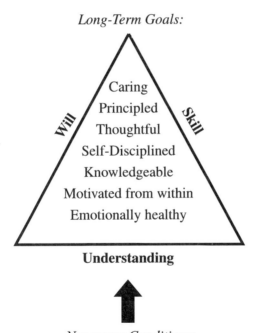

FIGURE 6.1. Elements of Schools that Promote Social Emotional Development

when students experience school as a community, they are motivated to care about its values—to engage in conflict resolution, perspective taking, and respectful conversation—and to use the other social and emotional skills they are learning.

The Child Development Project includes several program components that may be used singly or in combination. Each component attends to all three domains (skills, understanding, will). Skills are familiar components of many SEL programs and include, for example, taking turns in a conversation, eliciting the needs of both sides in a conflict, and checking that someone actually wants help before we engage in helping. Similarly, many SEL programs focus on building students' cognitive understanding of, for example, what it means to be "responsible," or of the situations that lead people to make choices they later regret. Discussion and reflection—thinking deeply about one's behavior and learning—are woven throughout our program components.

CDP's third emphasis, on will (motivation), is less common in SEL programs and flows from the experience of school as a caring community. When students feel supported and valued at school, they will be disposed to care about its values, such as kindness, helpfulness, responsibility, and so forth. Further, children's motivation to put social skills and understanding into practice will be greatest if the school emphasizes the *intrinsic* reasons to be kind, fair, and responsible—such as the good feeling it gives you or the need to make the world a better place—rather than relying on *external* rewards, recognition, praise, and so forth (Lewis, Watson, & Schaps, 1999). Why does a sense of community benefit students in these ways? Like a good family, a high-community school forges strong affective bonds that are essential to students' motivation, character, and citizenship.

In the 1980s and 1990s, the Child Development Project was chosen as a whole-school professional development focus in about 20 elementary schools across the United States. Teachers, administrators, and support staff in these schools spent 3 years building all of the program components described in the next section. In addition, these educators examined school policies, practices, and traditions to assess whether they fostered or undermined the goals or principles presented above, such as building supportive relationships among members of the school community, intrinsic motivation, and so forth.

PROGRAM COMPONENTS IN THE CLASSROOM

This section describes the four major components of the classroom program: classroom community building, cooperative learning, literature-based reading, and developmental discipline. Interspersed with descriptions of practices that can help teachers reflect on this child-centered approach to teaching are examples of how the needs of the two children profiled by Eisold in Chapter 2, Steven and Malika, might be met by a CDP teacher.

Classroom Community Building

Educators in CDP schools systematically deepen their practice in several areas in order to build classroom community:

1. *Unity-building activities.* Students share their experiences and ideas in a way that is enjoyable and accessible to students of all academic levels. This is done intensely at the beginning of the year, but continues throughout the year, especially when students are working in new groups.

2. *Teacher-student bonds.* Teachers share their own experiences—for example, their childhood joys and fears, their hobbies, their favorite books—in order to connect personally with students. Teachers make time to get to know each student.

3. *Regular informal collaboration.* Throughout the day, students have opportunities to hear each other's ideas. For example, a simple but powerful tool is "partner chats," in which students spend just a minute or so talking with a partner about the topic under discussion. This technique is particularly helpful when few students are volunteering ideas about the topic under discussion or, alternatively, when everyone wants to speak up.

4. *Peer help.* Sometimes there are also opportunities for students to help one another. Our approach emphasizes explicit teaching of the social skills and emotional context of helping, for example, thinking about and noticing the feelings of the person receiving help.

5. *Class meetings.* Students have the opportunity to take personal responsibility in helping to run the classroom. Our approach emphasizes the use of class meetings for a variety of purposes including building trusting relationships, building class norms (see developmental discipline, below), problem solving, and building a positive identity as a class. Students are explicitly taught the social skills of decision making, goal setting, and evaluating plans. These and other uses of class meetings are described in the book *Ways We Want Our Class to Be* (Developmental Studies Center, 1996b). Developmentally, our approach emphasizes ways to help students move from relatively concrete to more abstract ways of thinking about social interaction (e.g., from specific rules like "no pinching" to big ideas like "respect others") and from ego-centered understanding of events to an understanding of the perspectives of many other class members.

Although these practices may be present in today's classrooms, we must consider three factors in using them in a student-centered way to foster development:

- *Intensity*. Is this community pervasive and inclusive enough for students to feel its benefits?
- *Instruction*. Is the child supported so that he can negotiate the interactional demands of being a member of the community?
- *Need-satisfaction*. Are situational demands orchestrated in a way that builds on, rather than undermines, students' needs for Autonomy, Belonging, and Competence—the ABCs of intrinsic motivation?

It is through the lens of classroom community building that a teacher would examine ways to build relationships with students like Malika. Fundamental to making progress with such children is overcoming the barriers to establishing trust. For example, unity-building activities should avoid public "spotlighting." Thus class meetings might use prewrites so that Malika could contribute in writing without having to draw attention to herself. Unity builders could involve partner interviews to build shared understanding or partner products to contribute to a whole-class mural or display. The teacher might initiate a personal relationship with Malika through writing, using journals or pen pals. The teacher would carefully select partners for Malika's collaborative assignments, rather than use random assignment or student self-selection. Later, building on her positive relationship with Malika and on Malika's academic competence, the teacher could design safe opportunities for Malika to develop the ability to speak within a public forum. Involving Malika in setting a goal for class participation would help meet her need for autonomy. Using unity-building activities and class meetings, the teacher would systematically create an atmosphere of trust within which Malika's acceptance and her circle of friends would grow.

Cooperative Learning

In the early years of our work, cooperative learning was not yet widespread in the United States. Despite its recent spread, we believe that the potential value of cooperative learning to promote both academic and social emotional learning is seldom realized. Our approach to cooperative learning, outlined in *Blueprints for a Cooperative Classroom* (Developmental Studies Center, 1997), differs from many others in its focus on the following features:

- Choosing engaging, important tasks that enhance students' intrinsic motivation to learn, rather than relying on rewards or grades to encourage performance

- Emphasizing how students work together (e.g., how to show respect, responsibility, and helpfulness) as well as the academic task
- Asking students to reflect on how they worked together, so that they will develop a rich, concrete understanding of how to show qualities such as respect and responsibility in their group work and so that they will hear groupmates' perspectives

The importance of *how* students work together deserves to be highlighted. Some research suggests that cooperative learning benefits children socially, intellectually, and motivationally only if group members are helpful, friendly, collaborative, and concerned about each other. When small group members treat each other in a disrespectful, unfriendly manner, increased time spent in small groups is actually associated with *decreases* in liking for school, intrinsic motivation, academic achievement, and experience of the classroom as a caring community (Battistich, Solomon, & Delucchi, 1993).

CDP's approach to cooperative learning provides opportunities to build community, to hold up social interaction skills to the light of analysis, and to feel the benefits of having contributed to the success of the group. A new student in one sixth-grade class was clearly an "outsider": his shaved head and disconnection from any class discussion were outward signs of his alienation. He spent much time with his cherished Dungeons and Dragons notebook in which he had drawn characters and written elaborate descriptions of them. When the class studied mythology, the teacher assigned students to work in pairs to write a myth, assigning him to work with a boy who was friendly and academically skilled but lacked imagination. After their work was presented to the class, the new student received much recognition for his artwork and storytelling, speeding a positive connection to his classmates. This example might be instructive when applied to Steven. The teacher—recognizing that Steven is compensating for his problematic home relations (unmet needs for belonging) through his fantasy—might look for a way to help plug him into social relationships by helping him demonstrate his active fantasy (thereby meeting his need for competence). This talent could be turned to constructive use if the curriculum allows him to channel it. We assume he might focus attention more successfully in an activity he finds personally engaging.

Partnerships (rather than larger groups) may be preferable when students are young or new to the process of collaboration. As the challenge of managing decisions and dividing up tasks increases with group size, these children may become frustrated, unable to use their best social skills and unable to produce their best academic work. As children become older, tasks should be increasingly open-ended and roles increasingly flexible so that students are able to rise to their own level of meaningful challenge and learn to make their own decisions and evaluate them. With development, students need to move away from contrived ways of participating and toward natural, adult interactions.

For example, consider the common rule that each person takes a turn speaking before anyone can speak again. This makes for "smooth" interaction, but it doesn't help students develop the social competence to enter a conversation appropriately, to practice monitoring a conversation in order to encourage a quiet member to speak, or to withhold one's own comments until hearing what others have to say. This example points to the difference between practices that serve short-term goals (immediate social performance) versus long-term goals (mature social competence).

For both Steven and Malika, the teacher should carefully plan to engage their interest, provide preparation and structure to allow them to interact successfully, and provide instruction to develop self-awareness (metacognition) and disclosure. Malika would benefit from having female partners outside of her erstwhile African American circle of friends, in particular friends whom Malika could respect as writers. The teacher might monitor the partnerships, spending time with them to debrief their work process as well as to encourage them with positive feedback about the quality of their work.

Literature-Based Reading

Literature provides a rich arena for learning in the social, emotional, ethical, and academic areas. Through reading and discussing good literature, students can not only become eager, able readers, but they can also develop deeper understanding of human relationships, of experiences of people different from them, of humane values, and of their own part in a larger community.

The Developmental Studies Center has developed teacher guides for over 200 children's books, from wordless picture books to eighth-grade novels for adolescents. The books are high-quality children's literature, selected specifically to promote social and emotional learning, as well as academic development. Good children's literature often addresses issues that are developmentally salient for students—for example, insecurities about making friends for young children; bullying, gender roles, and prejudice for middle-grade students; cliques and gang membership for upper-grade students. Identifying with book characters who face such issues and discussing them can provide a safe arena to think deeply about problems students may encounter in their own lives at school or outside of school.

The literature offerings include read-aloud books at all grade levels. This enables all class members, whatever their reading abilities (e.g., Steven), to have access to the core curriculum and to engage in discussion about the chosen books. It also models how thoughtful readers work to comprehend important ideas in text, and it focuses children on what books have to say about relationships. This frame of "thinking and caring" is then carried over into the student-read books and their accompanying activities. The literature guides for each book provide cooperative activities, discussion prompts, related poetry and prose readings, and cross-disciplinary extension activities, thus easing the burden for teachers who want to use good literature to promote social and emotional, as well as intellectual, development.

Essential to social and emotional learning is the encouragement of perspective taking. In Steven's case, literature discussion could provide a forum for him to display his empathy (evidenced by his loving treatment of his sister), as well as to hear examples of children dealing with family difficulties. For Malika, hearing the experiences of story characters who have divided loyalties might offer a catalyst for expressing her situation in the follow-up writing activities. Later, class discussion and partner reading activities to create honest dialogue with white students in the context of these stories might provide ways for Malika (who seems developmentally ready to tolerate ambiguity) to move to a more complex understanding of human relations.

Developmental Discipline

When a second-grade teacher returned to her classroom after a break, she was surprised to find that her students had convened a class meeting and were intently discussing a problem that had come up during recess. They listened carefully to one another's ideas and solved the problem, while she observed from the sidelines (Kohn, 1990a).

Discipline, in most educational writing, connotes student obedience and the methods to elicit it; however, we mean something quite different, namely, the qualities of heart and mind that will enable children to sustain a humane, caring society. The second graders who spontaneously cut short recess to solve a class problem already show such qualities: a sense of responsibility for problems that threaten the common good, willingness to take initiative in solving these problems, and some skills (such as convening a community meeting and listening to each other) needed to work collaboratively toward solutions. How did the students develop these qualities?

Much of the answer to this question can be found in the qualities of the caring community of learners described early in this chapter: in the valued human relationships that make children *want* to behave responsibly; in the opportunities to understand what it means to be a kind, helpful member of the school community that occur throughout the curriculum and daily school life; in the emphasis on reflection and choosing to do right; in the models for social skills and for enacting positive relationships; and in the opportunities to practice these responsible behaviors. Practices central to developmental discipline are described in the sections that follow.

Build Trusting Relationships. When children begin the school year by getting to know one another as people, there is, in the words of one teacher "no opportunity for the picked-on child to emerge." As children have partner interviews (brief interviews in which, for example, each partner has one minute to talk about a favorite hobby while the partner listens), children discover common interests as well as learn what matters to others. (See Dalton & Watson, 1997, for many such unity-building activities.) Similarly, when children share titles of their favorite mysteries, fantasy stories, nonfiction, and so forth on butcher-paper graffiti boards, they build connections to other students *and* to reading.

When teachers embrace the goal of building trusting relationships, they may choose to discontinue common disciplinary practices (such as putting names of misbehaving children on the board) because of their ill effects on relationships among children. We know a 5-year-old who tearfully insisted on refusing a classmate's birthday party invitation because the friend's name had been put on the blackboard for talking out of turn: "I can't invite a *bad person* to my birthday party."

Even "rewards" can end up humiliating children and undermining the friendships among them, as top earners come to be envied and low earners to be seen as bad. (We know a teacher who stopped giving out daily "Good job!" slips because children who did not receive slips were derogated by their peers and even punished by some parents.) When children are persistently focused on their own performance—as they must be in classrooms where certificates, prizes, and points are the currency of self-worth—their attention is diverted from the needs and feelings of others, the very grist of social and ethical development. Even such seemingly benign standbys as "Look how nicely Darlene is sitting. Everyone should be sitting like Darlene" are invidious comparisons that over time erode relationships among students. Contrast it with "Everyone check yourself out. See if you're sitting like we agreed we should sit."

The goal of building trusting relationships means that practices found in other schools—for example, Special Person of the Week—are often modified to better promote human relationships; for example, each class member becomes a Special Person in turn, rather than as a reward for good behavior or grades. Many of the techniques that teachers traditionally use to maintain control—such as warnings and time-out—can be modified to avoid humiliating children. Instead of waiting until the teacher is ready for students to feel contrite in time-out, students are asked to take the responsibility to get themselves under control and decide when they are ready to return to the table group or discussion circle and participate. In this way the teacher sends a message that the children are competent and allows the students the autonomy to return. This not only maintains the children's dignity but avoids setting up a grudge.

To help students who have persistent difficulties with self-control, some teachers work with them to develop a private signal: some cue of body or voice that reminds them to control a disruptive behavior such as talking or getting up. Similarly, rather than calling the names of inattentive students, a teacher might issue the general request, Check yourself out! to cue all class members to notice whether their behavior is appropriate.

Clearly, Malika is not about to be motivated by a teacher who tries to manipulate her behavior. It is likely that both Malika and Steven may resist their teachers' efforts for a prolonged period of time: Steven, because of his lack of self-awareness of how his upset is shaping his behavior, and Malika, because of the sad combination of self-created protective behavior and her mother's admonitions. In these cases, it is essential to avoid becoming oppositional and risk creating a power struggle.

Allow Students to Help Establish and Maintain Class Norms. Students and teacher start the year not with a teacher-made list of rules and consequences, but by asking, What kind of class do we want to be? and discussing the rules that will allow them to live up to those aspirations (Developmental Studies Center, 1996b). Often, this is not a simple process. Students may come up with detailed prescriptions—no hitting, no cussing, no copying, no calling someone's mother a name—and need help seeing that these specific dos and don'ts suggest larger values such as respect and responsibility. When students are invested in these shared norms, the role of the teacher changes. The teacher is neither a boss who demands obedience, nor a manipulator who bribes and coerces students into compliance, but a moral guide and model who helps students ask, How does our current behavior live up to our aspirations for the class?

Once shared norms have been established, problems provide an opportunity for *all* students to think about their behavior—"not just the 5 or 10 names I might have arbitrarily chosen to put on the board in the past when most of the class was talking," as one teacher describes the change. Who among us, however well-behaved, wouldn't benefit from thinking about how our recent behavior fits our ideals of kindness, respect, and responsibility? An upper-elementary teacher notes how much self-direction her students developed as she shifted to developmental discipline. On their own initiative at a class meeting, students raised their concern that they had little time to play softball at lunchtime because they were wasting so much time choosing up teams. They decided to split the class into teams rather than choose teams daily, and to switch the team at bat at the halfway point. "They came up with that idea themselves. These experiences have shown them that they can do it for themselves. These solutions would not have worked if I had suggested them and imposed them."

When children help forge a solution to a problem, they are likely to try to make it succeed, and in the long run their personal investment can save a great deal of time. In schools where CDP has been established for several years, teachers often note that students come to them from lower grades with stronger problem-solving skills and a greater sense of responsibility; so the investment in children's motivation from within should not be measured over just one school year. Developmentally, students move from reliance on adult moral authority toward increasing reliance on peers; when the peer group has helped to shape norms of the classroom, students do not need to choose between adult and peer values.

After steps have been taken to build trust with Steven and Malika, the teacher would enlist other students to uphold the class norms and provide feedback to them in caring ways. This, of course, presumes that the teacher has worked on teaching the students respectful ways of disagreeing and being assertive, as well as how to respond without retaliation when others are disrespectful.

Adopt a Teaching Approach to Discipline. Many approaches assume that classroom discipline is something you must establish *before* learning can occur. We assume that discipline *is* learning and that disciplinary problems, like other learning problems, demand a careful effort to understand the cause of the problem and to help students build the understanding, skills, and commitment needed to remedy the problem. Just as a student's poor write-up of a science experiment may reflect many different root causes— from poor grasp of the scientific concept to poor writing skills to lack of motivation—misbehavior demands a careful differential diagnosis in the social, emotional, and intellectual domains. Students may not know what behavior is expected, or they may know but lack self-control skills, or they may be so wrapped up in their own needs that they don't grasp the needs and feelings of those around them. Each root cause demands a different solution. A teacher describes his shift to developmental discipline:

My approach to discipline has really changed. Now if students do something that's a problem, I'll say to them, "I think we need to talk. Can I have a little bit of your time, maybe at recess, to talk?" I'll tell them that I think they're not themselves that day, and ask them whether something's wrong. You find out an awful lot that way. Maybe their bird died last night. They really appreciate the time devoted to their needs.

"I'm worried about you. Can we talk after school?" conveys a very different message from "That's once too many. Stay after school." When teachers can take the time to ask the child why a problem is occurring, this often yields unexpected rewards. "The biggest difference in my discipline is that now I think: Why is this child acting up? What might be going on that would make the child act this way?" comments one teacher. Just listening to children can help them, by meeting their needs for attention, self-expression, and human connection. A child's problems do not excuse bad behavior; but understanding why children misbehave can help adults maintain their threads to the most trying children. A principal reflects on the change in her discipline to a teaching approach:

> I'm looking for solutions rather than just punishments. I'm asking students questions like, "What have you learned from this?" and "How can you solve this problem?" That's a big change for me. Instead of looking for the punishment that fits the crime, I'm looking to help the child grow.

In other words, a teaching approach means that teachers work to diagnose why misbehavior is occurring, and help children develop the skills, understanding, and human bonds that will help them avoid similar problems in the future.

Think about Steven. Given his age, it may be better first to work on his social competence to engage others successfully, rather than to target improving his ability to express his inner anxiety. He may not be developmentally ready to link his behavior and his inner states reflectively. This would suggest that skill instruction, such as role-playing problem situations or teaching him the rules for the games he avoids, could help him enter interactive activities. It would be useful to design learning or play situations where his nurturance could be displayed and appreciated by others.

While Malika is not disruptive, she needs to be part of planning and evaluating the social demands of collaboration. This would give her less reason to be argumentative. As she sees that there is opportunity for low-risk input, she may be able to grow into greater comfort with public speaking.

A further part of problem solving is finding ways for students who have transgressed to reestablish themselves as caring, responsible people by, for example, repairing the damage they have done or offering a genuine apology for a hurtful remark. Discipline requires will, skill, *and* understanding. Our discipline approach focuses on all three and on helping teachers diagnose problems and build the social and emotional skills, attachment to school, and understanding needed.

For practical strategies compatible with developmental discipline, some resources are *Beyond Discipline* (Kohn, 1996); *The Caring Teacher's Guide to Discipline* (Gootman, 1997); and *Moral Classrooms, Moral Children* (DeVries & Zan, 1994). While conflict resolution training is widely available, we suggest that all children, rather than just a few mediators, experience training in problem-solving processes that emphasize perspective taking and talking without blame. Resources in this area include the exemplary work of Educators for Social Responsibility including *Creative Conflict Resolution* (Kreidler, 1984).

SCHOOLWIDE ACTIVITIES

In addition to the classroom components, the Child Development Project has schoolwide activities designed to help build supportive relationships among members of the school community, to help students understand and practice important social behaviors such as helping, responsibility, and kindness, and to give students the joy of participating in something larger than themselves.

Students in American schools are typically tracked by age and often by academic achievement, native language, and other identifiers as well. Schoolwide activities can give students a chance to extend values of respect, fairness, and kindness beyond their immediate group of classmates. *At Home in Our Schools* (Developmental Studies Center, 1994) provides plans for many schoolwide activities as well as guidelines for smooth involvement of all members of the school community. A checklist for reflection on current schoolwide activities and a needs assessment enable educators and parents to assess whether their current activities are serving their long-term goals. For example, the redesign of a school science fair illustrates how teachers can reshape traditions to better support goals of building trusting relationships, fostering intrinsic motivation, teaching humane values, and teaching for understanding.

The Science Fair

Traditionally, the science fair at one California elementary school had been a time for upper-grade students to make projects and compete for schoolwide awards. In contrast, this year's "family science festival" transformed the school, for an evening, into a hands-on science museum. A record number of students and family members explored the mysteries of bubbles, magnets, and kitchen chemistry—activities planned and hosted by each class. As teachers worked to reconstruct the science fair, three aspirations guided them. First, they had been looking for ways to deepen and strengthen children's bonds to the school. With gang violence escalating sharply among the city's teenagers, these elementary teachers wanted to create a school that would be more appealing than gangs, by meeting children's needs for friendship, contribution, and belonging in a constructive way. Rather than pitting children against one another, the new science fair would join children in a shared, meaningful pursuit: to plan appealing, informative exhibits. Every child could gain, academically and socially, from contributing to this effort, and there would be no "losers."

Second, teachers had been seeking ways to make students' families feel more welcome at school—including the 50% of parents who spoke a first language other than English. They recognized that families play a critical role in children's development and were eager to provide an inviting and inclusive experience for as many family members as possible. The competitive science fair had provided mixed messages about family involvement: How much family help constituted cheating? By creating winners and losers, it had painfully reminded some parents of their own failures in school. In contrast, the new format unambivalently welcomed families. As others have noted, "Nobody flunks museum" (museum founder Frank Oppenheimer, quoted in Gardner, 1991).

Finally, teachers had become uncomfortable about using awards to motivate science learning. They had noticed that students were more interested in the awards than in the scientific content of the projects. Spurred on by research on the negative impact of rewards, the faculty chose to emphasize the inherent interest and challenge of designing hands-on science exhibits.

Buddy Programs

Buddy programs, in which younger and older classes regularly pair up for shared activities, have become common in recent years. Like our approach to cooperative learning, our approach to buddy programs is explicitly designed with goals of building relationships, practicing important social emotional skills, and the other goals listed at the outset of this chapter. *That's My Buddy* (Developmental Studies Center, 1996a) provides many activities for a buddy program designed with these goals in mind. We have a favorite group of slides that show fifth-grade and kindergarten "buddies' classes" going on a field trip together, touring a museum. A snapshot from the bus ride home shows a kindergartner fast asleep, snuggled up against the shoulder of his fifth grade buddy. Who can doubt that such experiences promote children's attachment to school? For children who have the benefit of a good buddy program or other schoolwide activities that help children know one another as people, contribute in meaningful ways to the welfare of others, and learn the excitement of creating something bigger than one can create alone, school is likely to become a motivating, valued place.

We might surmise that Steven would find some welcome stability in a one-on-one relationship with an older buddy. By contrast, Malika, who doesn't display empathy, might find expression for it in working with a younger child, since more highly charged interaction with other preadolescents would not be involved.

Homeside Activities

Another approach to building connections among members of the school community is to use homeside activities (volumes of material are available through the Developmental Studies Center): reproducible send-home activities for each grade level that engage students in meaningful conversation with parents or other significant adults. These activities help family members understand what students are learning at school and help students build their connections to adults—for example, the child interviews the adult about a childhood friendship and what it meant to the adult; the child interviews the adult about the ways social skills are important in the adult world; or a discussion takes place between the child and adult about childhood family traditions.

Both Steven's and Malika's parents need to be drawn into the effort to address their children's current issues. Even without outreach, the homeside activities could bolster each child. Steven could have a vehicle for maintaining his relationships with his parents and get to know the new man in his mother's life. Malika's mother might gain a more benign view of the intentions of the school, which would soften the distrust and disapproval that her daughter carries to class as a chip on her shoulder.

WHERE TO START

The Child Development Project can be seen as both a comprehensive intervention program and a set of curriculum resources that are grounded in a common vision of a child-centered learning community. As noted earlier in the chapter, the comprehensive CDP approach generally involves a 3-year commitment for an entire school faculty, with workshops and coaching focused on four classroom components (cooperative learning, literature-based reading, community-building, and developmental discipline), as well as schoolwide practices such as the buddy program, homeside activities, and reshaping of school traditions.

In the comprehensive approach, educators are introduced to the components at the beginning and revisit them in more depth in successive years as they gain experience in integrating CDP's key principles in their classroom work. This work is typically supported by grants, Title I funds, or Comprehensive School Reform (Obey-Porter) funds. For schools that want to start with a less intensive approach, or want to build on their own ongoing work with any of the CDP components, less intensive approaches to the creation of a caring community are also possible.

A second starting point is to concentrate on building community at the school level. This approach is offered as a federal model program by the Center for Substance Abuse Prevention. Schools can use Safe Schools funding to do this work. It involves a train-the-trainer approach to allow schools to do an introductory one-day workshop to guide their own year-long staff development. This schoolwide phase combines three components: implementing a program of buddy classrooms, creating a committee to design schoolwide activities that build relationships among students and adults, and using homeside activities to connect students to family members and to school. Schools can also just use curriculum materials and a package of collegial study videotapes to try each of these components.

A third approach is to select one classroom component—literature, math, cooperative learning, or classroom community—as an "entry point" to build community in the classroom. The Developmental Studies Center offers instructional materials, teacher guides, and collegial study videos for children's literature; replacement units for K–6 mathematics focusing on the "number sense" strand; class meetings; and cooperative learning. Whether a gradual or intensive approach is taken, it is essential that all pieces are tied to the caring community philosophy laid out at the beginning of this chapter.

EVIDENCE OF CDP'S EFFECTIVENESS

The Child Development Project has now been implemented and evaluated in three separate longitudinal studies, comparing project schools with demographically comparable nonproject schools. Research methods for these studies include classroom observations by trained observers who are unaware a program is going on as well as questionnaire and interview assessments of students and teachers. The findings suggest that good progress toward implementation can be achieved in a wide range of settings (e.g., high-poverty totally African American schools; affluent, suburban, largely European-American schools), given appropriate levels of district and site support (Battistich, Solomon, Kim, Watson, & Schaps, 1995). When teachers in a school move significantly toward CDP practices, students consistently show positive changes in a broad range of attitudes, feelings, and behaviors (Battistich, Solomon, Watson, Solomon, & Schaps, 1989; Solomon, Watson, Battistich, Schaps, Delucchi, 1996; Solomon, Battistich, Kim, & Watson, 1997). These include increases in the following:

- Commitment to democratic values (including commitments to interpersonal equality, assertion of opinions, and willingness to compromise)
- Conflict resolution skill (attending to the needs and wants of others as well as one's own)
- Concern for others
- Trust in and respect for teachers
- Prosocial motivation (doing positive things for internal reasons)
- Altruistic behavior
- Positive interpersonal behavior in the classroom (helpfulness, kindness, consideration)
- Sense of personal efficacy
- Academic motivation
- Active engagement in class
- Enjoyment of class
- Liking for school

There are decreases in the following situations:

- Loneliness in school
- Social anxiety
- Marijuana and alcohol use

CONCLUSION

In summary, establishing a caring community is important for the development of personal and social qualities (e.g., social competence, concern for others, conflict resolution skill, sense of autonomy, moral reasoning), academic orientations (e.g., liking for school, achievement motivation), and qualities that help students avoid the risk of problematic behaviors (Battistich & Hom, 1997).

It is becoming more and more apparent that creating caring communities in schools has good potential for helping to build students' social and emotional learning, their positive connections to others, their attachment to school, and their consequent resistance to problems such as drug and alcohol abuse, problems for which effective solutions have been remarkably hard to find. With some important exceptions (see Chapters 3, 10, and 11), most academic and social intervention programs—indeed, most educational practices—have been based entirely on models of individual change. Such models ignore the interdependence of the learner and the school environment and the inseparability of cognitive and social emotional development. Although prevention programs have often been provided *in* schools—through pull-out programs, special curricula, or extracurricular activities—in CDP *the process of schooling is itself the prevention program*, one that fosters skills, understanding, and motivation simultaneously.

REFERENCES

Battistich, V., Solomon, D., & Delucchi, K. (1993). Interaction processes and student outcomes in cooperative learning groups. *Elementary School Journal, 94*, 19–32.

Battistich, V., Solomon, D., Kim, D., Watson, M., & Schaps, E. (1995). Schools as communities, poverty levels of student populations and students' attitudes, motives and performance. *American Educational Research Journal, 32*, 627–658.

Battistich, V., Solomon, D., Watson, M., & Schaps, E. (1997). Caring school communities. *Educational Psychologist, 32*(3), 137–151.

Battistich, V., & Hom, A. (1997). The relationship between students' sense of their school as a community and their involvement in problem behaviors. *American Journal of Public Health, 87*, 1997–2001.

Battistich, V., Solomon, D., Watson, M., Solomon, J., & Schaps, E. (1989). Effects of a program to enhance prosocial behavior on children's social problem-solving skills and strategies. *Journal of Applied Developmental Psychology, 10*, 147–169.

Baumrind, D. (1967). Child care practices anteceding three patterns of preschool behaviour. *Genetic Psychology Monographs, 75*, 743–748.

Brody, C., & Davidson, N. (1998). Professional development for cooperative learning: Issues and approaches. Albany: State University of New York Press.

Brophy, J. (1999). Toward a model of the value aspects of motivation in education: Developing appreciation for particular learning domains and activities. *Educational Psychologist, 34*(2), 75–85.

Connell, J. P., & Wellborn, J. G. (1991). Competence, autonomy, and relatedness: A motivational analysis of self-system processes. In M. R. Gunnar & L. A. Sroufe (Eds.), *Minnesota Symposia on Child Psychology* (Vol. 23, pp. 43–77). Hillsdale, NJ: Erlbaum.

Dalton, J., & Watson, M. (1997). *Among friends.* Oakland, CA: Developmental Studies Center.

Deci, E. L., & Ryan, R. M. (1985). *Intrinsic motivation and self-determination in human behavior.* New York: Plenum.

Developmental Studies Center. (1994). *At home in our schools.* Oakland, CA: Author.

Developmental Studies Center. (1996a). *That's my buddy.* Oakland, CA: Author.

Developmental Studies Center. (1996b). *Ways we want our class to be.* Oakland, CA: Author.

Developmental Studies Center. (1997). *Blueprints for a collaborative classroom.* Oakland, CA: Author.

DeVries, R., & Zan, B. (1994). *Moral classrooms, moral children: Creating a constructivist atmosphere in early education.* New York: Teacher's College Press.

Elam, S. M. (1989, June). The second Gallup/Phi Delta Kappa poll of teachers' attitudes toward the public schools. *Phi Delta Kappan,* pp. 785–798.

Elam, S. M., Rose, L. C., & Gallup, A. M. (1993, October). The 25th annual Phi Delta Kappa/Gallup poll of the public's attitudes toward the public schools. *Phi Delta Kappan,* pp. 137–152.

Gardner, H. (1991). *The unschooled mind.* New York: Basic Books.

Gootman, M. E. (1997). *The caring teacher's guide to discipline: Helping young students learn self-control, responsibility, and respect.* Thousand Oaks, CA: Corwin Press.

Kohn, A. (1990a, January). The ABC's of Caring. *Teacher Magazine,* pp. 52–58.

Kohn, A. (1990b). *The brighter side of human nature.* New York: Basic Books.

Kohn, A. (1996). *Beyond discipline: from compliance to community.* Alexandria, VA: Association for Supervision and Curriculum Development (ASCD).

Kreidler, W. J. (1984). *Creative Conflict Resolution: More than 200 activities for keeping peace in the classroom.* Glenview, IL: Scott Foresman & Co.

Lepper, M. R. (1983). Social control processes and the internalization of social values: An attributional perspective. In E. T. Higgins, D. N. Ruble, & W. W. Hartup (Eds.), *Social cognition and social development: A sociocultural perspective* (pp. 294–330). New York: Cambridge University Press.

Lepper, M. R., Keavney, M., & Drake, M. (1996). Intrinsic motivation and extrinsic rewards: A commentary on Cameron and Pierce's meta-analysis. *Review of Educational Research, 66,* 5–32.

Lepper, M. R., Sethi, S., Dialdin, D., & Drake, M. (1997). Intrinsic and extrinsic motivation: A developmental perspective. In S. S. Luthar, J. A. Burack, D. Cicchetti, & J. R. Weisz (Eds.), *Developmental psychopathology: Perspectives on adjustment, risk, and disorder* (pp. 23–50). New York: Cambridge University Press.

Lewis, C. (1995). *Educating hearts and minds: Reflections on Japanese preschool and elementary education.* New York: Cambridge University Press.

Lewis, C., Schaps, E., & Watson, M. (1995). Beyond the pendulum: Creating challenging *and* caring schools. *Kappan, 76*, 547–554.

Lewis, C., Schaps, E., & Watson, M. (1996). The caring classroom's academic edge. *Educational Leadership, 53*, 16–21.

Lewis, C., Watson, M., & Schaps, E. (1997, March). *Conditions for school change: Perspectives from the Child Development Project.* Paper presented at the meeting of the American Educational Research Association, Chicago, IL.

Lewis, C., Watson, M., & Schaps, E. (1999). Recapturing education's full mission: Educating for social, ethical, and intellectual development. In C. Reigeluth (Ed.), *Instructional design theories and models* (Vol. 2). Mahwah, NJ: Erlbaum.

Rigby, C. S., Deci, E. L., Patrick, B. C., & Ryan, R. M. (1992). Beyond the intrinsic-extrinsic dichotomy: Self-determination in motivation and learning. *Motivation and Emotion, 16*(3), 165–185.

Schaps, E. (1997, January). Pushing back for the center. *Education Week*, p. 20.

Solomon, D., Battistich, V., Kim, D., & Watson, M. (1997). Teacher practices associated with students' sense of the classroom as a community. *Social Psychology of Education, 1*, 235–267.

Solomon, D., Watson, M., Battistich, V., Schaps, E., & Delucchi, K. (1996). Creating a caring community: Educational practices that promote children's prosocial development. In F. K. Oser, A. Dick, & J. L. Patry (Eds.), *Effective and responsible teaching: The new synthesis* (pp. 383–395). San Francisco: Jossey-Bass.

Solomon, D., Battistich, V., Kim, D., & Watson, M. (1997). Teachers' practices associated with students' sense of the classroom as a community. *Social Psychology of Education, 1*, 235–267.

Solomon, D., Battistich, V., Watson, M., Schaps, E., & Lewis, C. (2000). *A six-district study of educational change: Direct and mediated effects of the Child Development Project. A Social Psychology of Education, 4*, 3–51.

Sroufe, L. A. (1983). Infant-caregiver attachment and patterns of adaptation in the preschool: The roots of competence and maladaptation. In M. Perlmutter (Ed.), *Minnesota Symposia on Child Psychology* (Vol. 16, pp. 41–83). Hillsdale, NJ: Erlbaum.

Watson, M., Kendzior, S., Dasho, S., Rutherford, S., & Solomon, D. (1998). A social constructivist approach to cooperative learning and staff development: Ideas from the Child Development Project. In C. M. Brody & N. Davidson (Eds.), *Professional development for cooperative learning: Issues and approaches* (pp. 147–168). Albany: State University of New York Press.

Chapter 7

REACH OUT TO SCHOOLS:
A SOCIAL COMPETENCY PROGRAM

Pamela Seigle, M.S.
The Stone Center, Wellesley College

In 1987, I led a group of six public school teachers from two diverse elementary schools in Framingham, Massachusetts, in piloting a social competency project based at the Stone Center at Wellesley College. We used class meetings and a coordinated set of classroom activities (Schelkun, 1987) to address the social emotional learning needs of elementary school students. We hoped to improve the climate in elementary classrooms by teaching specific social competency skills, thereby increasing students' ability to work cooperatively and to solve interpersonal problems.

PROGRAM OVERVIEW

The success of our pilot effort and the enthusiasm of the participating teachers led to the creation of the Reach Out to Schools: Social Competency Program, a comprehensive multiyear social emotional learning program for elementary school children in kindergarten through fifth grade. At the heart of the program is the recognition of the important role that relationships play in the academic and social success of children and the challenge of supporting caring, respectful school communities with high expectations for all students.

The focus of the program's direct work with students is a yearlong, grade-differentiated social competency curriculum for elementary school classrooms. The *Open Circle Curriculum* (Seigle, Lange, & Macklem, 1999) has evolved in content and style over the years in response to the recommendations of participating teachers and observations by program staff, but the essence of the curriculum has remained constant, focusing on three areas: communication, self-control, and social problem solving. The curriculum is taught in the context of a class meeting known as Open Circle. Twice a week, students gather their chairs into a circle, always including an extra chair as a symbol of welcome and inclusion in the event that an unexpected guest comes to join them. For 15 to 30 minutes, teacher and students discuss a lesson on a topic such as being a good listener, including one another, speaking up, calming down, or problem solving, and do an activity, a role-play, or game that reinforces that topic.

In addition to being the setting for curriculum lessons, the Open Circle becomes a place to bring issues of importance for individuals or the entire class, and also a place to celebrate the classroom community. If there is a problem, such as how to prevent older kids from interfering with recess games, or a current teasing "epidemic" in the class, students and teachers can use Open Circle as a forum to solve problems. Students know that this time will be set aside to deal with their issues. As a school counselor noted, "Open Circle is a perfect forum for discussing difficult topics. The children have learned that it is a time to talk about things that are important to them but may not be easy to discuss and a time when they feel safe and dare to take risks."

Open Circle Possibilities for Malika and Steven

In light of such firsthand reports, we believe that the structure and philosophy of Open Circle provides a place for children like Malika and Steven, described by Eishold in Chapter 2, to feel more connected to their classmates and teachers and therefore less alone in facing their difficulties and challenges. The building of a caring community with clear norms offers consistency and a sense of safety, which would allow fifth grader Malika to talk honestly and openly about questions she might have concerning race and how people can get along, without fear of being judged for her opinions or queries. Likewise, Steven could develop a feeling vocabulary and be better able to identify and express feelings he may experience as a result of the turmoil in his family and the frustration he faces in learning to read.

Open Circle also provides support for teachers who face the challenge of helping students like Malika and Steven. The program provides new strategies for classroom management, thus buying back time for academics in the classroom. As one third-grade teacher commented, "I was definitely a dictator before I began using Open Circle. I now consider myself a sharer with the children. They trust me, and I trust them." All teachers are encouraged to carry over the social competency concepts from Open Circle into academic lessons and other parts of the school day. In this way, teachers of both Malika and Steven would have had the opportunity in training to learn about and reflect on the developmental issues and cultural factors that impact social emotional learning. In order to help students develop the emotional and social skills needed to face such complex challenges, Open Circle recognizes that their teachers, who have many additional responsibilities and unique challenges, must be strongly supported as well.

Theoretical Underpinnings of Open Circle

The Open Circle Curriculum integrates ideas from several different conceptual sources. The work of Jean Baker Miller (1986) and her colleagues at the Stone Center at Wellesley College provides a theoretical framework that emphasizes the importance of positive interpersonal relationships to the psychological and intellectual growth of both children and adults. According to Miller, growth-fostering relationships provide all involved with "a greater sense of 'zest'" (p. 5). Continuing, she explains how in the context of a growth-fostering relationship

> each person feels more able to act and does act. Each person has a more accurate picture of her/himself and other person(s). Each person feels a greater sense of worth. Each person feels more connected to the other person(s) and feels a greater motivation for connections with other people beyond those in the specific relationship. (p. 5)

In the classroom, growth-fostering relationships create a sense of community in which there is caring and respect. The relational skills taught in Open Circle help children, and the adults in their lives, develop the capacity to create and sustain growth-fostering relationships. Such feelings of connection, self-worth, and motivation allow students to be and feel known and supported in taking risks and working toward their greatest potential. We have also adapted our Open Circle methods from aspects of several well-researched programs in social competency skills development (Elias & Bruene-Butler, 1999; Elias & Clabby, 1989; Schelkun, 1987; Shriver, Schwab-Stone, & DeFalco, 1999; Shure & Glaser, this volume; Shure & Spivack, 1982; Weissberg, Gesten, Liebenstein, Doherty-Schmid, & Hutton, 1980).

TRAINING AND SUPPORT PROGRAMS

Since its beginnings in two schools, the Reach Out to Schools: Social Competency Program has trained over 2,850 teachers who have brought the Open Circle Curriculum to over 200,000 children in over 200 elementary schools and 67 diverse communities in New England and New Jersey.

Central to the program's success is our work with the classroom teachers who bring the curriculum to life with their students. We know that the way a teacher presents the curriculum and includes the concepts throughout the school day is critical to the program's effectiveness. Recognizing this, we ask that educators participating in our First Year Teacher Training Program, which introduces teachers to the Open Circle Curriculum, make a yearlong commitment to their training. Each teacher attends 4 full days of training at Wellesley College or at a site in their own community. Teachers attend 2 consecutive days of training in the summer or early fall, 1 day in January or February, and 1 day in March or April. We make an effort to help each training group become a community where participating teachers feel comfortable expressing their hopes and doubts and taking risks. Because our program model considers the classroom teacher's approach to classroom management, her use of inquiry or facilitation, and her attitude toward problem solving as central to effective program implementation, these skills are addressed throughout the training sessions.

In addition to providing an orientation to the curriculum, the training incorporates experiential activities that provide opportunities for teachers to connect to deeply held beliefs and to reflect on how these beliefs affect their classrooms and larger school community. As one teacher noted, "I had never thought about being nonjudgmental. From now on I will try to focus on what the child as an individual feels about himself or herself and not my opinion of what I am hearing" (Timko, 1998). Many teachers also comment that our experiential approach gives them an opportunity to "live" Open Circle and gain an understanding of the curriculum from their students' perspective (Timko, 1998). At the same time, the training gives teachers time to learn and practice the skill and art of facilitation, the primary pedagogy of the program, as well as time for personal reflection on their teaching practice.

Four Training Days

On their 1st day of training, teachers become part of an experience-based learning group in which they reflect on their own communication and problem-solving skills and begin to consider what it means to be a facilitator. As a group, they explore a variety of teaching techniques. The 1st day of training also includes observation of Open Circle lessons modeled by program staff and shown on videotape. This prepares the teachers for the 2nd day of training when they are given an opportunity to model lessons themselves and receive group feedback, to consider possible stumbling blocks, and to make an action plan that will help them begin to implement the program in their own classrooms. The 3rd day of training focuses on calming-down techniques and problem-solving steps as well as broader issues that include addressing challenges, considering the impact of culture on social competency, and the carryover of Open Circle concepts into a variety of contexts. The 4th day is set aside for reflection, evaluation, and opportunities to extend skills and create action plans for the next year.

A summary of teacher evaluations of the First Year Teacher Training included the following observation:

> Many participants, including veteran teachers, have commented on the positive impact the training has had on them personally as well professionally, indicating how it was an opportunity for personal as well as professional growth and learning. One experienced teacher noted, "Although I have taught for many years, I feel that using this program will help me grow as an educator and as a person." (Timko, 1998)

The personal and professional growth and development experienced by teachers in their training seem to reveal the power Open Circle concepts hold for adults as well as children.

On-Site Consultation and Coaching

In addition to the 4 training days, in-school consulting and coaching are critical to the success of the program. A program consultant comes to the school to model an Open Circle lesson, observe, and work with each teacher in his or her classroom. This one-on-one attention gives teachers and program staff an opportunity to assess progress and address the specific difficulties that individual teachers face in the classroom with their own students. Program consultants use a peer observation process and encourage teachers to observe each other as they facilitate Open Circle lessons and to share their expertise and challenges with their colleagues.

Collaboration and Feedback

This investment in training and one-on-one consultation helps ensure teacher buy-in and collaboration that are essential to the program's continued success. But we are also aware of the increasingly complex demands on teachers' time and the expanded expectations of the teacher's role in meeting children's needs. At the same time that they are seeking extra tools, teachers often feel pressured by an ever-escalating set of expectations. As reflected in their evaluations of training sessions, teachers in Open Circle training continually report a lack of time in the school day as a deterrent to program implementation. Since teacher attitudes about the program affect both the implementation and the likelihood of carryover of concepts into the school day, program staff continually seek feedback from teachers in order to amend aspects of training and the curriculum and to learn how we can better support them.

Training and Leadership Development for Other Members of the School Community

Over the years, we have learned that the social emotional learning needs of children cannot be addressed without also addressing the social emotional learning needs of all the adults in students' lives, not only their teachers, but also other school staff and students' parents or guardians. We have found that creating a socially competent classroom environment cannot occur in isolation from the rest of the school. In response, the program has expanded in scope over time to incorporate training and leadership development components that serve administrators, other professional and nonprofessional school staff, and parents, and also to employ strategies to support local training and consulting staff, schoolwide implementation, and long-term maintenance of the program.

Principals and Assistant Principals. One set of training activities targets school principals and assistant principals. School administrators who are new to the program are invited to participate in a workshop that introduces them to the concepts, structures, and language of the program and the Open Circle Curriculum. This workshop also presents them with strategies for supporting their teachers in the use of the program and for promoting effective schoolwide implementation.

In addition, our Whole-School Initiative Group brings together interested principals with teacher-leaders from their schools to form school-based leadership and advocacy teams. This network of leadership teams serves as a think tank to develop and exchange new strategies and approaches to support whole-school implementation of the program.

Specialists and Support Staff. A second set of training activities supports other adult staff members in the school. Many adults who do not work in the classroom interact with children throughout the school day and model behavior for them. In consideration of this, we have designed one-day workshops for specialists, nonclassroom professionals, and other support staff including secretaries, custodians, cafeteria staff, and bus drivers. These workshops provide these adults with concepts and Open Circle vocabulary that they can use to reinforce what children learn in Open Circle and to enhance their own interactions with students and other adults in the school community.

Parents and Guardians. A third set of training activities supports and informs the parents and guardians of participating students. Parent newsletters in both English and Spanish are provided, as well as short after-school presentations that introduce parents to the Open Circle Curriculum and describe its goals, concepts, and language. For parents who are particularly interested in the program, we have also developed a multisession training workshop model designed to encourage home use of the program's concepts and language. Such carryover of Open Circle concepts and practices reinforces the classroom experiences of students, encourages the use of the program in contexts outside the classroom, and supports participants' parenting skills. As one parent told us, "My child was surprised to hear me use the same language that he knows from school. This is providing the consistency that children need." The program works with local school social workers and psychologists in the use of this model so that schools and school systems can offer it to parents as needed and work with them within the structure of a community-based curriculum and philosophy.

AN OPEN CIRCLE LESSON

The *Open Circle Curriculum* has six versions, one each for kindergarten through fifth grade. The same concepts and skills are included in all six books in a developmentally appropriate way. Each year that a child participates in Open Circle, concepts are reinforced and skills are practiced with different activities at each grade level. The following is a scenario in which concepts and techniques previously learned in an Open Circle lesson are applied to smooth a transition period during a busy school day.

Ms. Morris's fifth-grade class has a particularly hectic schedule on Thursday mornings. Her class has gym and art, and several students go in and out of the classroom for special support. Five minutes before students are to leave for the lunchroom, Ms. Morris asks everyone to move their chairs to face the window, to sit in a comfortable position, and to get ready to do some calm breathing: "Breathe in slowly and deeply through your nose, filling your belly with air like a balloon. Then breathe out slowly through your nose. Let's take a few more calm breaths." After taking several calm breaths, students quietly line up and proceed to the lunchroom. Ms. Morris is helping students to practice and apply skills they have learned in Open Circle. Using breathing to calm down during transitions becomes a good habit that students can access at other times in their life when they need to calm down or exercise self-control.

These techniques used by Ms. Morris's class during transition periods are taught in the fifth-grade lesson "Being Calm" in which the objectives are to recognize the characteristics of a calm state, to learn and practice calming down, and to understand why being calm is useful and important. In the lesson, students think about a situation or time when they are extremely calm and peaceful and visualize themselves in that situation. Then both students and teacher share their calm situations and describe their breathing, activity level, heartbeat, and muscle tension during those times. Students practice several calm breathing strategies and then discuss times in school when they feel calm and times when they are not calm but might want to be. A subsequent follow-up lesson helps students identify for themselves the physiological and behavioral changes that signal that they are upset or too excited and need to calm down. This becomes important information that they can use to cope with stressful situations.

Lesson Benefits to Steven and Malika

One can imagine the many ways in which both Steven and Malika would benefit from explicitly learning strategies that help them calm down as a way of managing strong feelings and allowing them to be more focused, whether on academic tasks or in more positive social interactions. Such calming, focusing skills and techniques could be of tremendous help to Steven, who has difficulty working on group projects without being bossy, has difficulty focusing, and seems to handle anxiety by becoming immersed in his own preoccupations. Calming techniques could help him balance the personal preoccupations and worries that haunt his inner world with the important tasks and opportunities for learning and growth that surround him in the outer world of the classroom.

Malika, an otherwise energetic, dynamic child who has an anxious, fearful reaction to doing independent academic work and presenting it to the class, could also benefit greatly from such calming techniques. She could learn how to read her own level of anxiety, to recognize its manifestations, and to cope and work through these stressful states. A successful presentation to the class, for example, could bring her tremendous satisfaction and a boost in self-esteem, encouraging her to channel her energy toward achievements in class.

An Open Circle Lesson Plan

The specific lessons at different grade levels build on concepts that are introduced in kindergarten by using stories as a starting point for learning about being calm. They hold two objectives: (1) to understand what it feels like to be calm and (2) to learn and practice calm breathing techniques. The lesson plan follows these steps:

1. Ask students if they have been using feeling words to name their feelings. Ask a few students to share their experiences. Can they name two feelings they have had since they woke up this morning?

2. Ask how many students have a cat as a pet. How many students have ever seen a picture of a cat or read a story about a cat? Ask students to picture a cat in their minds.

3. Tell students that you would like them to imagine a cat sitting on a warm mat in the kitchen. It's a cold day, and the sun is streaming through the window onto the cat's back. Ask students to describe what the cat's body might look like. Have them show you (staying seated in their chairs) what the cat might look like. You may want to have one student come to the center of the circle and demonstrate. Ask students how the cat might be feeling. If the word *calm* doesn't come up, you can introduce it to students. Ask how the cat might be breathing (e.g., slowly, deeply).

4. Have students think about times during the school day or at home when they might feel calm and peaceful like the cat. Have students give examples. Explain that in those situations they are also breathing slowly and calmly. They are doing calm breathing.

5. Tell students that we are going to practice some ways to do calm breathing. First, they need to sit in a relaxed and comfortable position. Make sure that students aren't lifting or holding their shoulders in a tense way. Ask them to put their hands on their bellies. Begin by modeling calm breathing. Then lead them in the following sequence: Breathe in slowly and deeply, filling your belly with air like a balloon. Breathe out slowly.

6. After they have practiced a few times, introduce another calm breathing technique called "flower breathing" (Cheney, 1997): Breathe in through your nose, imagining the fragrance of a sweet-smelling flower. Breathe out with an "ahhh" sound. Have them practice flower breathing a few times.

7. Tell students that knowing and practicing calm breathing is important. When we are breathing calmly, we are able to be good learners, good friends, and good problem solvers.

8. Ask students for some ideas of times during the school day when it might be a good idea to practice calm breathing.

As the lessons build and expand upon one another in keeping with growth and development across the elementary grades, students develop an understanding and awareness of how calm breathing can help them be good learners, good friends, and good problem solvers during their elementary years and beyond.

AN EXAMPLE OF WHOLE-SCHOOL IMPLEMENTATION:
THE BROPHY SCHOOL

When students, faculty, and staff at the Brophy School in Framingham, Massachusetts, chose "Sharing One World at Brophy" as their theme in 1997–1998, they decided to make the Reach Out to Schools: Social Competency Program a schoolwide project. Students, teachers, school administrators, and parents joined together to extend Open Circle beyond the classroom to the entire school community.

Brophy School's whole-school project kicked off in the fall with a full-staff in-service workshop conducted by two Brophy teachers who serve as program peer consultants. At this workshop, adult members of the Brophy community spoke together about the Open Circle strategies that have been successful in the classroom, and they brainstormed ways to use these strategies outside the classroom to promote a caring, respectful community.

After this first workshop, staff followed up with a series of early-morning focus groups and now meet voluntarily before school to discuss Open Circle issues. Students at Brophy have also joined in the whole-school initiative by taking responsibility for an Open Circle bulletin board in the central hallway. Students take turns designing and installing the bulletin board each month. Their displays have included Open Circle vocabulary words, posted in a circle of Brophy faces drawn by the students during art class, and cutouts of children giving compliments to each other in both English and Spanish.

Parents visited their children's Open Circle during National Education Week, and Brophy School has translated Parent Workshop workbooks into Spanish.

Staff who facilitate an Open Circle have a standing invitation to visit other Open Circles throughout the school. A schoolwide Open Circle schedule is posted, and to boost awareness of Open Circle, many staff members wear Open Circle pins designed by a Brophy staff member.

Three Brophy staff members also attended an Advanced Training Workshop sponsored by the Reach Out to Schools: Social Competency Program and hosted by Project Adventure. They then returned to Brophy and shared the team-building activities they learned with the rest of the staff during an in-service day.

Finally, in order to accomplish the goal of complete Open Circle immersion at Brophy, Principal Maurice Downey is coordinating a special program for other members of the school staff. The program introduces school secretaries, custodians, nurses, support staff, and specialists such as art, music, and physical education teachers and librarians to Open Circle concepts, vocabulary, and schoolwide signals.

Creating school and classroom environments that value social emotional learning, growth-fostering relationships, and supportive communities is a complex, time-consuming process. There are no quick or easy fixes. As Maurice Downey says,

> This is hard work to be socially competent all the time. But it doesn't work if you don't internalize it, if you don't make it the way you do business all the time. I'm excited because I know it's going to be a bumpy road, but whenever it's uncomfortable, that's when good stuff is happening. Good stuff does not come easy. This is not fluff. What we're doing here is real and replicable.

PROGRAM EVALUATION

Since 1990, the Reach Out to Schools: Social Competency Program has conducted a series of evaluations (Black, 1995; Krasnow, Seigle, & Kelly, 1994) to document its impact on participating teachers, students, and parents and to better understand the changes occurring in classrooms and schools that use the Open Circle Curriculum. In general these evaluations conclude that the program promotes increased teaching and learning time and supports a caring and responsive community in the classroom.

According to evaluation results, significant gains among students from their participation in the program have occurred in specific areas including interpersonal skill development (including empathy and consideration for others), a greater sense of self-worth and empowerment, problem-solving skill development, individual responsibility, carryover of skills developed in Open Circle to the classroom and beyond, and a reduction in problem behaviors.

These evaluations have also found that the program creates an improved learning environment in participating classrooms and schools. Several specific changes contributing to this improvement include increased time on task for academics; increased ability of students to take risks, solve problems, focus their attention, support each other's learning, and make positive contributions; increased ability of students to share responsibility for the classroom learning environment, resulting in improvements in student discipline and classroom management; and a means to address problematic student behavior that affects children's ability to function successfully in the classroom. Finally, school community outcomes were evidenced in teachers' observations of changes in the classroom toward a more cohesive and egalitarian environment in which students share responsibility for class governance.

Evaluations also indicate that participation in the program improves teachers' relationships with students and leaves them better equipped to support students' social competency skills development. By incorporating program strategies and techniques, teachers improved their communication and teaching skills while coming to know their students better. At the same time, participation in the program led to changes in the ways teachers related to and worked among themselves as a group and in the development of a unified approach to student discipline.

In a study conducted in 1998 by Beth Hennessey of Wellesley College, using the Social Skills Rating System (SSRS) (Gresham & Elliot, 1990), fourth-grade teachers reported that students who participated in Open Circle had fewer problem behaviors and were more socially skilled than students who were not participants in the Program (Hennessey & Seigle, 1998).

A pilot assessment of the program conducted in 1997–1998 at the Stone Center at Wellesley College (Taylor, Liang, Tracy, Williams, & Seigle, 2000) evaluated social outcomes in middle school students based on student, teacher, and parent reports. The study suggests that students who participated in Open Circle for 2 years or more had better outcomes overall than students who had little or no experience with the program. Students, parents, and teachers completed the SSRS self-report survey and students also completed a survey on middle school adjustment including questions from the Survey of Adaptational Tasks—Middle School (Elias, Ubriaco, Reese, & Gara, 1992).

The composite social skill scores (including cooperation, assertion, empathy, and self-control subscales) from the student version SSRS were significantly higher for students who had participated in the program than for those who had not. Program students also faired better overall in middle school adjustment, according to both student and teacher reports. Among the middle school adjustment questions, students were asked to rate whether or not "getting into physical fights where someone is hit, punched, kicked, or something else" was a problem for them in middle school. Fewer students in the program group reported that fighting was a problem than those in the nonprogram group.

CONCLUSION

Overall, the results of these two studies strongly reinforce our earlier research. They demonstrate that the program has a positive impact among participating students on a range of social competency skills. Moreover, the most recent evaluation (Taylor et al., 2000) reveals that these positive benefits persist beyond students' direct participation in the program, which suggests that the program has a long-term impact. Such an impact could bring the hope and guidance that are so needed by students like Steven and Malika and the teachers who can make a difference in their lives. With the support and techniques of a social competency program like Reach Out to Schools: Social Competency Program and its Open Circle Curriculum, Steven, Malika, and children between and beyond can develop the skills and the capacity needed to be good learners, good friends, productive workers, and contributing citizens.

REFERENCES

Black, B. (1995). *Reach Out to Schools: Social Competency Program.* Wellesley, MA: Wellesley College, Stone Center.

Cheney, S. L. (1997). *Two flower breaths: The art of teaching yoga to children.* Unpublished manuscript.

Elias, M. J., & Bruene-Butler, L. (1999). Social decision making and problem solving: Essential skills for interpersonal and academic success. In J. Cohen (Ed.), *Educating minds and hearts: Social emotional learning and the passage into adolescence* (pp. 74–94). New York: Teachers College Press.

Elias, M. J., & Clabby, J. F. (1989). *Social decision-making skills: A curriculum guide for the elementary grades.* Rockville, MD: Aspen.

Elias, M. J., Ubriaco, M., Reese, A. M., & Gara, M. A. (1992, Spring). A measure of adaptation to problematic academic and interpersonal tasks of middle school. *Journal of School Psychology, 30,* 41–57.

Gresham, F. M., & Elliot, S. N. (1990). *Social skills rating system: Grades 3–6 social skills questionnaire.* Circle Pines, MN: American Guidance Service.

Hennessey, B. A., & Seigle, P. (1998). *Promoting social competency in school-aged children: The effect of the Reach Out to Schools: Social Competency Program.* Unpublished manuscript. Wellesley College, Wellesley, MA.

Krasnow, J. H., Seigle, P., & Kelly, R. (1994). *Project report 1990–1993: The social competency program of the Reach Out to Schools project.* Wellesley, MA: Wellesley College, Stone Center.

Miller, J. B. (1986). What do we mean by relationships? *Work in progress* (No. 22). Wellesley, MA: Wellesley College, Stone Center.

Schelkun, R. (1987, August). *QSL: A social system's intervention.* Paper presented at the 95th annual convention of the American Psychological Association, New York, NY.

Seigle, P., Lange, L., & Macklem, G. (1999). *Open Circle Curriculum, grades K to 5* (Rev. ed.). Wellesley, MA: Wellesley College, Stone Center, Reach Out to Schools: Social Competency Program.

Shriver, T. P., Schwab-Stone, M., & DeFalco, K. (1999). Why SEL is the better way: The New Haven Social Development Program. In J. Cohen (Ed.), *Educating minds and hearts: Social emotional learning and the passage into adolescence* (pp. 43–60). New York: Teachers College Press.

Shure, M., & Glaser, A. (2001). I Can Problem Solve (ICPS): A cognitive approach to the prevention of early high-risk behaviors. In this volume.

Shure, M., & Spivack, G. (1982). *Interpersonal cognitive problem solving.* Philadelphia: Hahnemann University, Department of Mental Health Services.

Taylor, C. A., Liang, B., Tracy, A. J., Williams, L. M., & Seigle, P. (2000). *Evaluation of an elementary school based social and emotional learning program: School adjustment, social skills, and physical fighting during middle school transition.* Manuscript submitted for publication.

Timko, M. (1998). *Reach Out to Schools: Social Competency Program summary of teacher training evaluations.* Unpublished manuscript.

Weissberg, R. P., Gesten, E., Liebenstein, N. L., Doherty-Schmid, K., & Hutton, H. (1980). *The Rochester Social Problem Solving (SPS) Program.* Rochester, NY: Primary Mental Health Project.

Chapter 8

I CAN PROBLEM SOLVE (ICPS): A COGNITIVE APPROACH TO THE PREVENTION OF EARLY HIGH-RISK BEHAVIORS

Myrna B. Shure, Ph.D. and *Ann-Linn Glaser*

MCP Hahnemann University

Social emotional learning can start in preschool. Research has now identified early high risk behaviors that can predict later violence, substance abuse, teen pregnancy, and some forms of psychopathology as early as age 4 (e.g., Parker & Asher, 1987). Those behaviors include physical and verbal aggression, inability to delay gratification and cope with frustration, inability to make friends, poor academic achievement, and lack of positive prosocial behaviors (Eron & Heusman, 1984). Research has also shown that social withdrawal, left unattended, can predict later internalizing problems such as depression, even suicide (Rubin & Mills, 1988).

THE ICPS THINKING SKILLS

In the late 1960s and early 1970s, George Spivack and Myrna Shure tested the hypothesis that there is a set of interpersonal thinking skills that may guide behavior; they began by identifying what they later called Interpersonal Cognitive Problem Solving (ICPS) skills that are associated with social adjustment and interpersonal competence as early as age 4 (Spivack, Platt, & Shure, 1976).

Alternative Solution Skills. From age 4 through adulthood, individuals who display forms of impulsive or inhibited behaviors, who lack awareness of, if not genuine concern for, others in distress, or who have few, if any, good friends are dramatically more deficient than their behaviorally adjusted peers in their ability to think of alternative solutions to real life problems. This applies whether it is a young child wanting the toy of another child, adolescent wanting a previously unobtainable date, or an adult wanting a neighbor to stop making noise late at night.

Consequential Thinking. From age 4 through 12, youngsters who display high-risk behaviors are also less able to think of different, alternative outcomes of what might happen next if, for example, a child grabs a toy from another. And high-risk adolescents are unlikely to weigh the pros and cons of transgressions, such as going to a party the night before an important exam.

Social Perspective Taking. Urberg & Docherty (1976) and Shure (1982) find behaviorally high-risk children to be less able to understand that others may feel and think differently about something than they do. For example, an impulsive or inhibited child who feels sad if his bike is run over by a car may not understand that another child may feel happy about that because he thinks now he can get a new bike.

Means-ends, or Sequential Thinking. Beginning at about age 8, behaviorally high-risk children are more deficient than their adjusted counterparts in their ability to plan ahead to reach a stated interpersonal goal (such as wanting to make new friends). High-risk children are less able to plan step-by-step means to reach that goal (such as wanting to visit the boy next door), to anticipate potential obstacles that may interfere (such as the possibility that the boy won't let him in because he doesn't know him), and to appreciate that problem solving can take time (such as waiting until they know each other and then asking the neighbor to come over to his house to play). In addition to realizing how long it takes to reach a goal, means-ends thinking also includes recognizing good and not-good times to act. In this example, competent means-ends thinkers will consider waiting until after dinner to call the boy because calling while the family is eating is not a good time to do that (Spivack et al., 1976; Spivack & Shure, 1982).

THE ICPS LINK TO EARLY HIGH-RISK BEHAVIORS

When Spivack, Platt, and Shure (1976) associated ICPS skills with specific behaviors, it wasn't yet known if the skills guided the behaviors or if the behaviors influenced the skills. For example, if educators and clinicians believed that by relieving our emotional tensions, we would be able to think straight, we could set out to test the reverse idea: by thinking straight, we would be able to relieve emotional tension. The rationale for ICPS was that an individual who thinks only of what he wants rather than how to go about getting it, who is not adept at thinking through ways to solve typical interpersonal problems, or who does not consider consequences and the possibility of alternative routes to the same goal may make impulsive mistakes, become frustrated and aggressive, or evade the problem entirely by withdrawing from people and from problems he cannot solve. On the other hand, an individual who thinks in terms of alternative possible solutions and who also has an appreciation of the consequences will be able to effectively evaluate and choose from a variety of possible solutions, turn to a different (more effective) solution in case of actual failure, experience less frustration, be successful in interpersonal relationships, and be less likely to exhibit behaviors that are now known to indicate risk for later, more serious problems.

Not only are solution and consequential skills associated with social adjustment and interpersonal competence as defined by the above-mentioned behaviors in inner-city, low-income 4-year-olds (Shure, Spivack, & Jaeger, 1971; Spivack & Shure, 1974; for data replicated by others, see Dimson, 1992; Turner & Boulter, 1981), but alternative solution thinking (consequential thinking has not been studied) is linked to these behaviors in the middle class as well (Arend, Gove, & Sroufe, 1979). In addition, alternative solution skills have also been significantly linked to social adjustment and interpersonal competence in children up to age 8 in both income groups (Johnson, Yu, & Roopnarine, 1980; McKim, Weissberg, Cowen, Gesten, & Rapkin, 1982; Richard & Dodge, 1982).

WHY SOCIAL EMOTIONAL LEARNING IN THE CLASSROOM?

Children preoccupied with interpersonal conflict, unable to make the friends they want, or consumed with other emotional tensions not only engage in maladaptive behaviors but also are less able to focus on the academic demands of the classroom (Elias, 1997). Do children who are failing at math really need more math, or do they just need to relieve whatever tension prevents them from focusing on the math they're getting? Do Steven and Malika, described by Eisold in Chapter 2, need more attention focused directly on their academic skills, or do they need to concentrate on learning skills to make friends? If they are better able to make the friends they so desperately want, would they be more interested in the task-oriented demands of the classroom?

Consider Steven, who is having difficulty reading at age 7. Although it is possible that he is experiencing genuine reading deficiencies, it is also possible that his preoccupation with classmates not paying enough attention to him, combined with his adjustment to his mother's new relationship and his intense desire to have friends, renders him unable to focus on reading. Disturbed by all his unmet needs, Steven is either unable, or unwilling, to think of different ways (alternative solutions) to resolve problems that do come up, as evidenced by his tendency to boss other kids around. His alternative—to bury himself deep in his own preoccupations when feeling anxious—only evades problems in the interpersonal arena and blocks responding to academic areas such as reading.

Although Malika, age 11, is from a background very different from Steven's, she also displays intense anger, albeit justifiably at times, and she is unable to control or redirect it. To a large extent, those overwhelming feelings of anger and frustration, which consume her waking moments, prevent her from achieving her potential in both her interpersonal and academic worlds.

It seems rather evident that neither Steven nor Malika will be able to get the necessary guidance from their parents that could help them meet their needs, at least not without formally engaging the parents in the process as well. If more teachers and administrators could recognize the importance of integrating social and emotional learning into their curriculum, perhaps Steven and Malika, and children like them, could learn skills that might prevent the very behaviors linked to later violence, substance abuse, teen pregnancy, some forms of psychopathology, and other serious problems as they move into their teen years and beyond.

THE "I CAN PROBLEM SOLVE" PREVENTION PROGRAM

Spivack and Shure (1974) asked whether children (like Steven and Malika) could reduce their anger, impulsivity, or tendency to withdraw into their own worlds, not by focusing directly on the behaviors themselves, but by involving them in the process of thinking about what they do in light of how they and others might feel and what other potential consequences to themselves and others might be. ICPS programming began by training teachers how to teach low-income African American children how to think the problem-solving way. The first intervention was designed as a formal research study to investigate a linkage between ICPS ability and social and emotional competence by experimentally enhancing ICPS skills (via inter-vention) and then observing changes in the children's display of behaviors characteristic of impulsivity and inhibition. The critical questions were whether those who would most improve in the trained ICPS skills would be the same youngsters who would most improve in teacher-observed behavioral adjustment and whether evidence of such linkage would be in-dependent of general intellectual functioning (IQ). The intervention, origi-nally called Interpersonal Cognitive Problem Solving (ICPS), now dissemin-ated as a service program called I Can Problem Solve (also ICPS), is a culture-free primary prevention program that teaches children from pre-school through age 12 *how* to think, not *what* to think, in ways that help them to solve everyday, interpersonal problems. ICPS intervention begins in the preschool.

Why begin in preschool? What behaviors and academic skills would Ste-ven and Malika be exhibiting today if they had had the opportunity to partic-ipate in a program such as ICPS early on? Shure and her colleague, George Spivack, believe that to reduce and prevent early high-risk behaviors it is best to start at the earliest possible age, which is age 4, and is indicated by their research (Shure, Spivack, & Jaeger, 1971). They set out to test whether social and emotional development during the years prior to kindergarten could set the stage for future behaviors as children move through school.

How does ICPS work? In order for children to become adept at solving problems using age-appropriate ICPS skills described above without con-stant adult intervention, certain prerequisite and problem-solving skills must first be learned. The following is a sample of lessons from the pre-school curriculum (Shure, 1992a).

An ICPS Vocabulary and Word Play. Specific words are helpful in bringing about an understanding and in the settling of disputes. Teaching children to use these words can begin as soon as the child becomes verbal. Although some of these words may seem quite elementary, continued interjection of the "problem-solving vocabulary," or "ICPS words," into games and exist-ing curricula will deepen the understanding of these terms, and they will also become associated with fun. For example, children play with the words *same* and *different* by first tapping their heads, then stamping their feet. After the teacher asks if head tapping is the *same* or *different* from foot stamping, the children then think of more body motions that are either the same or different. One boy often disrupted class lessons before the ICPS program was introduced and usually had to go to the back of the classroom until he was ready to rejoin the group. One day, after the class had started with the ICPS program, the children were all doing the same thing—jump-ing—when the boy disrupted the group. This time the teacher simply asked him if he was doing the same thing or something different from the others. Although he was initially doing something different, he enthusiastically chanted, "the *same* thing," and he began to jump like the others. No more needed to be said.

Is and *is not* are played first by pointing to a chair, asking what it *is* (a chair), and what it *is not* (a balloon). These words are later associated with real life by asking children to think about whether their idea to solve a problem is or is not a good idea, and if it is not, whether they can think of a *different* way? Play with words such as *or* help children think, I can do this *or* I can do that, and the words *some* and *all* help children recognize that one solution will be successful with *some* people but not *all* people.

Feelings. Some children who hurt others by hitting them claim to not care about being hit back. It is probable that before anyone can care about and develop empathy for others, they first have to care about themselves. Asking children how *they* feel, even though they may have initiated the conflict, sends a very important message. It tells children, "I care about you, and I want you to care about you." Then they are asked how they think the other child might be feeling in conflict situations. Shure's preschool curriculum focuses upon the feeling words *happy, sad, angry*, and *afraid*. Children enjoy hearing children say what makes them feel *happy*, for example, and remembering one, two, three, or more things each child says. This memory game not only helps children focus on the emotions, but helps them listen and pay attention, and often they learn something about others that they may not already know. Building upon the ICPS vocabulary, children come to recognize that *different* people can feel *different* ways about the *same* thing, and it is important to find out people's preferences as part of solving a problem.

Sequencing. Children cannot solve problems without a firm understanding about what happens before the conflict and what might happen after various strategies are attempted. They cannot know what the problem is without being aware of the sequence of events. As a precursor to the more advanced ICPS skill of means-ends, or sequential thinking, children are shown a series of pictures and asked to point to which event probably happened first, followed by the question, "And then?" For example, a child kicking another may have started a sequence, *and then* the child who was kicked cries. And *then* the child who was kicked tells the teacher, *and then* the teacher talks to the boy who kicked his friend.

Alternative Solutions. This key skill is introduced as early as preschool, not only because research suggests that lack of ability to think of solutions to problems is associated with impulsive and inhibited behaviors, but also because thinking of alternative solutions encourages children very early on to be open to the concept that there is more than one way to solve a problem. Because impulsive and inhibited youngsters are stuck on one or two solutions, they either fly off the handle in the face of frustration or give up too soon. Children as well as adults will profit from the understanding that there is no one correct solution to any conflict and that the solution that works for one person at one time may not be suitable for the same or a different person at a different time. Creatively seeking a myriad of possible solutions is the keystone to successful "ICPS-ing."

Consequential Thinking. Playing with new ICPS words *might* and *maybe* and the phrase *if-then*, children think about what *might* happen next *if*, for example, Jane teases Beth. After children think of many things that might happen next, including how they and others might feel, they decide if the solution *is* or *is not* a good one. As time and interest permit, the group repeats the process with other solutions and then picks the solution they think is best; then they discover why.

ICPS IN REAL LIFE

Early pilot field tests in the late 1960s and early 1970s suggest that the curriculum has an impact on behavior only if the teachers help children apply in real life the skills practiced in fictitious situations (Shure, Spivack, & Gordon, 1972). When Shure observed teachers in preschools, she noticed that they became quite skilled at *asking* children ICPS questions about fictitious situations, such as "What's the problem?" "How do the people in the picture feel?" "What can they do to solve the problem?" "What might happen if they do that?" However, once the lesson ended, teachers reverted back to *telling* their students what to do when, for example, one child shoved another. Therefore, we wanted to know what impact fictitious ICPS lesson-games would have if teachers continued the same line of questioning when problems came up in real life, in other words, if teachers helped children associate how they think with what they do. That is how ICPS dialoguing was born.

Over the years, we divided the way adults talk to children into four levels of communication (Shure, 1992a, 1992b, 1992c; 1996a, 2000a). Of course everything we say to children might not fall into one of these four groupings, but these groupings help to clarify the difference between ICPS dialoguing and other forms of communication.

Level 1: Power Assertion. Power assertion includes any form of negative demands, commands, or even time-outs when used to humiliate children in front of their classmates. In this form of time-out, children are not thinking about their actions; if they are thinking at all, it may be on how to revenge the child who they think got them into trouble in the first place. Some children may feel anger and frustration, and their emotions may escalate because they have no control in the resolution of the problem. Other children, such as those who don't care if they get hit back by peers, may also become immune to being overpowered by adults with commands and demands, thereby making their behavior next to impossible to control.

Level 2: The Positive Alternative. A more positive approach advanced by Haim Ginott (1965) is to tell children what *to* do, instead of what *not to* do. For example, instead of saying "Don't hit" say "Ask for what you want" or "Play nicely. Share your toys."

Level 3: Explanations and Reasons. By the 1970s, researchers had added explanations and reasoning (also called induction) to the mix (e.g., Hoffman & Salzstein, 1967). For example, "If you hit, you might hurt her" or "If you grab toys, you'll lose a friend." Shure classifies the popular *I*-message into this grouping, such as "I feel sad when you hurt your brother" (Gordon, 1970).

Although Levels 2 and 3 are more positive approaches than Level 1, and the *I*-message does include talk about feelings in a way that does not produce guilt, teachers and other adults who use these approaches are still doing the thinking for children. We are still telling children rather than asking. By age 4, they are likely to have heard these suggestions and explanations many times and therefore often tune out, making the adults frustrated and exasperated.

Level 4: Problem Solving. Problem solving changes a statement into a question, thereby involving the child in the conversation and engaging them in a dialogue instead of a monologue. Instead of telling a child not to hit, or even explaining why, an ICPS teacher asks, "What's the problem?" "How do you think your friend feels when you hit him?" "What happened next?" "How did you feel when that happened?" "Can you think of something different to do so that won't happen?" The child's answers to these questions will likely lead him to the conclusion that his friend feels angry, sad, and hurt and won't play with him anymore. One child, when asked how he feels when his brother tells his mom when he hits him, replied, "I feel sad when I hurt my brother." What a different outcome from children who don't care!

ICPS WITHIN A DEVELOPMENTAL PERSPECTIVE: EDUCATIONAL DOMAINS

It is established that young children learn best in a developmentally appropriate environment. Although much is known about developmental stages and how children develop, these considerations are not always applied in the preschool classrooms or later in the elementary grades. According to Carol Catron and Jan Allen (1993), young children learn best with an appropriate curriculum that includes the following skills or domains of knowledge: language development, perceptual development, cognitive development, social emotional development, and motor development.

Let us see how each ICPS skill area dovetails with developmentally appropriate domains of instruction for preschool-age children.

ICPS and Language Development. Language development is the starting point for ICPS. The initial introduction is a critical part of young children's learning. The concrete way that ICPS activities reinforce vocabulary needed to solve fictitious problems provides an excellent model for introduction to other vocabulary, such as the more sophisticated concepts of *before/after* and the feeling words *proud* and *frustrated* introduced in later grades. ICPS dialoguing with word pairs, such as *is/is not, same/different,* and *might/ maybe,* and words describing people's feelings, such as *happy, sad, angry,* and *afraid,* also encourages the development of language skills. When children are *asked* what they can do to solve an actual problem that arises, they are given the opportunity to participate with language, not just to passively stand by, perhaps not even hearing what is being said.

ICPS and Perceptual Development. The perceptual domain is involved when teaching children to use visual and auditory clues as to the state of mind of others. As early as preschool, ICPS children learn to assess body language and tone of voice to determine "good times" and "not good times" to approach someone about a need or a problem, such as whether it *is* or *is not* a good time to approach someone who is looking sad. In developmentally appropriate ways, ICPS children also learn to assess whether things are what they appear to be, such as how to interpret statements made by others as "anger" or "not anger"—interpretations that research has shown can influence children's behavior (e.g., Dodge & Feldman, 1990).

ICPS and Cognitive Development. The cognitive domain is particularly developed through ICPS activities. As early as preschool, children use the interpersonal cognitive skills of solution and consequential thinking. They are also able to engage in understanding sequences of events, a precursor to both understanding potential consequences (what might happen next) and the more developmentally advanced skill of means-ends thinking that involves planning sequenced steps toward a goal. In addition, the interpersonal concepts are integrated into developmentally appropriate impersonal concepts the children are already learning, such as helping them think of *different* sizes, shapes, and colors, whether the sun comes out in the day *or* in the night, how someone feels when the sun does *not* come out in the day (it rains), what a fireman does that a nurse does *not* do, and what *might* happen if someone drops a rock into a bowl of water.

ICPS and Social Emotional Development. Although there are continual opportunities for "teachable moments" to encourage social and emotional growth, ICPS is a curriculum that concretely and developmentally teaches children how to develop in their interactions with other people and become sensitive to their own and others' emotions. With increasing awareness of social emotional development as a predictor of later life's success (e.g., Goleman, 1995), it is becoming more imperative for teachers to incorporate these kinds of activities as part of their day. As one teacher said, "It is becoming just as important to solve people problems as it is to solve problems in math."

ICPS and Motor Development. Although motor development per se is not a goal of ICPS, motor activities are nonetheless included as a concrete mechanism for linkage with other domains. For example, motor activities are used as one way to practice language concepts, such as when children tap their heads and stamp their feet to demonstrate the vocabulary words *same* and *different*.

ICPS AS A PART OF THE EVERYDAY CURRICULUM

Good educational curricula include use of as many modalities as possible in any lesson, with various domains overlapping. ICPS is not distinct from educational goals and reinforces existing educational domains in a new way. Integration of ICPS into the everyday curriculum is a natural and appropriate extension of typical experiences in an educational setting. Each of the blocks of time in a balanced preschool program can provide opportunities for ICPS skills to be practiced.

Story Time. The ICPS concept of sequencing can be practiced when children retell a familiar story or go back through the pictures of a book and use visual clues to recall the story. Children can be asked how the characters feel at various points in the story, using both verbal and nonverbal cues, such as the pictured body language. To develop empathy for others, children can think not only about how, for example, the victim of teasing might be feeling, but also about how the child who is doing the teasing might be feeling. As problem situations arise, children can brainstorm lots of different solutions, as well as potential consequences if those solutions are carried out.

Snack or Meal Time. Relaxed social time such as snack or meal time is an opportunity for children to practice ICPS vocabulary. For example, children can be asked, "Who *is* at our table?" "Who *is not* at our table?" The teacher can say, "I have peanut butter. Does Peter have the *same* thing or something *different*? Do *all* the children have peanut butter or *some* children?"

Music Time. Teachers can play different types of music and allow students to respond with their own movements and interpretations. Use of scarves and rhythm instruments can allow children to see that there is no one right way to respond to music, just as there is no one right way to solve a problem. Children can also come to appreciate that different people can like different types of music. Although one child might especially enjoy "Eensy Weensy Spider," another might enjoy "The Wheels on the Bus." An important ICPS skill is for children to appreciate that different people have different feelings about the same thing, as well as appreciating that different people have the same feelings about different things.

Free-play Time. As children make choices of activity, some of the ICPS games can be played or reenacted. Puppets might be available for children to act out conflict situations. Art activities can encourage children to think of different ways to use the materials, fostering creativity. The block corner is an ideal environment to concretely discover lots of different ways to build a structure. Sometimes block play leads to problematic situations such as how to maintain balance or fit pieces together in a way that allows the structure to stand; working together to solve these problems is excellent ICPS practice. Also, by using ICPS vocabulary with questions as, "Who *is* painting?" "Who *is not* painting?" "Who is doing the *same* thing as Daniel?" "Who is doing something *different*?" teachers are not only reinforcing the words, but also helping children notice and pay attention to others in the classroom. In addition, it is during free play that a child might begin to cry over something, and children can be asked how that child feels, and what are different ways they can try to make that child feel happy.

Outside Time. In addition to use of ICPS concepts during indoor free play, outdoor play often provides other opportunities for ICPS. One 4-year-old, practicing his skill at tying a rope, chose the door of the gate that opened to the playground. The boy was simply asked, "Is that a good place to tie your rope? Can you think of a different place to tie your rope?" Smiling, the boy took his rope elsewhere. No long explanations were needed. He already knew.

POTENTIAL PRESCHOOL AND ELEMENTARY SCHOOL ICPS LINKAGES

Fortunately, present-day practices will make interventions for children prior to kindergarten more accessible than previously possible. In the coming years, with increasing frequency, preschools will be associated with and housed in elementary school systems. This trend is fueled by several factors. Current research suggests that the early years are crucial for brain development, and lack of appropriate stimulation during the first years of life creates deficits that cannot be overcome. These critical periods of development must be attended to in order for children to enter the elementary years on the same playing field as children who have received the stimulation and practices associated with a quality early education setting.

Also, recent changes in the welfare system have created a need for more child care slots for the children of mothers who are now being placed in the workforce. These factors have encouraged school systems to become increasingly involved in providing early education. Since ICPS affects the very behaviors that can foster or hinder later success in school (and in life), and since there is the possibility of teamwork between preschool and kindergarten teachers, facilitated by preschool intervention and by physical proximity, it seems reasonable to hope that ICPS intervention could become an integral part of the educational system.

ICPS AFTER PRESCHOOL

After several research investigations (see "Outcome Evaluations" later in this chapter), Shure created separate ICPS curricula for kindergarten and the primary grades (Shure, 1992b) and for the intermediate elementary grades (Shure, 1992c). Exact grade levels are not identified because of the variability of skill levels around the country, but generally the kindergarten/primary manual goes up to Grade 3 and the intermediate manual covers Grades 4 through 6. Children with early ICPS experience, however, are generally ready for the ICPS intermediate curriculum by Grade 3.

With developmentally appropriate activities, ICPS for kindergarten and beyond follows the problem-solving approach conducted with preschool children—namely, involving youngsters in the process of thinking about what they do and why—and teaching them the skills to do that. More sophisticated feeling words, such as *proud, frustrated, worried,* and *relieved,* are added, and the intermediate curriculum introduces the ICPS skill of means-ends thinking (sequenced planning) through fictitious storytelling techniques. Also, children exposed to the intermediate curriculum are taught to understand that people don't always do things for reasons that appear on the surface, but that there might be hidden and underlying motives for why people do what they do. For example, a child who comes to understand that a peer bullies others because he's upset about his parents' divorce may treat him differently than if he thought he was just being "funny," or "bossy."

In addition to thinking of solutions to problems and consequences to acts that come up in real life, ICPS dialoguing now includes elements of means-ends thinking, such as "What can you do first?" "What will you do next?" "Will there be any obstacles that could get in the way?" "What will you do then?" "How long do you think that might take?" and "When is the best time to do that?"

ICPS AND PARENT INVOLVEMENT

To the extent that parent involvement involves activities that parents do to help their children learn, and to the extent that school counselors, school psychologists, or other student support personnel can work with parents, ICPS can serve as a viable addition for schools to offer to parents to help their children at home. *Raising a Thinking Child* (Shure, 1996), a modification of the I Can Problem Solve program, is designed for families with children ages 4 to 7. The *Raising a Thinking Child Workbook* (Shure, 2000a) provides an interactive set of exercises and games for parents to conduct with their children, also for ages 4 to 7. The workbook also includes "ICPS ladder" pages so that parents can see how they are handling problems between themselves and their children. Using the same four levels of communication described earlier for teachers, parents can easily see whether they are on Rung 1 (power assertion), Rung 2 (positive alternatives/suggestions), Rung 3 (explanations), or Rung 4 (problem-solving style of talk).

Raising a Thinking Preteen (Shure, 2000b) includes ICPS exercises and activities for families with children ages 8 through 12. Even parents and children who have never experienced the ICPS program can benefit from the activities before normal adolescence sets in. Steven's and Malika's parents could, with the help of a parent educator, learn to reinforce the social emotional ICPS concepts presented at school. And parents who have implemented the program from *Raising a Thinking Child* can continue to expand their children's ICPS skills with new, more complex ones.

In addition, because the exercises in the books for families are designed for use with individual children, school counselors and psychologists who work one-on-one with high-risk children can use exercises from the age-appropriate parent books to supplement ICPS classroom programs.

IMPLEMENTING ICPS IN THE SCHOOLS

Teachers can implement ICPS at any time of day they find convenient. Preschool and kindergarten teachers find it helpful to conduct ICPS lessons every day at a time when the children are already gathered. Some teachers prefer to organize small groups of 10 to 15 children to allow for maximum participation. Others find it possible to conduct the lessons with the entire class. In the grades after kindergarten, teachers have found it feasible to substitute ICPS for language arts, three times a week, for about 4 months. Our research indicates that the children do not lose academic information (actually, ICPS is a form of language arts): Since ICPS supports the impact of social emotional learning on academics, standardized achievement test scores in social studies, math, and reading substantially improve (Shure, 1980, 1984, 1993).

ICPS schools report that a very feasible way to add ICPS programs to their curriculum is to phase them in slowly. They find it most effective to start with enthusiastic teachers in the same grade level, who can network with each other. The school counselor, school psychologist, and other on-site personnel can play a key role in maintenance of the program in their schools. In addition to using the approach with individual high-risk children, they can support classroom teaching by helping out when needed and by training incoming teachers.

OUTCOME EVALUATIONS

Research Studies. Low-income African American 4- and 5-year-olds trained by teachers or by their parents could, compared to comparable controls, dramatically reduce negative impulsive and inhibited behaviors and increase positive sharing and caring behaviors. Importantly, trained youngsters not showing behavior problems in preschool were less likely to begin showing them in kindergarten and first grade, suggesting important implications of this cognitive approach to prevention. That the same youngsters who most improved in the trained ICPS skills also most improved in the measured behaviors, regardless of IQ, supports ICPS as significant mediators of behaviors (Shure & Spivack, 1978, 1979a, 1979b, 1980, 1982; Spivack & Shure, 1974). Compared to never-trained controls, children trained for 2 years by their teachers in kindergarten and in first grade were superior in ICPS skills and positive and negative behaviors 3 years later in grade 4. Children trained by parents who best learned how to use the problem-solving dialogue techniques when real problems arose had children who showed the most ICPS gains and behavioral improvement at the end of grade 4 (Shure, 1993).

For youngsters first trained in grade 5, positive behaviors increased before negative ones, and the latter took longer to change than in younger children. However, nontrained comparison groups actually showed more impulsive behaviors from grade 5 to 6. Positive outcome also occurred in the area of academic achievement. As mentioned earlier, standardized achievement test scores of ICPS-trained children improved, both in children first trained in kindergarten and in those first trained in grade 5, suggesting that children whose behaviors improved could better concentrate on the task-oriented demands of the classroom.

Service Evaluations. In addition to the formal research of Shure and Spivack, independent service evaluations have been conducted in several schools. In diverse ethnic and income groups, about equally distributed between Hispanics, African Americans, and Caucasians, Aberson (1987) found that ICPS-trained kindergarten children significantly decreased impulsive and inhibited behaviors and increased in the areas of peer acceptance, concern for others, and classroom initiative (findings that held through a 6-month follow-up). Teachers of Hispanic youngsters reported that the early ICPS vocabulary helped them learn the English language and may have contributed to enhanced self-confidence and ability to get along with others.

Similar findings were shown by the Mental Health Association in Illinois in Chicago Public Schools (Callahan, 1992) and in the Memphis Public Schools (Weddle & Williams, 1993), with behavioral impact in both studies having been the greatest among children whose teachers not only implemented the formal lesson-games, but most systematically used the problem-solving dialoguing techniques during the day. One school, serving over 800 lower- and middle-income Caucasian, African American, and Asian American youngsters (kindergarten to grade 5), reported a reduction in the number of incidents of children seen for disruptions in nonstructured settings (e.g., playground, school bus) since ICPS began there in 1994, from over 60 incidents a year down to 8 to 12.

Regarding parent training, Aberson (1996) found that ICPS enhances social emotional development in special needs youngsters (e.g., those with ADHD, Aspergers disorder), decreases depression and impulsivity, and increases ability to plan and to utilize verbal mediation skills. Her 3-year follow up of ADHD youngsters is showing maintenance, and even further gains (B. Aberson, personal communication, June 1999).

CONCLUSION

If Steven and Malika, and other children like them, can learn through ICPS and other social emotional programs to solve problems important to them now, they will be better able to solve problems important to them later. As they learn to care about themselves, they will come to be more caring about others. They will be more successful at making friends and better able to make responsible decisions in light of their potential consequences, and they will feel pride in their successes instead of frustration in their failures. Most importantly, they will more likely grow up to be thinking, feeling human beings who won't want to hurt themselves or others, either physically or emotionally.

REFERENCES

Aberson, B. (1987). *I Can Problem Solve (ICPS): A cognitive training program for kindergarten children* (Technical Report). Miami, FL: Dade County Public Schools.

Aberson, B. (1996). *An intervention for improving executive functioning and social/emotional adjustment of ADHD children: Three single case design studies.* Unpublished doctoral dissertation, Miami Institute of Psychology, Miami, FL.

Arend, R., Gove, F. L., & Sroufe, L. A. (1979). Continuity of individual adaptation from infancy to kindergarten: A predictive study of ego-resiliency and curiosity in preschoolers. *Child Development, 50,* 950–959.

Callahan, C. (1992). *1991–1992 evaluation report for the Mental Health schools project* (Technical Report). Chicago, IL: Mental Health Association in Illinois.

Catron, C. E., & Allen, J. (1993). *Early childhood curriculum.* New York: MacMillan.

Dimson, C. (1992). *Interpersonal cognitive problem solving and behavioral adjustment in preschoolers.* Unpublished master's thesis, California State University, Hayward.

Dodge, K. A., & Feldman, E. (1990). Issues in social cognition and sociometric status. In S. R. Asher & J. D. Coie (Eds.), *Peer rejection in childhood* (pp. 119–155). New York: Cambridge University Press.

Elias, M. J. (1997, December 1). "The missing piece": Making the case for greater attention to social and emotional learning. *Education Week*, pp. 36–37.

Eron, L. D., & Heusman, L. R. (1984). The relation of prosocial behavior to the development of aggression and psychopathology. *Aggressive Behavior, 10*, 201–211.

Ginott, H. G. (1965). *Between parent and child*. New York: MacMillan.

Goleman, D. (1995). *Emotional intelligence*. New York: Bantam Books.

Gordon, T. (1970). *Parent effectiveness training*. New York: Wyden.

Hoffman, M. L., & Salzstein, H. D. (1967). Parent discipline and the child's moral development. *Journal of Personality and Social Psychology, 5*, 45–57.

Johnson, J. E., Yu, S., & Roopnarine. J. (1980, March). *Social cognitive ability, interpersonal behaviors, and peer status within a mixed age group*. Paper presented at the meeting of the Southwestern Society for Research in Human Development, Lawrence, KA.

McKim, B. J., Weissberg, R. P., Cowen, E. L., Gesten, E. L., & Rapkin, B. D. (1982). A comparison of the problem-solving ability and adjustment of suburban and urban third grade children. *American Journal of Community Psychology, 10*, 155–169.

Parker, J. G., & Asher, S. R. (1987). Peer relations and later personal adjustment: Are low-accepted children "at risk"? *Psychological Bulletin, 102*, 357–389.

Richard, B. A., & Dodge, K. A. (1982). Social maladjustment and problem solving in school-aged children. *Journal of Consulting and Clinical Psychology, 50*, 226–233.

Rubin, K. H., & Mills, R. (1988). The many faces of social isolation in childhood. *Journal of Consulting and Clinical Psychology, 56*, 916–924.

Shure, M. B. (1980). *Interpersonal problem solving in ten-year-olds*. (Grant No. MH27741). Washington, DC: National Institute of Mental Health.

Shure, M. B. (1982). Interpersonal problem solving: A cog in the wheel of social cognition. In F. C. Serafica (Ed.), *Social-cognitive development in context* (pp. 133–166). New York: Guilford Press.

Shure, M. B. (1984). *Problem solving and mental health of 10- to 12-year-olds*. (Grant No. 35989). Washington, DC: National Institute of Mental Health.

Shure, M. B. (1992a). *I Can Problem Solve (ICPS): An interpersonal cognitive problem-solving program* [preschool]. Champaign, IL: Research Press.

Shure, M. B. (1992b). *I Can Problem Solve (ICPS): An interpersonal cognitive problem-solving program* [kindergarten/primary grades]. Champaign, IL: Research Press.

Shure, M. B. (1992c). *I Can Problem Solve (ICPS): An interpersonal cognitive problem-solving program* [intermediate elementary grades]. Champaign, IL: Research Press.

Shure, M. B. (1993). *Interpersonal problem solving and prevention*. (Grant No. 40801). Washington, DC: National Institute of Mental Health.

Shure, M. B. (1996). *Raising a thinking child: Help your young child to resolve everyday conflicts and get along with others*. New York: Pocket Books.

Shure, M. B. (2000a). *Raising a thinking child workbook*. Champaign, IL: Research Press.

Shure, M. B. (2000b). *Raising a thinking preteen: The I can problem solve program for 8- to 12-year-olds.* New York: Henry Holt.

Shure, M. B., & Spivack, G. (1978). *Problem solving techniques in childrearing.* San Francisco: Jossey-Bass.

Shure, M. B., & Spivack, G. (1979a). Interpersonal cognitive problem solving and primary prevention: Programming for preschool and kindergarten children. *Journal of Clinical Child Psychology, 8,* 89–94.

Shure, M. B., & Spivack, G. (1979b). Interpersonal problem solving thinking and adjustment in the mother-child dyad. In M. W. Kent & J. E. Rolf (Eds.), *The primary prevention of psychopathology: Vol. 3. Social competence in children* (pp. 201–219). Hanover, NH: University Press of New England.

Shure, M. B., & Spivack, G. (1980). Interpersonal problem solving as a mediator of behavioral adjustment in preschool and kindergarten children. *Journal of Applied Developmental Psychology, 1,* 29–43.

Shure, M. B., & Spivack, G. (1982). Interpersonal problem solving in young children: A cognitive approach to prevention. *American Journal of Community Psychology, 10,* 341–356.

Shure, M. B., Spivack, G., & Gordon, R. (1972). Problem solving thinking: A preventive mental health program for preschool children. *Reading World, 11,* 259–273.

Shure, M. B., Spivack, G., & Jaeger, M. A. (1971). Problem-solving thinking and adjustment among disadvantaged preschool children. *Child Development, 42,* 1791–1803.

Spivack, G., Platt, J. J., & Shure, M. B. (1976). *The problem solving approach to adjustment.* San Francisco: Jossey-Bass.

Spivack, G., & Shure, M. B. (1974). *Social adjustment of young children.* San Francisco: Jossey-Bass.

Spivack, G., & Shure, M. B. (1982). Interpersonal cognitive problem solving and clinical theory. In B. Lahey & A. E. Kazdin (Eds.), *Advances in clinical psychology* (Vol. 5; pp. 323–372). New York: Plenum.

Turner, R. R., & Boulter, L. K. (1981, August). *The validity of the PIPS.* Paper presented at the meeting of the American Psychological Association, Los Angeles, CA.

Urberg, K. A., & Docherty, E. M. (1976). Development of role-taking skills in young children. *Developmental Psychology, 12,* 198–203.

Weddle, K. D., & Williams, F. (1993). *Implementing and assessing the effectiveness of the Interpersonal Cognitive Problem-Solving (ICPS) Curriculum in four experimental and four control classrooms* (Technical Report). Memphis, TN: Memphis State University.

Chapter 9

PATHS IN YOUR CLASSROOM: PROMOTING EMOTIONAL LITERACY AND ALLEVIATING EMOTIONAL DISTRESS

Carol A. Kusché, Ph.D.

University of Washington

Mark T. Greenberg, Ph.D.

Pennsylvania State University

Over the past few decades, our culture has been changing at an unprecedented rate. Thus, raising children, even under the best of conditions, has been complex not only on a daily basis, but also because parents have not been able to rely on their own childhood experience or predict the future for which they are preparing their children. In addition, the gene pool has become far more heterogeneous than was typical for the small groups that existed for most of our evolutionary history, which adds another level of complexity (e.g., when children inherit the propensity for traits such as intense nervous system sensitivity, strong desire for risk-taking, and so on that are foreign to the caregivers). Thus, professionals often hear perplexed mothers expressing such things as, "I don't understand her at all. She's just like her father." or "No one has ever been like that in my family."

For most of human evolution, people lived in small, homogenous groups, where the culture and genetics apparently changed relatively little from one generation to the next. This began to change with the advent of agriculture several thousand years ago and then far more rapidly with industrialization a century ago. Now we have computers, global warming, worldwide travel, a six-fold population increase since 1900, and other un-precedented changes that are leading us into new and uncharted territories. In order for the new generations to cope adaptively, education must keep pace.

THE NEED FOR EMOTIONAL LITERACY FOR ALL CHILDREN

Two hundred years ago, education for the average child (who grew up under agricultural conditions) consisted largely of teaching by parents and the church, followed perhaps by an apprenticeship for a son. Formal education and literacy were not crucial for economic or social well-being. A hundred years later, as industrialization began to take hold, it became necessary to provide formal education for all children, especially with regard to reading literacy. In today's world, an adult who is illiterate is at a distinct disadvantage. Similarly, in the past, formal social and emotional education outside of religion were apparently unnecessary for adequate adult functioning, but this is no longer the case. In the next century, individuals who are emotionally illiterate will be at a distinct disadvantage. Further, many parents readily admit that they did not have effective social emotional experiences as children and therefore are not well-equipped to provide the optimal social emotional learning context for their own children. Thus, it has become crucial for educators to be able to teach these to their students.

During the past few decades, it has grown increasingly more apparent that many children grow up in chronic distress (Wolchik & Sandler, 1997). Although we know many of the reasons for this—including poor parenting skills, abuse, family fragmentation, parental stress, disintegration of community support networks, urbanization, economic changes, overexposure to graphic violence, and overcrowded living conditions—this knowledge by itself does little to help these children with their emotional pain. Moreover, not only does chronic emotional suffering interfere with the ability to learn (Kusché, Cook, & Greenberg, 1993), but also it is unconscionable to allow children to suffer when this can be corrected.

MAJOR GOALS FOR DEVELOPING PATHS

These needs for optimal social emotional development, prevention, and intervention provided much of the motivation 15 years ago when we began to develop the PATHS Curriculum (Kusché & Greenberg, 1994) and continue to inspire us to promote its dissemination. We wanted to fill the need for a comprehensive, developmentally based curriculum that could be taught by elementary school teachers from Grades K through 5, so that all elementary-school-age children could have the opportunity for high-quality social and emotional education.

Our major goals for developing PATHS (*P*romoting *A*lternative *TH*inking *S*trategies) were multifocused and included all of the following:

- Promote emotional literacy
- Improve social competence
- Optimize developmental growth
- Alleviate and prevent emotional distress
- Prevent behavioral and emotional problems
- Reduce risk factors related to later maladjustment
- Improve classroom atmosphere and teacher-student relationships

Thus, PATHS was designed to be a curriculum that would benefit all children, those who are normally adjusted, at risk, or in need of intervention. We also felt strongly that social emotional instruction needed to be taught on a regular basis throughout every school year and that instruction from one year to the next should be increasingly more complex as the children matured; that is, social emotional instruction should be based on and grow from previous learning, just like reading and arithmetic. We also wanted to provide a curriculum that would be comfortable for teachers to use, enjoyable for children to learn, and generalizable for use throughout the classroom day and throughout the school environment. Finally, we wanted to include material for use with parents so that PATHS could be generalized to the home environment as well. PATHS went through several evolutions and considerable research before we were able to reach all of these goals.

THEORETICAL BACKGROUND OF PATHS

When we first started to develop the PATHS Curriculum for use with deaf children, we naively thought that we would be able to simply adapt curricular material from regular education so that it could be used with deaf children. To our surprise, we found that there were no available comprehensive models. In order to develop such a model, we reviewed the literature as well as the leading theoretical models of development, so that we could utilize what was best in each of them. Our review included psychoanalytic developmental theory, attachment theory, developmental neuropsychology, developmental social cognition, cognitive developmental theory, cognitive social learning theory, and an ecobehavioral systems model. Two of these models were of special importance, so we will review them in greater detail.

Psychoanalytic Developmental Theory

Psychoanalytic developmental theory was central to the development of PATHS, and its incorporation distinguishes PATHS from the vast majority of other social learning curricula. One aspect of this, for example, involves the emphasis on the centrality of emotions. Instead of encouraging children to repress or stifle their feelings in order to focus exclusively on cognition, children are encouraged to become aware of and verbally express their feelings in a safe manner. Emotions are an integral part of daily life and profoundly affect learning in a dynamic manner regardless of whether a child or teacher is aware of them. Part of the value that awareness brings to the learning equation is in allowing children and adults to have more understanding and control over subsequent behaviors. Encouraging the expression of emotions in a controlled manner ultimately enhances the educational process, promotes healthy integration, and improves classroom atmosphere. In addition, with PATHS we have shown that emotional knowledge can be taught to children, like all of the other important areas in a child's basic education.

Psychoanalytic education is derived from a developmental theory and aims to coordinate social, emotional, and cognitive growth (Jones, 1968). Special emphasis is placed on respect for the integrity of each child, as well as on the encouragement of active student participation and interaction in the learning process. In other words, this model is not one of teaching *to* children or of shaping children to conform to external adult expectations, but rather one of providing conditions that will result in optimal internalization, integration, and growth. Like John Dewey's educational philosophy and Piaget's cognitive theory, psychoanalytic theory asserts that children attain their optimal propensities when they experience interactive environmental conditions of respect, caring, empathy, and knowledge. Further, by promoting the development of internal self-control and self-motivation along with healthy standards for behavior, children develop an optimal sense of autonomy and ability to make decisions while simultaneously considering the needs and feelings of others.

For example, in the PATHS subunit on manners, the emphasis is not on simply teaching the rules of etiquette. Rather, students contemplate and discuss the consequences of having good versus bad manners and evaluate why good manners are important (e.g., the way we act affects how other people feel; caring about other people's feelings is beneficial for everyone). In this way, children come to "own" the concepts as belonging to themselves (i.e., they internalize them), and they voluntarily choose to use good manners because they want to use them and believe that it is the right thing to do. As a result, children do not have to be externally controlled or monitored; this is especially important in today's complex world where teachers, police, and other authority figures are not continually available to oversee behavior or to provide for safe living conditions.

Psychoanalytic education is intended to enhance developmental growth, promote mental health, and prevent emotional distress (Kusché, in press). In addition, it provides a greater appreciation of such things as emotions, the development of the defensive repertoire, and internalization. Moreover, psychoanalytic theory invites us as educators and parents to seek a greater understanding of the unrecognized thoughts and feelings that dynamically influence our children's behavior, self-esteem, awareness of self and others, social competence, problem solving, decision making, and so on. Once we become aware of unconscious factors that affect daily functioning, we can begin to explain these phenomena to our students.

In addition, teachers are powerful role models for children, and the information that teachers impart is often given the status of absolute truth, especially during the elementary school years. When teachers express an interest in children's feelings and emotional experiences or show respect for children's opinions, their students can be impacted in a profound manner. Students also develop a healthy sense of self-esteem from observing the positive reactions of others towards them. This promotes positive relationships between teachers and students, encourages respect among students for one another, enriches the classroom atmosphere, and enhances academic learning.

In summary, some of the long-range goals of psychoanalytic education include the development of a positive sense of self, a kind but fair sense of prosocial internal control, respect for self and others, healthy internal motivation, and curiosity and love for learning that operate independently of the external environment. These, in turn, enhance developmental growth, improve school functioning, and optimize mental health, and at the same time, prevent negative outcomes such as antisocial tendencies, violent behavior, and substance abuse.

Developmental Neuropsychology

Another model, developmental neuropsychology, also greatly influenced us during the development of PATHS, and we believe that the utilization of this model further distinguishes PATHS from other programs. Among other things, developmental neuropsychology includes such areas as the evolutionary understanding of brain development; developmental considerations of brain maturation; organization of the brain; structuralization of neuronal networks; integration of processing between different areas of the brain; differences between unconscious, preconscious, and conscious processes; and ways in which emotions are processed.

For example, we have recently come to better understand the important role of neuronal networks between the prefrontal cortex and the limbic system with regard to self-control (Kusché & Greenberg, in press-a). Moreover, research strongly suggests that this neuronal wiring or structuralization does not automatically occur; rather, adequate environmental input within the context of a caring relationship seems to be crucial for this to develop in an optimal manner (Schore, 1994). Based on this information, we teach younger children in PATHS a motor-inhibiting response (i.e., "doing Turtle," originally conceptualized by Robin, Schneider, & Dolnick, 1976) to calm down and gain self-control. Older children, on the other hand, are taught to practice consciously mediated strategies for self-control that include self-talk (i.e., verbal mediation and the Control Signals Poster, adapted from the concept originally developed by Weissberg, Caplan, & Bennetto, 1988).

Another major area of importance in developmental neuropsychology involves the specialization of different areas of the brain for different types of functions. With the exception of positive emotional expression, to become consciously aware of how we are feeling, neuronal networks must be able to transmit the information from the right to the left side of the brain via the corpus collosum (a bridge-like structure that links the left and right hemispheres), so that it can be translated into language.[1]

Thus, in PATHS we emphasize verbal identification and labeling of affects (e.g., with use of Feeling Face cards that include the drawing of each affect expression with its printed label) to assist with affect management, control over behavior, and improved hemispheric integration (Kusché, in press). We also use a color-coded differentiation of comfortable (yellow) versus uncomfortable (blue) feelings (the pleasure/displeasure dichotomy originally identified by Freud, 1915/1957). In addition, encouraging children to talk about emotional experiences (both at the time they are occurring and in recollection) further strengthens intercortical integration.

In summary, research strongly suggests that learning experiences in the context of emotionally meaningful relationships during childhood strongly influence the development of neural networks within and between different areas of the brain which, in turn, affect such psychological phenomena as self-control and emotional awareness. Thus, we incorporated strategies in PATHS to optimize the nature and quality of teacher-child and peer-peer interactions that are likely to impact brain development as well as learning. A more comprehensive review of our neuropsychological model of brain organization and integration can be found in Greenberg and Snell (1997) and in Kusché and Greenberg (in press-a).

The ABCD Model of Development

Based on what we felt was the best of all of the theoretical models that we reviewed, we developed our own ABCD (Affective-Behavioral-Cognitive-Dynamic) model that places primary importance on the developmental integration of emotion, behavior, language, and cognitive understanding as they relate to social and emotional competence. The stages of developmental integration in the ABCD Model, as well as further information on this and the other theoretical models, can be found in Greenberg & Kusché (1993, 1998a).

OVERVIEW OF THE PATHS CURRICULUM

The complete PATHS Curriculum consists of six volumes of lessons, a teacher's instructional manual, several posters, a set of photographs, Feeling Face cards, and all of the pictures needed for each lesson. There are a total of 131 lessons, but any particular lesson can last one to five or more sessions, depending on the needs of the specific group of children. In addition, although the content itself is valuable, it should be stressed that the process and generalization throughout the classroom day are at least of equal importance. Supplementary material for parent education, homework assignments, classroom activities, and so on can be utilized as desired.[2]

PATHS provides teachers with systematic, developmentally based lessons and materials for teaching emotional literacy, self-control, social competence, healthy relationships, positive self-esteem, empathy, and interpersonal problem solving. PATHS lessons target the key active ingredients for effective prevention and emotional intelligence programs identified by the W. T. Grant Consortium on the School-Based Promotion of Social Competence (1992). These include instruction in identifying and labeling feelings, expressing feelings, assessing the intensity of feelings, managing feelings, understanding the difference between feelings and behaviors, delaying gratification, controlling impulses, reducing stress, using self-talk, reading and interpreting social cues, using steps for problem solving and decision making, understanding the perspectives of others, developing awareness of behavioral norms, having a positive attitude toward life, developing self-awareness, using nonverbal communication skills, and using verbal communication skills (Goleman, 1995). In using PATHS, teachers also become more aware of their students' emotional issues and other dynamic factors that affect behavior. We believe that all of these factors contribute to the growth of productive, creative, well-balanced children and facilitate the development of a strong, healthy foundation prior to the onset of adolescence.

Using and Adapting PATHS in Different Classrooms

PATHS is designed to be used in a flexible manner. Thus PATHS will be taught differently in a self-contained class for developmentally delayed children than it will be taught with children in a regular education classroom. It is also likely, however, that even in two regular education classes, teachers will want to make adaptations to address the needs of their particular students. Similarly, the scope and sequence of PATHS will differ if it is begun in kindergarten or in a later grade. In other words, because schools and classrooms have disparate needs, we recommend adapting PATHS as needed, and the best way to know how to adapt PATHS for your particular classroom will be to get to know PATHS.

The PATHS Process

Finally, although this review of PATHS has emphasized content thus far, the PATHS process is at least as important (Kusché & Greenberg, in press-b). As teachers learn the material to teach to their students, they also begin to understand more about emotions and their importance in the classroom. Engaging in the PATHS process and the use of empathy begins to positively influence the manner in which teachers interact with their students throughout the day, a phenomenon we have repeatedly observed and teachers have reported. This, in turn, improves teacher-student relationships, as well as overall classroom atmosphere.

USING PATHS WITH STEVEN AND MALIKA

Rather than give a comprehensive description of PATHS (available in Greenberg & Kusché, 1998a; Kusché & Greenberg, 1994), we will describe the use of PATHS in the hypothetical context of working with Steven and Malika, the two children introduced in Chapter 2 who are not actualizing their potentials in school for different reasons. Using the background information provided, we will continue their stories, hypothesizing about the following year in their respective lives, a year in which PATHS is used in each of their classrooms. To this purpose, we introduce two new characters, Ms. Sugar, Steven's second-grade teacher, and Mr. Spice, Malika's sixth-grade teacher. Both of these teachers are well aware of the challenges that each of their students is facing and both also understand the need for social emotional learning for all children. These teachers attended a 2-day workshop on PATHS and both feel excited about using PATHS in their classrooms this year.

Steven in the Second Grade

After reviewing the records of her incoming second graders and discussing their histories with their first-grade teachers, Ms. Sugar decided that she would introduce the Turtle story and play, along with the PATHS Kid paradigm (which includes complimenting), at the beginning of the school year. Even though her students were in second grade, they had never had PATHS or any social emotional program before. Moreover, there were a number of children who were still displaying problems with self-control (including Steven), and Ms. Sugar liked the metaphor of a turtle going into its shell to calm down. She also felt that the Turtle story and the PATHS Kid paradigm would foster a bonding process to help the classroom environment feel safer and would introduce her students to role-playing. However, she didn't feel that her students needed the reinforcement system or the early language lessons, so she elected to skip these. Following Turtle, Ms. Sugar planned to continue with the feelings lessons, along with the friendship and manners lessons.

When Steven heard the Turtle story, it was clear that he identified with the feelings of Little Turtle, and he was very proud to play the part of Wise Old Turtle who gave advice and help to the younger turtle. When he had a turn to take home the video that Ms. Sugar had made of the class play, he reported to Ms. Sugar that both of his parents had told him that they felt proud of him. Ms. Sugar also was impressed with Steven's ability to memorize the lines in the play; this observation, along with testing data showing considerable skill in phonemic processing, letter decoding, and so on, suggested to her that Steven's problem with reading was not due to a cognitive learning disability.

At about this same time, Ms. Sugar learned from a parent conference that neither parent had ever spent much time reading to Steven, because they had both been so busy with their careers. Since love for reading (within the context of a loving relationship) had never been established (recall that Steven frequently voiced that he "hated reading"), Ms. Sugar felt that this, along with his low self-esteem, were the emotional vulnerabilities that needed to be addressed before cognitive progress could proceed.

Steven responded very well to the structure of using Turtle and the procedure for calming down. He loved the Turtle story and repeatedly asked Ms. Sugar to read it again to the class. To promote generalization, Ms. Sugar gave a copy of the Turtle story to Ms. Cinnamon, Steven's reading resource teacher, so that she could use it with him as well. At first Steven only wanted to be read to, but after several sessions, Steven said he wanted to read the story himself. Since he had memorized the story by this time, he was able to "read" it almost flawlessly, and as a reward, Ms. Cinnamon gave him his own copy of the Turtle story to take home and read to his sister. Steven did so proudly, and his mother was so impressed that she called the school to thank Ms. Cinnamon.

By this time, Ms. Sugar had introduced the Feelings Unit, and the two teachers discussed the idea of Steven bringing his box of Feeling Faces to discuss his feelings about reading with Ms. Cinnamon. Ms. Cinnamon, of course, would have her own set of Feeling Faces too. Steven was excited about this, as he was already happily displaying and discussing his feelings in Ms. Sugar's class. Ms. Cinnamon also chose other stories with problems and emotions that Steven could identify with so that he could talk about his feelings via identification with the characters.

The first day that he used his Feeling Faces with Ms. Cinnamon, Steven put his confused face into the pocket. "I see you're feeling confused today," Ms. Cinnamon remarked to Steven.

"Yes," he replied. "I used to hate reading, but now I think maybe I like it, so I'm confused."

Ms. Cinnamon smiled and said, "Yes, it can be confusing when our feelings change, can't it?" Ms. Cinnamon put her delighted face into her Feeling Strip and told Steven that she felt delighted to learn that maybe he now liked reading.

Progress in reading continued throughout the year. Steven loved to discuss the feelings of the characters, and after learning the basics of informal problem solving in Ms. Sugar's class, he began to conjecture about potential consequences and endings to the stories he read with Ms. Cinnamon. "Sometimes," Steven told Ms. Cinnamon one day, "my endings are better than the ones in the book! Why didn't they think about the consequences?"

Ms. Sugar also watched Steven progress during the year. He paid close attention during the PATHS lessons and was eager to share examples of his own experiences and feelings. In addition, the other children had also developed better self-control and emotional understanding, and a communal sense of bonding and mutual support was palpable in the classroom atmosphere.

When it was Steven's turn to be the PATHS Kid, virtually all the children in the room raised their hands to give him a compliment.

"You are a good friend," said the first child Steven picked.

"You are fun to play with and you always help me," said the second.

"I am proud of all of the hard work you have done this year and at how much you have grown," said Ms. Sugar.

And for his own compliment, Steven stated, "I am a good friend and I am a good reader."

As always, the class applauded loudly.

At the end-of-the-year PATHS party, the class had much to celebrate. Steven and his classmates were ready, emotionally and academically, for the third grade. Fortunately, Mr. Cardamom, Steven's third-grade teacher, was eager to continue to use PATHS the following school year.

Malika in the Sixth Grade (Last Year in Elementary School)

Mr. Spice had taught sixth grade for the past dozen years, and every year he made it his personal goal to see that all of his students were ready for middle school by the time that they left his classroom. This year, Mr. Spice was even more optimistic, because now for the first time, he had an actual curriculum, as well as social emotional training.

With regard to Malika, Mr. Spice had read over her student file, in which her fifth-grade teacher had written: "Malika is a very bright child with leadership qualities, who, unfortunately, will probably drop out of school within the next few years."

"Not if I can help it," Mr. Spice had thought to himself.

Following a phone consultation, Mr. Spice decided to begin PATHS with the class discussion and creation of class rules, followed by the PATHS Kid, a review of basic feelings, anger management with the Control Signals Poster, more feelings lessons, friendship, manners, and informal problem-solving sessions. Mr. Spice also opted to use the Feeling Faces even though his students were sixth graders because they had received no previous instruction involving emotional understanding.

During the first week of school, Mr. Spice found that his 35 sixth graders were eager to participate in the creation of class rules, and they clearly liked the PATHS Kid paradigm. At the end of their first week, they were given their first homework assignment to go home and give compliments to all of the members of their family.

To introduce the Feelings Unit, Mr. Spice decided to combine the introduction to feelings with a lesson on diversity. First he talked about how we all feel the same set of feelings, regardless of race or gender. Mr. Spice further noted that in spite of the fact that all humans everywhere in the world have the same feelings and show the same facial expressions for them, different people can feel differently about different things. Mr. Spice spent two more weeks on diversity and feelings (in which he incorporated geography) and further expanded the topic to include the handicapped and the elderly. Mr. Spice noted that Malika began to voluntarily participate in some of these class discussions.

After introducing the basic feelings, Mr. Spice spent another two weeks on introducing anger, the difference between feelings and behaviors ("All feelings are OK to have. Behaviors can be OK or Not OK."), and the Control Signals Poster. It was clear that Malika liked the Three Steps for Calming Down; she frequently walked up to the poster, touched the red light, and calmed herself down. Malika told Mr. Spice that she was a Pikachu from the Pokémon game who went inside her Poké Ball so she wouldn't shock other people whenever she felt upset. Mr. Spice wasn't really familiar with Pokémon, but he soon learned, when his students, modeling after Malika, took on the identities of other characters. Malika was secretly proud of having started this trend, but when Mr. Spice complimented her on her leadership skills, as well as her great idea, she was surprised that he felt proud of a girl for being a leader.

The class readily took to Informal Problem Solving and soon the Problem Box was stuffed full of problems that needed to be solved. In addition, with the help of parent volunteers, the children were able to discuss and share their feelings in smaller groups. The only complaint was, "There is never enough time!" Even Malika became an active participant. When classroom situations arose that required intervention, Mr. Spice turned them into class problem-solving sessions or met individually with the students to discuss their feelings and possible resolutions to their problems. Mr. Spice also added writing assignments involving feelings and encouraged the use of the PATHS Feelings Dictionaries. Sharing these stories with the class became a tradition during language arts.

Following the lessons on belonging and rejection, Mr. Spice integrated history with PATHS by adding a lesson on Susan B. Anthony. The class learned that less than a hundred years ago, women in the United States were not considered equal to men, and they did not even have the right to vote. Ms. Anthony felt furious about being told that women were inferior to men, and she knew that this wasn't true. So every year for 37 years, she appeared before the U.S. Congress to try to get an amendment to the Constitution so women could have the right to vote. In 1920, fourteen years after she had died, women finally achieved this right. Although Susan B. Anthony never got to vote herself, her diligent work was very important, and she had helped other people; the Nineteenth Amendment was unofficially named after her. Malika, as well as the rest of the class, showed so much interest that Mr. Spice added more of these biographies to his history lessons.

When the class began their community project (a problem-solving lesson), Malika was chosen as one of the two student leaders. She encouraged the class to start a food drive, "because," she said, "not everyone has as much as we do." Malika's actual circumstances hadn't changed, but now she felt empowered to take charge and implement change, which enabled her to master her feelings of anxiety, anger, and helplessness.

Problem solving, feeling discussions, and other lessons continued. Soon spring would be coming with placement testing for middle school. Two months before the testing date, Mr. Spice began to hold mock test-taking role-plays and practices, and the students discussed their feelings of anxiety, fear, anger, and so on. They also discussed why these tests were important, which led to a discussion about why education was important, what kids would be doing in the future, and so on.

Although test-taking anxiety was almost paralyzing for Malika during the first role-plays, she practiced her three steps for calming down in her imaginary Poké Ball, and she expressed her feelings about these experiences. Malika also received strong support from the class when she discussed how embarrassed she felt when she did well because she thought that girls were not suppose to stand out or be special or, especially, do better than boys.

"If you work hard and do well," said one of the boys, "then you should feel proud of yourself, no matter what other people are doing—like Susan B. Anthony did!" The rest of the class, boys and girls, agreed.

Malika soon began to master her test-taking anxiety, and by the time the real placement test came, she did well. She displayed her proud Feeling Face when Mr. Spice told her the results.

June came all too soon, as it always does, but Mr. Spice felt that he had been successful in reaching his goal of preparing his students for middle school. And Malika, the proud leader who now stood up for herself and her ideas, had changed profoundly from the angry, frightened little girl that she had been the year before.

EFFICACY: RESEARCH EVIDENCE DOCUMENTING THE EFFECTIVENESS OF PATHS

Obviously, the stories of Steven and Malika are fictional, although largely based on actual experiences with real children. But science demands a more rigorous collection of data, and to this end, the present authors have conducted three controlled studies with randomized control versus experimental groups, using one year of PATHS implementation with pre-, post-, and follow-up data (Greenberg & Kusché, 1993, 1996, 1998b; Greenberg,

Kusché, Cook, & Quamma, 1995; Kusché, 1984).These studies involved three different populations: (1) deaf or hearing impaired, (2) regular education, and (3) special education–classified children. A summary of these researches is provided in the next section, but a more comprehensive review of this research can be found in Greenberg and Kusché (1998a).

Increasing Protective Factors

In all three clinical trials, the use of the PATHS Curriculum significantly increased the following abilities:

- Recognizing and understanding emotions
- Understanding social problems
- Developing effective alternative solutions to problems
- Decreasing the percentage of aggressive or violent solutions

Similarly, in all three groups of children, teachers reported significant improvements in children's prosocial behavior in the following domains:

- Emotional understanding
- Self-control
- Ability to tolerate frustration
- Use of effective conflict resolution strategies

Cognitive testing indicated that PATHS led to improvements in the following skills:

- Ability to plan ahead to solve complex tasks with normal and special needs children (not tested in the deaf or hearing impaired group)
- Cognitive flexibility and lower levels of impulsivity (coding from the WISC-R)
- Improved reading achievement for young deaf children

Reducing Maladaptive Outcomes

Teachers (in regular and special needs classes) reported the following reductions in behavioral difficulties at one-year post intervention:

- Decreased internalizing symptoms (sadness, anxiety, and withdrawal)
- Decreased externalizing symptoms (aggressive and disruptive behavior)

Students (in regular and special needs classes) reported the following reductions in behavioral difficulties at one-year post intervention:

- Decreased symptoms of sadness and depression (Child Depression Inventory)
- Decreased report of conduct problems

Initial Findings from the National FAST Track Demonstration Program

The FAST Track PATHS Curriculum is a revised version of PATHS which maintains the critical components of the original curriculum, with additional material provided primarily for the older grades (i.e., third through fifth grades). It was utilized in four American locations (Seattle, Nashville, Durham, and rural Pennsylvania). Findings at the end of first grade, after one year of implementation (Bierman, Greenberg, & Conduct Problems Prevention Research Group, 1996; McMahon, Slough, & Conduct Problems Prevention Research Group, 1996), indicated that in schools in which PATHS was operating, there was improved social adaptation (as compared to matched control schools) as indexed by more positive reports on the following dimensions:

- Lower peer aggression scores based on peer ratings (sociometrics)
- Lower peer hyperactivity scores based on peer ratings (sociometrics)
- Lower teacher ratings of disruptive behavior (teacher report)
- Improved classroom atmosphere (assessed by independent observers)

Research from Independent Replications

During the past decade, the PATHS Curriculum has been implemented in numerous schools and classrooms throughout the United States and around the world, in such countries as Canada, Great Britain, Australia, New Zealand, Holland, Belgium, Norway, Israel, and Thailand. Most of these uses have not included formal research, although informal reports have all been positive. In Texas, however, three cities (Laredo, Austin, and Lufkin) collaborated in data collection and analysis. The evaluation report showed significant improvement for each city, as well as for all the cities combined, in all areas tested, including emotion vocabulary and aspects of classroom behavior, after one year of PATHS implementation (Russell, 1998). In addition, nonverbal intelligence (measured only in Laredo through the use of Block Design and Mazes from the WISC-R, Wechsler, 1974) also showed significant improvement. The significant improvement on Block Design replicates a similar finding with our regular education population and supports the hypothesis that use of PATHS improves cortical integration.

Another replication of PATHS, conducted with deaf children in Great Britain, similarly showed significant improvement in emotional understanding, behavior, self-image, and emotional adjustment after one year of PATHS lessons (Hindley, Reed, Jeffs, & McSweeney, 1998). PATHS has also been used successfully, but not formally researched, with elementary-school-age children in after-school care settings. An adapted version of PATHS was beneficial when used with preschool children and assessed through the use of a quasi-experimental design (Denham & Burton, 1996).

Reports from Independent Research Review Projects

A number of research review projects have been conducted in the area of social emotional learning. PATHS has received top ratings from all of these independent review panels including *Positive Youth Development* (Catalano, Berglund, Ryan, Lonczak, & Hawkins, 1998), *Safe Schools, Safe Students* (1998), *Blueprints for Violence Prevention Project* (1997–1998), and *Promising Approaches* (Wong, Catalano, Hawkins, & Chappell, 1996). All of these review panels searched through numerous programs to find the few that met their stated criteria.

Summary of Program Effectiveness for Positive Youth Development, Prevention, and Intervention

PATHS has been shown to improve protective factors and reduce behavioral risk across a wide variety of elementary-school-age children, even after only one year of implementation. Effectiveness has been demonstrated with normally functioning children of both genders in regular education (private and public schools), as well as children in special education (deaf, hearing impaired, gifted, learning disabled, mildly mentally retarded, and serious emotional and behavioral disorders). In addition, these findings have shown cross-rater validity, as they have been reflected in teacher ratings, self-reports, child testing or interviewing, and independent ratings by classroom observers (Greenberg & Kusché, 1998a).

Successful implementations of PATHS have been undertaken with entire schools as well as with selected grades of elementary-school-age children, in both mainstreamed and self-contained classrooms. We have also found beneficial results with a wide diversity of ethnic, cultural, socioeconomic, and family backgrounds. It seems that difficulty with growing up in today's world is affecting all children and is not limited by economic, racial, cultural, or family backgrounds. We also believe that this is a reflection of the universal importance of social and emotional learning.

Findings indicate that PATHS is effective for positive youth development, prevention, and intervention. This is especially of practical value to educators, since the average classroom generally includes a mixture of children who are in need of intervention as well as those who are normally functioning but can nevertheless benefit from positive youth development. In other words, PATHS is a universal program that improves the quality of development for all elementary-school-age children (Kusché, in press).

WHY DOES PATHS WORK?

Research has shown that PATHS is very effective and beneficial for children, but does not clearly demonstrate which of the many factors make PATHS work so well. As noted in the theory section, we believe that the dynamic integration of emotion, cognition, behavior, and language, which in turn promotes cortical integration and personality maturation, is crucial to the success of our program. In addition, PATHS meets all of the specifications of the core principles described in this volume by Cohen (see Chapter 1), components that are hypothesized to promote social emotional growth.

1. *PATHS helps to establish a safe, caring, and responsive classroom.* The ecological process factors targeted in PATHS are believed to serve multiple protective functions. First, improved training and emotional awareness for teachers positively alter the quality of relationships between school personnel and students. Second, in using PATHS, teachers become more knowledgeable about dynamic factors that affect behavior, as well as about the specific emotional needs of their particular students, and thus can be more empathic and better able to intervene in more effective ways. Third, children become better able to understand their teachers, respect their teachers' feelings, and identify with their teachers' prosocial values, which also helps to diminish anxiety and anger that can interfere with attention and learning.

Finally, when children feel listened to and are shown respect by their teachers and peers, they feel valued, cared for, appreciated, supported, respected, and part of a social group. This, along with empathy from teacher and peers, motivates children to value, care for, appreciate, and feel prosocial toward themselves, their environment, the social groups to which they belong, other people, and their world. To become truly socialized, children must internalize and embrace prosocial values as their own and must feel that their society is a group that they respect, belong to, and toward which they want to contribute in positive and responsible ways. All of this is best achieved through nurturance and mutual respect.

2. *PATHS promotes self-awareness.* When children talk about their feelings and experiences, they become more aware of who they are. Getting feedback from others, participating in role plays, and so on, further enhance the process of self-awareness. Moreover, many children (e.g., bullies) receive attention from teachers and peers primarily for negative behaviors rather than for prosocial actions or for verbally communicating their feelings and experiences. Given human nature, they feel that any attention is better than no attention at all; thus negative and aggressive behaviors are often inadvertently reinforced, that is, we unwittingly end up encouraging the development of behaviors that we don't want rather than the prosocial behaviors that we really do want. With PATHS, we reverse these contingencies, so that prosocial behaviors are reinforced and negative behaviors are not.

3. *PATHS improves awareness of others.* Empathy, respect for others, and the ability to understand how one's behaviors affect others are all important factors for being aware of others, as well as for the self-prohibition of antisocial behavior. It has been shown, for example, that the recidivism rate for delinquents is significantly reduced when these adolescents are made to role-play and to take the perspectives of their victims. Furthermore, awareness of others helps to improve interpersonal skills, which, in turn, facilitate the ability to form positive, adaptive relationships with others. As a result, there is an increased likelihood that individuals will feel a sense of belonging to prosocial groups and a decreased need to join groups of individuals who feel alienated from society (e.g., gangs). In addition, prosocial coping styles (problem-solving skills) and positive peer relations have both been shown to act as protective factors for children under stress.

4. *PATHS promotes social emotional problem-solving abilities.* The development of self-control, the ability to calm oneself when frustrated or upset, and the capacity to utilize effective problem solving are all crucial skills for optimal functioning. Research suggests that the development of more complex and accurate plans and strategies (social cognitions) regarding emotions has a major influence on children's social behavior. Moreover, recognizing, labeling, and thinking about feelings, and the use of other social emotional problem-solving capacities, make it more likely that feelings will not be automatically translated into action-oriented responses (i.e., there will be more cortical as compared to limbic system control over responses to strong emotions).

5. *PATHS promotes the ability to use awareness of self and others to create useful processes.* Emotions are an integral aspect of daily functioning

and serve many different functions. Among other things, feelings provide information and facilitate our very survival. In fact, when we consider all of the many important uses of emotion, it is not surprising that it helps for children to learn about them, but it is surprising that we have not been more active until recently in promoting emotional literacy in the classroom (Kusché & Greenberg, 1998). Improving self-esteem in children is also a crucial goal, and one that has been largely misunderstood in the past (due to the use of former methods that did not achieve effective results).

6. *PATHS furthers collaborations between educators, parents, and the community in short- and long-term implementation planning.* PATHS is only one component with regard to furthering collaboration, but certainly it can be an important one. For example, when PATHS was implemented in Laredo, Texas, children's behaviors improved so markedly at home that parents called to ask the teachers what they were doing that was working so well. They also asked if they could learn PATHS so that they could use it at home. Parenting workshops were offered and had enthusiastic attendance. Certainly programs designed to enhance community involvement in short- and long-range planning (e.g., *Communities That Care,* Hawkins, Catalano, & associates, 1992) have endorsed PATHS as one of the promising components.

CONCLUSION

In conclusion, the rapid and complex cultural changes of the past few decades, as well as those predicted for the foreseeable future, make emotional and social competency crucial requirements for the adaptive and successful functioning of children in both their current life situations and for their lives as adolescents and adults. Although emotional literacy has never been considered to be a necessary component of education in the past, we feel that it has become as critical for the basic knowledge repertoire of all children as reading, writing, and arithmetic (Kusché, Riggs, & Greenberg, 1999). We believe that PATHS provides a comprehensive, developmentally based social emotional curriculum for teachers to use every year with elementary-school-age children from Grades K to 5 to promote optimal development in these areas.

NOTES

1. This description is somewhat simplified and refers to the majority of people who process language in the left hemisphere. This includes the vast majority of

men, but it has been estimated that approximately 40% of all women process language to some extent in both hemispheres. Thus, a large percentage of women (though still the minority) may be more aware of their uncomfortable emotions than the majority of people where asymmetry in language processing is more definitive. In addition, all children younger than three appear to process language in both hemispheres; however, thinking in language is rarely found at this age and the corpus collosum is also very immature, so that cross-hemispheric processing is not yet developed. For a more in-depth exposition of brain functioning and emotional literacy, see Kusché & Greenberg (in press-a).

2. For a more complete summary of the PATHS Curriculum, see Greenberg & Kusché (1998a, pp. 24–33). The tables of contents from all the volumes are reprinted in this same reference (Appendixes B & C, pp. 73–81), in addition to a division of PATHS lessons into developmental units (Appendix D, p. 83), a copy of a sample lesson on guilt (Appendix E, pp. 85–93), an example of a parent informational handout (Appendix F, pp. 95–97), and a sample homework assignment (Appendix G, pp. 99–100).

REFERENCES

Bierman, K., Greenberg, M. T., & Conduct Problems Prevention Research Group (1996). Social skills in the FAST Track Program. In R. DeV. Peters & R. J. McMahon (Eds.), *Prevention and early intervention: Childhood disorders, substance abuse, and delinquency* (pp. 65–89). Newbury Park, CA: Sage.

Blueprints for violence prevention (Books 1–10). (1997–1999). D. S. Elliott (Series Ed.). Boulder: University of Colorado at Boulder, Center for the Study and Prevention of Violence.

Catalano, R. F., Berglund, M. L., Ryan, J. A. M., Lonczak, H. C., & Hawkins, J. D. (1998). *Positive youth development in the United States: Research findings on programs that promote positive youth development* (Final report submitted to the U.S. Department of Health and Human Services, Office of the Assistant Secretary for Planning and Evaluation). Seattle: Social Development Research Group.

Denham, S. A., & Burton, R. (1996). A socio-emotional intervention program for at-risk four-year-olds. *Journal of School Psychology, 34,* 225–245.

Freud, S. (1957). The unconscious. In J. Strachey (Ed.), *The standard edition of the complete psychological works of Sigmund Freud* (Vol. 14, pp. 159–215). London: Hogarth Press. (Original work published 1915)

Goleman, D. (1995). *Emotional intelligence: Why it can matter more than IQ.* New York: Bantam Books.

Greenberg, M. T., & Kusché, C. A. (1993). *Promoting social and emotional development in deaf children: The PATHS project.* Seattle: University of Washington Press.

Greenberg, M. T., & Kusché, C. A. (1996). *The PATHS project: Preventive intervention for children* (Final Report, Grant No. R01MH42131). Washington, DC: National Institute of Mental Health.

Greenberg, M. T., & Kusché, C. A. (1998a). *Blueprints for violence prevention: Bk. 10, The PATHS project.* Boulder: University of Colorado at Boulder, Center for the Study and Prevention of Violence.

Greenberg, M. T., & Kusché, C. A. (1998b). Preventive intervention for school-aged deaf children: The PATHS Curriculum. *Journal of Deaf Studies and Deaf Education, 3,* 49–63.

Greenberg, M. T., Kusché, C. A., Cook, E. T., & Quamma, J. P. (1995). Promoting emotional competence in school-aged children: The effects of the PATHS Curriculum. *Development and Psychopathology, 7,* 117–136.

Greenberg, M. T., & Snell, J. L. (1997). The neurological basis of emotional development. In P. Salovey (Ed.), *Emotional development and emotional literacy* (pp. 93–119). New York: Basic Books.

Hawkins, J. D., Catalano, R. F., & associates (Eds.). (1992). *Communities that care: Action for drug abuse prevention.* San Francisco: Jossey-Bass.

Hindley, P., Reed, R., Jeffs, J., & McSweeney, M. (1998). An evaluation of a social and emotional intervention for deaf children. Unpublished manuscript, St. Georges Hospital, London.

Jones, R. M. (1968). *Fantasy and feeling in education.* New York: New York University Press.

Kusché, C. A. (1984). *The understanding of emotion concepts by deaf children: An assessment of an affective curriculum.* Unpublished doctoral dissertation, University of Washington, Seattle.

Kusché, C. A. (in press). Psychoanalysis as prevention: Using PATHS to enhance ego development, object relations, and cortical integration in children. *Journal of Applied Psychoanalytic Studies.*

Kusché, C. A., Cook, E. T., & Greenberg, M. T. (1993). Neuropsychological and cognitive functioning in children with anxiety, externalizing, and comorbid psychopathology. *Journal of Clinical Child Psychology, 22,* 172–195.

Kusché, C. A., & Greenberg, M. T. (1994). *The PATHS (Promoting Alternative Thinking Strategies) Curriculum.* Seattle: Developmental Research and Programs.

Kusché, C. A., & Greenberg, M. T. (1998, October). Integrating emotions and thinking in the classroom: The PATHS Curriculum. *Think Magazine,* 32–34.

Kusché, C. A., & Greenberg, M. T. (in press-a). Brain development and social-emotional learning: An introduction for educators. In M. Elias, H. Arnold, & C. Steiger (Eds.), *Fostering knowledgable, responsible, and caring students.* New York: Teachers College Press.

Kusché, C. A., & Greenberg, M. T. (in press-b). Teaching emotional literacy in elementary school classrooms: The PATHS Curriculum. In M. Elias, H. Arnold, & C. Steiger (Eds.), *Fostering knowledgable, responsible, and caring students.* New York: Teachers College Press.

Kusché, C. A., Riggs, R. S., & Greenberg, M. T. (1999). Using analytic knowledge to teach emotional literacy. *The American Psychoanalyst, 33,* 20–21.

McMahon, R. J., Slough, N. M., & Conduct Problems Prevention Research Group (1996). Family-based intervention in the FAST Track Program. In R. DeV. Peters & R. J. McMahon (Eds.), *Prevention and early intervention: Childhood disorders, substance abuse, and delinquency* (pp. 90–110). Newbury Park, CA: Sage.

Robin, A. L., Schneider, M., & Dolnick, M. (1976). The Turtle Technique: An extended case study of self-control in the classroom. *Psychology in the Schools, 13,* 449–453.

Russell, T. (1998). Final evaluation report for project year 1997–1998: Seattle Social Development Model. Laredo, TX.

Safe Schools, Safe Students. (1998). Washington, DC: Drug Strategies.

Schore, A. (1994). *Affect regulation and the origins of the self: Neurobiology of emotional development.* Hillsdale, NJ: Erlbaum.

Wechsler, D. (1974). *Manual for the Wechsler Intelligence Scale for Children—Revised.* New York: The Psychological Corporation.

Weissberg, R. P., Caplan, M. Z., & Bennetto, L. (1988). *The Yale-New Haven middle-school Social Problem Solving (SPS) Program.* New Haven, CT: Yale University Department of Psychology.

Wolchik, S. A., & Sandler, I. N. (Eds.). (1997). *Handbook of children's coping: Linking theory and intervention.* New York: Plenum Press.

Wong, S. C., Catalano, R. F., Hawkins, J. D., & Chappell, P. J. (1996). *Communities That Care prevention strategies: Promising approaches. A research guide to what works.* Seattle: Developmental Research and Programs.

W. T. Grant Consortium on the School-Based Promotion of Social Competence. (1992). Drug and alcohol prevention curricula. In J. D. Hawkins, R. F. Catalano, & associates (Eds.), *Communities that care: Action for drug abuse prevention* (pp. 129–148). San Francisco: Jossey-Bass.

Chapter 10

IMPROVING THE SOCIAL AND INTELLECTUAL CLIMATE IN ELEMENTARY SCHOOLS BY ADDRESSING BULLY-VICTIM-BYSTANDER POWER STRUGGLES

Stuart W. Twemlow, M.D., *Peter Fonagy*, Ph.D., *Frank C. Sacco*, Ph.D., *Martin L. Gies*, M.Ed., and *Debora Hess*, M.S.

The Menninger Clinic and The Topeka Public Schools

As all schoolteachers and counselors know, children are often cruel in their behaviors in social situations. Although the spine-chilling novel *Lord of the Flies* exaggerates the cruelty of children, it should be remembered that the author, William Golding, had been a public school teacher!

The negative impact of bullying on students is of growing concern to elementary school educators and counselors (Olweus, 1991, 1992; Twemlow, Sacco, & Williams, 1996). Although power struggles are an expected part of developmental milestones (Coie, Dodge, Terry, & Wright, 1991), bullying is a pathological variant of power struggles that fosters absenteeism, poor academic achievement, and other possible consequences of an unsafe environment in elementary schools, including violence.

The intellectual development of elementary school children in the latency years has, as Eisold points out (see Chapter 2), a solid ground in certain developmental milestones; for example, from the capacity to inhibit and sublimate aggressive impulses comes the emerging capacity to abstract, symbolize, and self-reflect. This volume and its predecessor (Cohen, 1999) highlight the critical role of psychological development as a necessary precondition for intellectual learning. With these facts in mind, we developed and tested a whole-school focused intervention to reduce power struggles and improve the atmosphere for social growth and intellectual learning in an elementary school in the Midwest: C.A.P.S.L.E.: Creating a Peaceful School Learning Environment (Twemlow, Fonagy, Sacco, Evans, Gies, & Ewbank, 2000).

A REVIEW OF RECENT LITERATURE

The last seven years has seen an explosion of published articles on bully and victim issues. The pioneer in that research is Dan Olweus (1991, 1992, 1994, 1995), a psychologist who conducted several large-scale studies of bullies and victims in Norway. He found that bullies are usually physically large and fascinated with dominance; they are impulsive, lack empathy, and have a proclivity for negative actions. He identified victims as weaker and smaller than bullies, as well as insecure, depressed, and suffering from low self-esteem. Olweus also found that younger students are more likely to be bullied than older students especially in the earlier grades, with this tendency leveling off in middle school. In a study in Italian schools, Genta and colleagues (1996) used questionnaires similar to those used by Olweus and found that boys are more likely to admit to bullying than girls, and that bullying occurs between children in the same social class. In a Canadian study, Bentley and Li (1995) also found that victims tend to be younger or close in age to the children who bullied them. This study of fourth through sixth graders found that 21.3% of the children were bullied and 11.6% admitted to bullying others. The playground is the main location for bullying, and the bullies tend to be older boys.

Boulton and Underwood (1992) reported on a study of 9-year-old British schoolchildren in which both bullies and victims are rated as unpopular by their peers. Slee (1995) found that both bullies and victims in Australian schools have poor health status, often with severe depression. Slee and Rigby (1993) also found that bullying episodes last 6 months or more and that victims are less popular, have low self-esteem, and feel unsafe at school, whereas bullies do not like school.

Victimization in the elementary grades may create a role that can last for life. For example, Bernstein and Watson (1997) report that victims remain victims for most of their lives with readily identifiable characteristics. For example, victims stand out as easy targets, and once targeted, they tend to remain targets regardless of the situation.

Boulton and Underwood (1992) found that boy bullies tend to bully both males and females, but for the most part tend to favor same-sex victims. Also, this British study hinted that girls bullying boys may be an underreported activity at school, a position with which we strongly agree. Power, Dyson, and Wozniak (1997) interviewed young Scottish offenders in institutions and found that victims tend to be convicted of less violent offenses than bullies. They also found that the longer an offender remains in an institution, the greater the chance of becoming a bully.

Bowers, Smith, and Binney (1994) and Austin and Joseph (1996) discovered that there is a distinct group that they call bully-victims, representing a mixed group of children who both bully and are victimized, similar to a group that Olweus calls provocative victims (Olweus, 1992). Lowenstein (1995), using interview techniques, found that bullies are often targets of bullying themselves and are perceptive about what makes them easy targets for bullying.

Salmivalli (1995) studied hundreds of Finnish school children and identified several other roles including reinforcer of the bully, assistant to the bully, defender of the victim, and outsider. Boys are more associated with the roles of bully, reinforcer, and assistant. Girls are associated with the roles of defender and outsider. Thus, current research highlights the complex nature of the bully-victim-bystander relationship, with these roles being fluid and heavily dependent on the social climate.

Batsche, George, and Knoff (1994) found that the incidence of bullying in elementary schools is increasing, with less prosocial behavior and respect for others in the schools examined. This research supports the notion that students believe that adults in the school environment do little to discourage bullying and that students are poorly equipped to handle bullying. Menesini and colleagues (1997) found that children rarely intervene in bullying situations; instead teachers are seen as the responsible party who are entrusted to intervene. They found that girls are more empathic toward victims and are more likely than boys to respond to help a victim.

The problem of bullying has its roots in the family. Berdondini and Smith (1996) studied families of identified bullies in Italian elementary schools and found an increased absence of fathers, with more broken marriages in families of bullies. Rican (1995) studied Czech children and reported that parents' increased tolerance of aggressive behavior is a key determinant of problems in the families of bullying children and that self-centeredness is prominent in families of both bullies and victims. Rigby (1994), studying a cohort of 856 Australian children, found that the families of bullies function less well than other families and that female bullies have the most dysfunctional families. Oliver, Oaks, and Hoover (1994) describe the families of bullies as emotionally cool, limited in structure and rules, and high in social isolation; with increased parental conflict, positively reinforced aggression, punished nonaggression, and increased rigidity. Victims' families are mostly overinvolved and enmeshed.

Programs to address bullying in schools are proliferating, but vary in degree and sophistication in the evaluation of their effectiveness. Several programs are summarized in Annette and Walsleben (1998). School conflict resolution programs are currently in wide use in schools, but differ significantly in their approach from C.A.P.S.L.E., the approach discussed in this chapter. Although conflict resolution efforts use peer mediation as we do for some aspects of our program, the central focus of C.A.P.S.L.E. is on the group as a whole, with a focus on school climate rather than individual problems and conflicts. We emphasize a nonpathologizing approach to power struggles, rather than extracting the problem children from the classroom context for special attention.

THE BULLY-VICTIM-BYSTANDER MODEL

Psychoanalytic group theory, including Adlerian, helped inform the conceptualization for our model (Dreikurs & Soltz, 1964). Adler describes a healthy attitude as a sense of oneness and identification with the community, with concern for others and their welfare, that is without power struggles within the community group (school). A student who is excluded from belonging to the school group either becomes an outsider (victim) with attendant psychological effects or instead strives to find a place in the group by "proving" him- or herself in order to belong (bully). This bully-victim-bystander interaction interrupts the healthy identification with the school group by creating a power struggle for the child resulting from the asymmetrical coercive power relationships and leading to the exclusion of some children from the group. There is attendant disruption of the whole school climate and a consequent reduction in the optimal atmosphere for learning.

An alternative bully-victim-bystander model is one that sees bullying as part of an interactional process that has three principal social roles and a limited number of subtypes. This model was developed by Twemlow, Sacco, and Williams (1996) and follows the pioneering work of Olweus (1991), who worked in Scandinavian schools. This bully-victim-bystander model creates a metaphor that can be used as a schoolwide nonpathologizing psychoeducational model addressed to all participants in this drama. As a result, the school counselor is not so often in the position of having to identify individuals and create solutions for them, but instead facilitates a prevention focused schoolwide model of education that addresses the impact of the misuses of power relationships between students, between students and teachers, and between parents and school personnel.

This model also suggests a three-dimensional process with a stage upon which students and teachers, administrative personnel, support personnel, and parents enact the various dramas that can be understood as changing combinations of the roles of bully, victim, and bystander. Thus, any individual act of bullying or victimization has by definition a third participant—an audience, the bystander. This bystander group is an intricate facilitator of the evolution of the problem within the school and in the community. Bystanders can have bully, victim, avoidant, or ambivalent dispositions and can be identified by their passive (victim-bystander and avoidant) or active (bully-bystander and ambivalent) participation in any ongoing interaction between a bully and a victim.

Bullies

Bullies are individuals who misuse their power over others to create negative consequences and discomfort for another. Our typology of bullies divides them into three general categories (Twemlow, Sacco, & Williams, 1996). The first is the *sadistic bully* who typically orchestrates much of the trouble within the school. This student often has high self-esteem, low anxiety, excellent social skills, and a rather cold-hearted proclivity to engage other students in harmful acts. The second is the *agitated bully* who is commonly given the diagnosis of ADHD. This bully is easily activated by a sadistic bully into pushing other kids around. The third type of bully is the *depressed bully* who has low self-esteem, whines and tattles, and engages adults and peers in negative actions. The depressed bully is usually not liked by teachers and is most often caught in the act of bullying by teachers or is scapegoated by peers.

Victims

Victims are characterized by a submissive and passive attitude. These students often fail to make a place for themselves within the group and usually suffer from low self-esteem. A provocative subtype masks the passivity with cycles of submission and aggression (Olweus, 1992). These children are the natural targets for bullies because their submissive stance attracts the sadistic or aggressive element. Two further subtypes are described among high school students where victims tend to crystallize into martyr and rescuer clusters also (Twemlow, Sacco, & Williams, 1996).

Bystanders

Bystanders include the vast majority of the student population. This "audience" consists of children who can be characterized as different types depending upon their relationship with the bully (or vicarious identification with the bully): victim type (a frozen, frightened bystander); avoidant type (denying the existence of a problem with power struggles in the school); and ambivalent type (unsure of what to do and not yet in fixed pathological roles) (Twemlow, 1999). This is the population from which new bullies and victims arise should the school adopt a procedure of expulsion and remove the identified bully or victim from the school in an attempt to solve the larger disruptive influence of their interactions. Thus, the bystander population is essentially a rather diverse combination of potential bullies and victims in a dormant or passive state.

A great deal of emphasis in the literature has been placed on the role(s) of the bully especially. School counselors have often been trained to identify both victim and bully roles and to understand the relationship between them. They know that both bullies and victims can change roles: Sometimes a victim bullies and vice versa. Bystanders do not get their attention. Afterall, it is human nature to want to watch or peek. The most disciplined of us find it difficult not to watch a fight on the street or to slow down to peek at an accident on the road. People are naturally curious and experience vicarious thrills from observing high-stimulation activity.

The bystander, however, is the invisible engine in the cycle of bullying. If bully and victim are social roles for the drama of bullying, then bystanders are the audience. As such, the nature of the bully-victim interaction, or desired drama, is shaped and maintained by the demand of the audience of bystanders. Unlike theater, bystanders do not stay passive and remain in their seats while the drama unfolds.

In an environment that does not target the role of the bystander, the bully has the advantage. No adult blames the audience, just the players. As long as there is a demand for a show and the audience watches for free, the show will go on. The phenomenon of bystanding becomes even more central as the student progresses through the elementary grades and into middle and high school. In the later grades, the phenomenon of talking about who will fight whom after school can become a preoccupation. Roving "cockfights" can dominate the social climate and exert a very destructive force on the school.

In the early grades, the bystanders are open to suggestion and can be easily lured into one of these roles. The longer the bystander is allowed to watch and not be considered part of the problem, the more experience the bystander has in assuming and trying on new and dysfunctional social roles at school. The innocence of the observer is maintained when the focus is on only the players of bully and victim.

The bystander role is very catchy. When one person stops to look, a crowd is sure to follow. There is safety in numbers. When the class clown acts up, the teacher is forced to enter the drama. If the teacher becomes a bystander, then the clown becomes the star and everyone else becomes the audience and learning stops. If the teacher engages the clown, then the clown is calling the shots if the teacher cannot immediately regain control. If a principal does not support the teacher and the clown continues to plan, then the principal becomes a bystander, the teacher the victim, and the clown the bully.

POWER STRUGGLES IN SCHOOLS: SOME EXAMPLES

The effect on the overall school climate of subtle and not so subtle power struggle can be illustrated by a series of examples.[1]

Bullying of Students by Teachers

The assistant principal of a Denver, Colorado, middle school suspended some 97 students over a 3-day period for a variety of nonviolent infractions. In defense of his action he argued, "The troublemakers weren't doing us any good. They were just interrupting the educational process for good students who come to school every day" (Davila, 1995, p. 18). Within a few days the school was in a state of virtual anarchy with direct confrontation of teachers by students, and many angry phone calls from parents to local politicians and school administration. The problem with teachers who bully students is a highly sensitive one that is relatively unexplored in the literature; we will address this issue in a later publication.

Bullying of Teachers by Students

This was well illustrated in a school in which the teachers decided to allow the school classes to be organized around local indigenous gangs rather than by age and academic achievement. What was striking in this particular intervention was that the teachers, including the principal, did not see the process as bullying and instead viewed the suggested interventions as constructive. Outside consultation revealed a pattern by which the staff identified with the aggressor, reflecting deep fears of the gangs and their impact on the school. During a staff consultation, the staff, including the principal, became quite emotional and were ultimately able to reflect on the irrationality of their proposal.

Complex Bully-Victim-Bystander Interactions

The incident that crystallized the pervasive bully-victim-bystander interaction was one in which a window was broken in a fifth-grade classroom and the incident was blamed on an innocent student. The situation was a result of collusion between the sadistic bully and other class members, who were threatened with serious trouble if they did not lie about who had broken the window. The submissive victim simply acquiesced and agreed that he had done it. The bully involved had a history of following through with his threats, including physical mistreatment of other children, vandalizing property, painting graffiti on school property, damaging library books, and so on. The submissive child victim eventually ended up in psychiatric care.

Through a circuitous route from counselor to parent and later a complaint to the school principal, the whole issue was brought to the foreground. The school had had increasing problems with out-of-school suspensions and other disciplinary referrals, yet all took place in an apparently quiet school environment. The children rarely looked happy, and there was little laughter in the corridors or on the playgrounds. The principal had difficulty in dealing with this particular incident because of the long history of trouble with the family of the bullying child.

Both parents of the bully had a history of frequent complaints to the school board and school administration members about the ill treatment of their children in previous schools. The parents had several severely dysfunctional children and difficulties with money and employment, thus eliciting sympathy. While neither parent participated in any school activities or worked within the PTO structure, they were frequent visitors to the school with complaints about how their children were being treated; this included accusations of racial, religious, and other forms of discrimination. Interactions between the mother and the principal involved thinly veiled threats to the principal, for example, "You don't have to worry, I'm not going to hit you. I don't do things like that"—a provocative response on the mother's part to presumably nonverbal submissiveness.

It became apparent that the bullying boy in the classroom was actually the instrument of his older sister's bullying. He performed the dirty work for his sister. In this instance, the class of children became victimized bystanders to the sadistic manipulations of the bully and the submissive victim child became the casualty or scapegoat. The staff of the school, led by the principal, were already in the position of victim bystanders to a bullying family who encourage highly ambivalent feelings complicated by threat of litigation against the school. The school administration's unconscious denial of this threat caused them to delay action until a crisis occurred. The intervention to be outlined later was successful particularly because it did not pathologize the bullies concerned and in fact ended with the parents of the bullying children becoming involved with the program and becoming instructors and promoters of the program. Although the submissive victim continued to need psychiatric treatment, the treatment was made more effective, we believe, by the interactional approach to the school climate as a whole.

Roles of Administrative Staff and School Board

The particular roles of administrative staff within the school and on the school board are also very important for the overall effectiveness of this model (*C.A.P.S.L.E.*). What's good for the goose is good for the gander, is a maxim that is important in this context. Bullying behavior by any personnel acts as a negative model for children in that regard. For example, it is not uncommon for there to be overt conflict between school administration and staff over issues like salary and conditions of employment, in which the administration are seen as bullying and unreasonable. Staff who become depressed and angry about these issues transmit their feelings to their students, even if they are not discussed in their presence. Similarly, the influence of school secretaries and school custodial and janitorial personnel have a time-honored role as part of the informal process that can create a bully-victim-bystander atmosphere. Special problems in such school personnel that are not discussed openly often exert an indirect influence on school climate, reflected for example in failing academic achievement and increasing disciplinary referrals.

C.A.P.S.L.E. PROGRAM DESCRIPTION

This program has two core and two support components. The core components that should be used in all schools are Zero Tolerance for bullying, bystanding, and being a victim and the Gentle Warrior martial arts–based program. The two support programs that can be used if the conditions of the school warrant it are Peer Mentorship and the Bruno Program, an adult membership approach.

Zero Tolerance for Bullying, Bystanding, and Being a Victim

Specifically, posters are placed at strategic points around the school depicting desirable behaviors to reenforce the central theme of the program: zero tolerance. The posters cover the following topics:

- Nine ways to handle bullies
- Are you a bully?
- Are you a victim?
- Are you a bystander?

- Right speech (a way of interacting with people noncoercively)
- The manners and social skills of a good elementary school student
- What is a gentle warrior? (emphasizing service to others and empathy)
- Are you getting angry?
- The self-protective response (a quick way of relaxing the body)

Next, the posters are supported by regular classroom discussions about the bully-victim-bystander relationship, either in half-hour segments or in one full period each semester. Teachers continue reinforcement with such techniques as a joke of the day, keeping conscious the importance of dealing with power struggles.

Once each semester a 6-session Family Power Struggles workshop is conducted collaboratively between parents and the coordinator of the C.A.P.S.L.E. Program. The workshops use role-play to help bring about an understanding of power struggles and also offer solutions to family conflicts. Several rewards are developed for each class when the class succeeds in keeping fighting and conflict out of the classroom or school, including a special flag for each grade and a school Peace Flag. Children who cause a disruption take the flag down, but if a school has 150 consecutive days of peace, a visit from a local dignitary is suggested. Many other forms of reinforcement are included: patches, buttons, magnets, and stickers depicting various aspects of the bully-victim-bystander relationship.

In each monthly school newsletter, an article is written by one of the program workers on some aspect of how the school is responding. The C.A.P.S.L.E. leadership group meets monthly, which could also be the school mental health team. At a minimum this team should include the principal of the school, a designated mental health worker (usually a school counselor), and representatives from each aspect of the program including older children when appropriate. The main purpose of this support group is to monitor the Zero Tolerance for bullying since it is most important that the issue never be allowed to become routine.

The Gentle Warrior Program

Each school year, two 12-week training modules are conducted, either by outside martial artists or with a trained P.E. teacher or other interested person. One session a week is used and all children in the classroom should participate without pathologizing them. The lesson plan includes the following elements: a relaxation period; a question and answer period around a discussion of self-respect, self-control, and respect for others; stretching and muscle strengthening exercises; and certain martial arts techniques. Although no kicking or punching techniques are used, balancing, falling safely, defensive positioning, and blocking and release techniques are taught. In addition, there is fun-style role-playing to illustrate bully-victim-bystander relationships and, where possible, reading of stories chosen from classics such as Aesop, Plato, and Thomas Jefferson to illustrate aspects of the code of conduct. A variety of tips for parents is circulated each week with the child's take-home folder to suggest that parents go over the issues with their children to reinforce the social and physical skills learned. Parents and teachers are encouraged to participate in the program.

It should be noted that martial arts is the metaphor used to engage the whole school in an ongoing discussion of power struggles and the bully-victim-bystander interaction. Other techniques can be equally effective, for example, sports, dance, theater, and debate.

The Bruno Program

The importance of the containing metaphor or adult protective shield (Sacco & Twemlow, 1997; Twemlow & Sacco, 1996) evolved from our work in Jamaican schools and communities. We adopted the name "Bruno" for these adult mentors, a term applied to them by Jamaican children, to describe a loyal "yard dog" who is not vicious, but is helpful, protective, and caring. This warm, gentle, and "can do" attitude is a metaphor for a way to communicate within the culture of the school that there is control and order that alters the atmosphere.

Adult mentors, preferably male, are recruited from surrounding districts and sometimes retirement homes and assisted by older students to monitor the power dynamics of the school climate. They are specifically most functional during recess, lunch hour, and before and after school, with minimum involvement in the actual classrooms and intellectual activity. The adult mentor is paired with an honor patrol, a fifth-grade child who assists the mentor, especially to informally assist with the creation of rules for games, especially problematic games like basketball and the use of play equipment.

Peer Mentorship Program

For this program students are recruited from the high school to which many of the children at the elementary school will eventually go. The high school students benefit from the involvement since they often have had trouble with disruptiveness and are given credit for the work done. Several times a week they assist students in academic learning and in conflict resolution, and to a lesser extent, they help children identify personal problems and issues. Some formal training is given to the mentors, but the majority of the training takes place during ongoing weekly supervision. They are trained to deal gently with children's secrets and confidences and to help children solve physical violence problems. An emphasis is placed on the importance of keeping one's word; not acting superior; and being forgiving, compassionate, honest, and sincere. Mentors are trained with role-playing scenarios for situations that they may come across, for example, a child who won't stop crying, an uncooperative child, a withdrawn child, and so forth.

RESULTS OF A CONTROLLED STUDY OF C.A.P.S.L.E.

The results of a 4-year controlled study of this program are reported in Twemlow et al. (2000). There is a dramatic reduction of informal notifications to the principal about serious infractions, compared to the control school, and a significant reduction in out-of-school suspensions (OSS) over the 4-year period of the study. For the 1997–1998 school year the difference between experimental and control schools was at $p < .004$ level for OSS with the difference between experimental and control school getting more and more significant over time. (A full report on statistics can be requested from Stuart W. Twemlow.) Dramatic improvement in academic achievement is demonstrated in comparing the standardized Metropolitan Achievement Test scores of third and fifth graders. The difference on composite test scores show an improvement in the experimental school from the 40th percentile to the 58th percentile, with especially strong improvement in the reading scores ($p < .0001$ level).

These analyses indicate that the school's overall performance improved as well as individual students' performance improving more significantly in the experimental school than in the comparison school. As expected, the primary improvement in these academic achievement test scores are in the children who did not have particular problems, that is, they are not classified as bullies, victims, or bystanders by school teachers. It is these children who, in fact, suffer the most when classrooms are disruptive. One teacher commented that by the 2nd year of the program in an average classroom period of 45 minutes usually 20 minutes were spent settling the children down. After the program became effective the full period was available for teaching. General measures of school safety show that older children are quickest to benefit and feel safer at school especially. The younger children are the slowest to improve.

Teacher-rated problem behaviors in children of the Gentle Warrior program also show a significant change with a reduction in dependency, tendency to be withdrawn, and victimized behavior. In general, this more outwardly directed program results in the most significant and observable changes in children who tend to be quiet, withdrawn victims who have the poorest academic achievement of any group, much poorer than, for example, the bullying children. These "wall flowers" show a dramatic shift in an ability to be assertive with an ameliorating effect on the bully, necessitating less direct intervention by the disciplining teacher.

A SUCCESSFUL PSYCHOEDUCATIONAL MODEL
WITH THE SCHOOL COUNSELOR AS FACILITATOR

School counselors have traditionally been the identified resource to assist teachers in managing disruptive students. Every school has a disciplinary code and is led by a principal with certain values and attitudes toward discipline. Thus, a counselor may be in the position of having to respond to a principal who is authoritarian or submissive and hands-off with student aggression. Traditional counselor responses target either the victim or the bully in aggressive acting out, or respond to a teacher's request to remove a child because of a series of incidents that result in one student being identified as the problem.

The alternative suggested in this chapter involves an intervention strategy that places the counselor in a dual role. In addition to the traditional individual approach, the counselor becomes a change agent targeting the entire school climate. This social interventionist role requires the counselor to develop and manage a schoolwide program to educate students, support staff, teachers, and parents on the negative aspects of such power struggles since disruptiveness in the school is seen as a direct result of the ongoing interactions of social roles, including the bully, victim, and bystander, and the results from unmanaged coercive power interactions between bullies and their victims under the watchful eyes of the bystanders.

Often the counselor can identify these roles, but there is usually no systematic approach in place for everyone in the school to be proactive and learn how to manage the harmful roles of bully-victim-bystander. The younger the child, the more impressionable they are to simple and positive messages. Programs that target these social roles can encourage positive behavior by illustrating the undesirability of being a bully, victim, or bystander and by providing a socially acceptable language with behavioral skills to manage these struggles.

The school counselor in this dual role of consultant-monitor of the school climate and helper for individual problem students fits very well with the Comer model school development program (Comer, 1993), now in use in over 800 schools around the nation. This model uses a participant management, child-centered focus with the school counselor in a counseling and preventive role on the mental health team. This program encourages in-depth parent and community involvement in school governance and a mental health team that is responsible for school climate also. Widespread involvement of the community surrounding the school, from which the children come, is encouraged in line with the findings of Elias and colleagues (1997).

Besides Comer, other recent writings also suggest that school counselors shift their role from "counselor as clinician" to a more preventively focused approach (Nystul, 1993). It is impossible to create this type of intervention without the full cooperation of the school leadership and administration, parents, and outside volunteers. These programs only work when the change agent is successful at engaging all levels of the school in solving this problem, since the specific interventions are metaphors to engage all levels of the school in the process. For example, in the C.A.P.S.L.E. Program, martial arts is used as such a metaphor; however, others such as art, music, dance, drama, or sports could be used equally successfully, provided that multiple levels of staff and students are engaged in a process that targets the misuse of the power relationship in a nonpathologizing way. Bell and Suggs (1998) propose a sports metaphor to promote resiliency in children. *Heart* is defined by them as that extra mile needed to master a sports drill or technique. They feel that such achievement inoculates the child against stress and low self-esteem, similar to the extra self-confidence that Gentle Warrior training confers especially on victimized and bystanding children.

The first action step, therefore, is to engage interest from all levels of the school in a project targeting the bully-victim-bystander interaction. Since there is considerable denial in many school systems regarding violence and disruptive power struggles, prevention is greatly enhanced when the school counselor engages the principal in exploring an intervention for the entire school rather than just targeting problem students. The principal as the leader needs to be convinced that this is the appropriate direction and then commit the staff resources to proceed.

The second step is to create a plan that reflects the input of all levels of the school and surrounding community. These programs work best when a concept is kept simple and the school is allowed to express its own cultural values in the design and implementation of an intervention. The message needs to be kept the same: Power struggles are intolerable; standing by and watching someone being bullied is not acceptable; and victims need to learn to be assertive and reach out for the resources they need. Once this message is etched in the minds of the change agents, then the specific vehicle becomes less important than maintaining the purity and the consistency of the message. When a majority of the school staff and students practice the language of the bully-victim-bystander interaction, then a peaceful and creative school learning environment can become a reality.

How would Steven and Malika, the children introduced by Eisold in Chapter 2, fare in such a school? There would be considerable potential gains for each child. Steven would likely develop greater comfort with his peers and struggle less to gain their attention with boastfulness, since his class would be having discussions about showing off as a potential put-down to others (bullying). Steven might also become more expressive and assertive about his serious concerns about both his troubled parents, insisting that they develop skills to interact with him about these important matters.

Malika is about to enter middle school where bullying behavior peaks. In her unsafe school environment this program could help her develop self-defense skills, and, in addition, a variety of ways to handle the numerous power struggles she will encounter. Malika seems to be developing some bullying behaviors herself, including gossiping and tattling, as well as outbursts of rudeness. C.A.P.S.L.E. would likely help her become more self-aware, self-reflective, and thus self-correcting. The program could help both these children whose opportunities and backgrounds are so different.

CONCLUSION

In this chapter we have outlined the philosophy and techniques of an intervention to reduce violence in schools and to create a peaceful learning environment. The intervention focuses on the school climate and not on mentally ill children. By its attention to the dialectical relationship between bully, victim, and the bystanding audience, all students, staff, and parents become part of the problem and thus also part of the solution. Once coercive power struggles are settled, the climate usually becomes conducive to both academic learning and a happy and stress-free environment for teachers and students.

Acknowledgments. This paper is part of a research project involving the staff and students of several elementary schools in Topeka, Kansas. It is to the staff and students that this paper is dedicated.

This research is supported by the Peaceful Schools Project, Child and Family Center, Menninger Clinic, Topeka, Kansas.

NOTE

1. Examples used in this chapter are either composite examples or have the permission of the individuals concerned.

REFERENCES

Annette, J., & Walsleben, M. (1998). *Combating fear and restoring safety in schools.* Washington, DC: U.S. Department of Justice, Office of Juvenile Justice and Delinquency Prevention.

Austin, S., & Joseph, S. (1996). Assessment of bully/victim problems in 8- to 11-year-olds. *British Journal of Educational Psychology, 66*(4), 447–456.

Batsche, G. M., George, M., & Knoff, H. (1994). Bullies and their victims: Understanding a pervasive problem in the schools. *School Psychology Review, 23*(2), 165–174.

Bell, C. E., & Suggs, H. (1998). Using sports to strengthen resiliency in children: Training heart. *Child and Adolescent Psychiatric Clinics of North America, 7*(4), 859–865.

Berdondoni, L., & Smith, P. K. (1996). Cohesion and power in the families of children involved in bully/victim problems at school: An Italian replication. *Journal of Family Therapy, 18*(1), 99–102.

Bernstein, J. Y., & Watson, M. W. (1997). Children who are targets of bullying: A victim pattern. *Journal of Interpersonal Violence, 12*(4), 483–498.

Bentley, K., & Li, A. (1995). Bully and victim problems in elementary schools and students' beliefs about aggression. *Canadian Journal of School Psychology, 11*(2), 153–165.

Boulton, M. J., & Underwood, K. (1992). Bully/victim problems among middle school children. *British Journal of Developmental Psychology, 62,* 73–87.

Bowers, L., Smith, P. K., & Binney, V. (1994). Perceived family relationships of bullies, victims, and bully/victims in middle childhood. *Journal of Social and Personal Relationships, 11*(2), 215–232.

Cohen, J. (Ed.). (1999). Educating minds and hearts: Social emotional learning and the passage into adolescence. New York: Teachers College Press.

Coie, J., Dodge, K., Terry, R., & Wright, V. (1991). The role of aggression in peer relations: An analysis of aggression episodes in boys' play groups. *Child Development, 62,* 812–826.

Comer, J. P. (1993). *School power.* New York: Free Press.

Davila, F. (1995, January 20). Denver debates school ousters. *The Washington Post,* p. 18.

Dreikurs, R., & Soltz, V. (1964). *Children: the challenge.* New York: Hawthorn Books.

Elias, M., Zins, J. E., Weissberg, R. P., Frey, K. S., Greenberg, M. T., Haynes, N. M., Kessler, R., Schwab-Stone, M. E., & Shriver, T. P. (1997). *Promoting social and emotional learning: Guidelines for educators.* Alexandria, VA: Association for Supervision and Curriculum Development.

Genta, M. L., Menesini, E., Fonzi, A., Costabile, A., et al. (1996). Bullies and victims in schools in central and southern Italy. *European Journal of Psychology of Education, 11*(1), 97–110.

Lowenstein, L. F. (1995). Perception and accuracy of perception by bullying children of potential victims. *Education Today, 45*(2), 28–31.

Menesini, E., Eslea, M., Smith, P. K., Genta, M. L., Giannetti, E., Fonzi, A., &

Costabile, A. (1997). Cross-national comparison of children's attitudes towards bully/victim problems in school. *Aggressive Behavior, 23*(4), 245–257.

Nystul, M. S. (1993). A comprehensive developmental model for guidance and counseling. In *The art and science of counseling and psychotherapy* (pp. 302–305). New York: Maxwell Macmillan International.

Oliver, R., Oaks, I. N., & Hoover, J. H. (1994). Family issues and interventions in bully and victim relationships. *School Counselor, 41*(3), 199–202.

Olweus, D. (1991). Bully/victim problems among schoolchildren: Basic facts and effects of a school-based intervention program. In D. Pepler & K. H. Rubin (Eds.), *The development and treatment of childhood aggression* (pp. 441–448). Hillsdale, NJ: Erlbaum.

Olweus, D. (1992). Bullying among schoolchildren: Intervention and prevention. In R. Peters, R. McMahon, & V. Quincey (Eds.), *Aggression and violence throughout the lifespan* (pp. 100–125). London: Sage.

Olweus, D. (1994). Annotation: Bullying at School: Basic facts and effects of a school based intervention program. *Journal of Child Psychology and Psychiatry and Allied Disciplines, 35*(7), 1171–1190.

Olweus, D. (1995). Bullying or peer abuse at school: Facts and interventions. *Current Directions in Psychological Science, 4*(6), 196–200.

Power, K. G., Dyson, G. P., & Wozniak, E. (1997). Bullying among Scottish young offenders: Inmate's self-reported attitudes and behavior. *Journal of Community and Applied Social Psychology, 7*(3), 209–218.

Rican, P. (1995). Family values may be responsible for bullying. *Studia Psychologica, 37*(1), 31–36.

Rigby, K. (1994). Psychosocial functioning in families of Australian adolescent schoolchildren involved in bully-victim problems. *Journal of Family Therapy, 16*(2), 173–187.

Sacco, F. C., & Twemlow, S. W. (1997). Brief reports: school violence reduction: a model Jamaican secondary school program. *Community Mental Health Journal, 33*(3), 229–234.

Salmivalli, C. (1995). Bullies, victims and those others: Bullying as a group process. *Psykologia, 30*(5), 364–372.

Slee, Philip T. (1995). Bullying: Health concerns of Australian secondary school students. *International Journal of Adolescence and Youth, 5*(4), 215–224.

Slee, P. T., & Rigby, K. (1993). Australian schoolchildren's self appraisal of interpersonal relations: The bullying experience. *Child Psychiatry and Human Development, 23*(4), 273–282.

Twemlow, S. W. (1999). A psychoanalytic dialectical model for sexual and other forms of workplace harassment. *Journal of Applied Psychoanalytic Studies, 1*(3), 249–270.

Twemlow, S. W., Fonagy, P., Sacco, F. C., Evans, R., Gies, M. L., & Ewbank, R. (2000). Creating a peaceful school learning environment: A controlled study of an elementary school intervention to reduce violence. *American Journal of Psychiatry.*

Twemlow, S. W., & Sacco, F. C. (1996). Peacekeeping and peacekeeping: The conceptual foundations of a plan to reduce violence and improve the quality of life in a midsized community in Jamaica. *Psychiatry, 50,* 156–174.

Twemlow, S. W., Sacco, F. C., & Williams, P. (1996). A clinical and interactionist perspective on the bully-victim-bystander relationship. *Bulletin of the Menninger Clinic, 60*(3), 296–313.

Part IV

CURRENT ISSUES AND FUTURE DIRECTIONS

Part IV of this volume provides an overview of the "next steps" for educators as well as collaborative groups of teachers, parents, and concerned citizens.

Chapter 11 by Ronald J. Areglado details concrete steps that teachers and administrators can and need to consider in effective implementation of SEL efforts. Areglado is an experienced educational administrator who has worked in many schools, and on the national scene through the National Association of Elementary School Principals. Teams of educators, who are invested in programmatic efforts in this area, will also learn about considerations that enhance effective school reform.

Chapter 12 by Jonathan Cohen suggests that we think about what it means to be socially and emotionally literate. Being able to "decode" the self and others and then use this information in order to solve real problems and learn is as important as decoding phonemes and using this information to be a language learner. But what can—and should—we expect of our children at, say, the 3rd or 10th grade level? This chapter suggests steps that we can take on a local—as well as a national—level to helpfully consider what we can expect from our children and ourselves.

Chapter 11

SOCIAL AND EMOTIONAL LEARNING: THE FUTURE IS NOW

Ronald J. Areglado

Potowomut School, Warwick, RI

Let [young people] remember that there is meaning beyond absurdity. Let them be sure that every little deed counts, that every word has power, and that we can—everyone—do our share to redeem the world in spite of all absurdities and all frustrations and all disappointments. And above all, remember that the meaning of life is to build a life as if it were a work of art.

—Abraham Joshua Heschel

After a 14-year self-imposed sabbatical from an elementary school principalship, I elected to return to a school setting and to once again experience firsthand the joy and excitement of guiding the overall social, emotional, and intellectual growth of young people. I was also motivated by the many conversations I had with countless school principals whom I had met in my former position with the National Association of Elementary School Principals. I had been alternately fascinated and troubled by their stories about the day-to-day events of school life in the 1990s. Apart from their collective problems with ever-decreasing financial resources, lack of public confidence in the success of schooling, and greater demands on their time, talents, and energy, I found the spiritual and emotional dimension of their work with children, families, and staff compelling. When I probed and examined this aspect of their work, I learned about the serious condition and fragility of so many of the children they strive to serve.

In my prior role, I participated in the writing of several national studies on the conditions of children and families. I had read the sobering reports from several leading child advocacy groups such as the Children's Defense Fund and the Annie Casey Foundation. I felt I had a solid intellectual understanding of what my colleagues were experiencing. And that was the deeper problem for me—the disconnect between the visceral and intellectual understanding of educating young students. It reminded me of a comment made to me many years ago by a wise counselor who talked about the significance of integrating "the head with the belly button" when trying to understand another's point of view. It was the impetus I needed to return to the "sacred work" of schools as so aptly described by a mentor and friend, Tom Sergiovanni (1992).

YOUNG LIVES AT STAKE

A casual observer of education knows that a school's mission is to guide the intellectual, social, and emotional development of children commensurate with their talents and abilities. It is fundamental to the business of education, but more important to the development of able, decent people. In his highly acclaimed work, *Seven Habits of Highly Effective People*, Steven Covey (1992) discusses the need for a balance in the character and competence of successful people. This simple but profound message has captured the interest of millions of people who are concerned with the character traits and issues of personal integrity we both possess and hope to impart to others, especially our children. However, there are competing forces both external and internal to schools that jeopardize this balance.

Since the infamous 1983 educational summit held in Charlottesville, Virginia, during Reagan's presidency and its rebuke of public education, politicians, business leaders, educational policy makers, and especially certain advocacy groups singled out our nation's schools as the focus of their time, resources, and talents. Under the guise of educational reform, we have witnessed a proliferation of national standards and mandated state and national tests unprecedented in the annals of American education. The educational landscape is now covered with incalculable volumes of academic standards and the concomitant verbiage of frameworks, accountability, and high-stakes testing. Emboldened business leaders such as IBM's CEO Louis Gerstner and President Clinton, during the National Education Summit of 1997 held in Palisades, New York, advanced the notion of meaningful standards that would require a test for children to move from elementary school to middle school or from middle school to high school. This "get tough" approach replete with consequences for academic failure such as grade retention has become the mantra for many governors who have worked to advance such thinking in the schools in their respective states.

What is both incredible and ironic about the Palisades Summit is its timing and location. At the same time the President, business moguls, and other high-ranking politicians and academics were discussing the future of education in resplendent surroundings, Jonathan Kozol's breathtaking book, *Amazing Grace* (1995), had begun to capture the minds and hearts of a multitude of people. Based on interviews with the residents of the Mott Haven section of South Bronx, New York, the poorest congressional district in the country, Kozol poignantly depicts the overwhelming struggle of families and the faith and hope of children juxtaposed against the squalor and horrifically dangerous conditions of their immediate surroundings. It would have been instructive for the Summit's attendees to board a yellow bus and travel the relatively short distance from the Palisades to the South Bronx to work and live for a time amid these courageous residents. I cannot help but wonder what tone their pronouncements might have taken, especially if they and their teachers had been respectfully asked to join the conversation.

Many of us are familiar with the ambitious and bipartisan educational goals of both the Bush and Clinton administrations. While cosmetic changes have been made in *Goals 2000* and *America 2000*, one component remains clear: that by the year 2000 *all* children ages 3–4 would come to school ready to learn. We are now in the twenty-first century, and we are no closer to that goal now than we were over a decade ago. If anything, we are moving further away from it. Disturbing reports about the increasing numbers of children in poverty abound. The Columbia School of Public Health's National Center for Children in Poverty (NCCP) concluded that the young child poverty rate has grown at an alarming pace. Between 1979 and 1997 the number of children under 6 years of age living in poverty in the United States grew from 3.5 million to 5.2 million and the percentage of young children living in extreme poverty increased from 6% to 12% between 1975 and 1994.

This study underscores the grim facts that life in near poverty is almost as detrimental to children's health and development as living just below the poverty line and that extreme poverty in early life is especially deleterious to children's future life chances. The scepter of economic stress looms large in the capability of educators to achieve the desired academic achievement all of us want for all our nation's children. The problem is exacerbated by the elimination of the spiritual and emotional capacity of our most vulnerable youth. The net effect does not bode well for them or our society. And the evidence is sobering. Proportionately we are spending more money to build prisons and warehouse society's "failures" than we spend on school construction.

The purpose of illustrating the pervasive economic and health-related issues facing millions of youth is to make clear that they enter public schools and are expected to compete academically with more fortunate students who, by their more advantaged backgrounds, have a greater chance to achieve the benchmarks as delineated in the academic standards that schools are creating at a frenetic pace.

But the problems of education are not merely a function of dollars. The tragedy of Columbine High School has underscored that lesson all too well. Young people's alienation from places called schools and their correspondingly frightening reactions are numbing. Although it is impossible either to understand or to address all the psychosocial and economic causative factors troubling many young people, it is clear that our behaviors as a society are not aligned with the sense of compassion and the social and emotional competence necessary to both prevent and solve a number of the social injustices that have spawned unthinkable violence and a siege mentality that greets us in the twenty-first century.

The plight of our most vulnerable citizens and the concomitant effects on our society are unsettling. Quick-fix solutions are not forthcoming. However, the beginning of this new millennium may hold promise for adults and children. If we work to make our world a kinder, gentler, and safer place, we can improve the quality of life for many people. Central to this vision is the field of social and emotional learning.

Social and emotional competence is the ability to understand, manage, and express the social and emotional aspects of one's life in ways that enable the successful management of life tasks, such as learning, forming relationships, solving everyday problems, and adapting to the complex demands of growth and development (Elias et al., 1997). Research on its significance is growing. We are learning that social and emotional competence is the key to helping young people make responsible decisions and aspire to positive opportunities for personal growth and development.

THE ROLE OF SCHOOLS

Walk into any public school and ask the principal for a copy of the school's mission statement. No doubt you will read language common to any such mission. They are interspersed with high expectations for learning and virtuous behavior. I do not question the sincerity or enormous effort of parents, students, and staff to accomplish the balance of competence and character. But if one spends appreciable time in schools and district meetings and reads the endless communication from state departments of education, one realizes that intentions and realities are not evenly aligned. Indeed, many school districts are now tying teachers' and administrators' salary increases to increased student academic achievement solely. And as far as measuring student character achievement is concerned, there are no meaningful assessments available. Furthermore, these same districts have increased security in the form of armed guards, metal detectors, video surveillance, and zero tolerance policies, and there are no financial incentives for teachers and administrators who raise the emotional quotient of their students by introducing conflict resolution and character-building programs.

A Call for Reason

As part of my return to the principalship in 1998, I had to meet with a district's school board for a final interview. During that meeting I was asked by a board member what I saw as my major responsibilities as a principal. I spoke about the need to build a community of learners that valued both intellectual and social growth. It was not the answer that she had hoped to hear. She was quick to point out that it was her position that the district's focus was fundamentally academic.

Based on my conversations with many principals, my experience is not atypical. There is enormous and pervasive pressure to emphasize academic content and to administer national, state, and district tests at a staggering rate in an effort to assess scholastic performance. Yet we know that such practices are developmentally and pedagogically unsound. In Massachusetts, fourth-grade students spend more hours in testing situations than aspiring attorneys do for the state bar examination. Is it any wonder that we are witnessing a dramatic increase in young people diagnosed with the learning disability of the 1990s, attention deficit disorder, along with its quick-fix solution, Ritalin. I think I will insist that any aspiring principal whom I counsel must read *The Emperor's New Clothes*! It is going to take a concerted effort to bring reason, compassion, and courage of conviction to challenge those who ignore the clear and growing message that our schools are becoming hostile and insensitive to the social and emotional needs of students.

Daniel Goleman's book *Emotional Intelligence* (1995) crystallized for legions of people the impact of social and emotional learning. It underscored and reassured for many of us that effective children and adults are the result of a meaningful integration of "hand and heart." The implication of Goleman's work for educators is that to achieve schools' lofty missions, careful attention must be given and time allocated to honing skills essential for meaningful social and emotional learning. In turn, these skills play out in their immediate lives at school and at home. They are also foundational to leading productive lives as adults.

In order to advance the tenets of social and emotional learning, our schools need educational leaders who posses what Tom Peters and Bob Waterman described in the impassioned book *In Search of Excellence* (1982) as monomaniacs who will not be distracted or deterred from doing what is morally and ethically right for children, their faculties, and staffs. It will take that level of resolve to influence others in creating schools that become safe harbors or sanctuaries for the most vulnerable of our children. It will take leaders who resist the surreptitious motives of pretenders but bring about meaningful and responsible educational reform.

A Call for School Principals to Lead

There is a rapidly growing body of impressive research that supports the absolute necessity for balancing the school curriculum to include social and emotional learning. But anyone who has spent time working in schools knows that change is slow and, at times, nearly impossible. Valuable educational programs and innovations have failed because school leaders have not understood how to successfully address and implement a meaningful change process. Unless school principals have a working knowledge of effective change models and employ the sensitivity to assist staff throughout the process, attempts to infuse social and emotional learning into the instructional program of the school will fail.

A MODEL FOR CHANGE: THE COMPETENCE SIDE OF SOCIAL AND EMOTIONAL LEARNING

Principals' leadership is fundamental to creating an outstanding school. Their knowledge, skills, and disposition are key to inspiring others to take risks, exercise creativity, and transform schools into places of joy, curiosity, and high achievement. Changing and creating such a powerful school culture has long been the interest of researchers dedicated to the study and analysis of organizational life. Their studies have focused on a myriad of intellectual and interpersonal dynamics that foster and instill a high degree of overall effectiveness. For example, Saranson (1996) contends that the change process used by principals has more impact on the success or failure of an innovation than the innovation itself. Therefore, it is important for principals to possess and demonstrate insight into this critical aspect of leadership. One such approach is John Kotter's (1996) eight stage change process that provides ways to approach effecting change and overcoming individual or group resistance. Each of the eight steps will be described within the context of embedding social and emotional learning into a school's culture.

Step 1: Establishing a Sense of Urgency

A school staff needs a reason to change, and whole-school change is achieved when there is a perceived sense of legitimate urgency. In short, principals can be catalysts for establishing a sense of urgency that is grounded in fact, not in unsubstantiated claims. For instance, principals can collect both quantitative and empirical information regarding student behavior, administer school climate inventories, and conduct parent and student interviews to build a basis for the need to improve social and emotional literacy in their schools.

Principals must proceed with caution in two areas. First, they must convince staff that there is a sense of urgency, otherwise reluctant staff will not be convinced of the need to change. Second, there must be earnest and broad-based agreement among all administrators and a significant majority of staff that change is necessary or else the process will falter and be ultimately abandoned.

Step 2: Creating a Guiding Coalition

The process of change is an interdependent relationship between principals and their staffs. Staff members have a key role in helping to advance new ideas or instructional practice. Those individuals become part of a guiding coalition and are selected to be part of the group because of this personal and position power, their expertise, credibility among community members and staff, and their proven leadership within the staff.

It will be vital to the group's success that time and resources are available to help them to build trust among themselves and to establish agreed-upon ground rules for them to work and make decisions as a team. Although principals are active participants within the coalition, they must also be resource gatherers and providers. Specifically, they must work to find common, uninterrupted time for meetings and to secure the needed materials and resources to help members develop appropriate goals and related tasks for sustaining the process to fruition.

Step 3: Developing a Vision and Strategy

Kotter contends that a vision of the future is an essential component to bring about change. Members of the guiding coalition play an important role in "painting a picture" of the future based on the changes that need to occur in order to get there. This aspect of visioning must be accompanied by developing a set of strategies before the vision can be achieved. In turn, the strategies will enable the coalition to plan goals and objectives, and develop a budget to achieve the vision. In the case of implementing a social and emotional learning program, the principal and coalition members must conceptualize and articulate how everyone can benefit. For example, teachers will spend less time in mediating disputes among students and more time on instruction. Students' self-esteem will improve. The combination of the two are known variables that positively affect student achievement. Principals will see a diminution in the time they spend on schoolwide discipline and enable them to focus more time and energy on improving curriculum and instruction throughout the school. Significant research supports the positive relationship between the role of principals as a visible presence and academic improvement (Smith & Andrews, 1989).

Step 4: Communicating the Vision

The true strength of the vision is realized when all staff members are aligned with its goals and direction. Principals communicate the vision in ways that help others understand and embrace the changes recommended and developed by the guiding coalition. Kotter suggests that to be effective, communication must:

> Be simple
> Use metaphor, analogy, and examples
> Be presented in multiple forums and repeated frequently
> Be communicated through actions consistent with words
> Offer explicit explanation of seeming inconsistencies
> Include meaningful dialogue to improve the vision

Step 5: Creating a Climate for Broad-Based Action

Principals play a key leadership role in creating a climate for meaningful change by working with the guiding coalition to remove obstacles that impede reaching the school's vision. Part of the group's role is to examine closely existing practice, overall training and development needs, reallocation of human and fiscal resources, and the alignment of supervision and evaluation processes to validate new behavior. If school systems want to implement social and emotional learning, the aforementioned behaviors are indicative of staff consensus and serve as symbols and tangible evidence of an abiding commitment to change.

Step 6: Generating Short-Term Wins

Changing existing practice in a school is a long process that happens only when short-term successes occur and are celebrated. Again, symbolic gestures are essential to effect meaningful change. A key component of exceptional principal leadership is being a symbolic leader (Deal & Peterson, 1994). The principal's behavior sends a strong institutional message of support, encourages risk taking, reinforces the desired behavior, and affirms the coalition's vision as one that is possible. This step is a transformational and crucial one. If the planning and implementation have been well designed, positive results will follow and the change process can accelerate.

Step 7: Consolidating Gains and Producing Additional Change

Initial success is important, but momentary. Impetus is needed to involve others in more active planning with the guiding coalition and to broaden the scope of the goals and objectives of the project throughout the school. At this point, principals must monitor clarity of purpose, and work with the coalition to keep urgency levels high. Their role in support of this dynamic is vital at this point. A function of human behavior is to erroneously assume that short-term accomplishments are indicators that success has been achieved and one's work is done. The reality is that the change process is not a means to an end, but a means to other means. Modifications are a necessary by-product of any planned change. As new ideas or research emerge, as staff changes take place, principals must assimilate these realities into the work of the coalition. For instance, the integration of social and emotional learning into the school's curriculum is a relatively new idea for many schools. The emerging research on best practice will be invaluable to producing better ways to strengthen initial efforts.

Step 8: Anchoring Change in the Culture

The last step in the process is to bank or institutionalize the changes by reinforcing the new and desired behaviors. Kotter points out that systemic cultural change exists when people's prior behaviors have been modified, their new behaviors have produced benefits to the system and themselves over time, and results have become tangible. Principals will know quickly whether new behavior is evident by watching classroom instruction, pupil-to-pupil interaction, and listening to conversations between and among staff and children. Both qualitative and quantitative assessments will help principals assess the success of the planned change and to share the results with staff. The priority principals place on monitoring and supporting the change will, in large measure, determine the extent to which the new be-havior will become an integral part of the school's culture.

GETTING FROM THERE TO HERE

The previous section addressed dynamics of organizational change and of-fered principals a theoretical perspective on what steps to consider as they initiate and implement a model for change with staff. As a principal, I find these aspects of leadership considerations most helpful. When I begin the transition from theory to practice, I also appreciate having access to quality information about the concept or program that I wish to introduce to my staff. So often, we as principals fall victim to the "one day wonder" syn-drome of attending a conference or seminar and imposing it on students and staff without regard for careful analysis and applicability to our pres-ent circumstances. We do a disservice to everyone, including ourselves, if we do not do the intellectual work in preparing for change.

With respect to social and emotional learning, there are examples of excellent resources available to guide thinking and to expand understand-ing of and appreciation for both pragmatic and proven information to help launch social and emotional learning programs in schools. In tandem with these resources, here are five suggestions to help in your journey.

1. *Do your homework.* It happens in most instances that we don't get a second chance to make a good first impression. If you plan to implement social and emotional learning in your school, become familiar with the topic and implications for including it in your school. At the same time assess your school's readiness for it. Oftentimes, a school has undertaken a major reform project that diminishes the time, energy, and resources to begin something new. Although your staff may not be ready to begin, your initial work will stand you in good stead when the time is right.

2. *Self-examine.* The subject of social and emotional learning is a func-tion of appropriate child and adult behavior. Before asking others to change their behavior, we must examine our own behavior and determine to what extent we model what we are preparing to ask others to do. Think about how you deal with parents, staff, and students. Are your belief symptoms aligned with the beliefs of social and emotional learning? Seek feedback from others and make changes in your daily behavior that epitomizes what you expect to see and hear among members of your school community.

3. *Conduct a social and emotional school audit.* Assess your environ-ment carefully. This will include a close examination of the physical facili-ties inside and outside. Does your school reflect care and suggest to every-

one that it is a safe, inviting, and nurturing place? Are the interactions between adults and children positive, especially in matters of conflict or discipline? Is classroom life marked by high academic and behavioral standards and recognition of individual and group contributions? Are children actively engaged in meaningful problem-solving situations? Do members of your community and school personnel feel valued and respected? Keeping anecdotal information of this nature will be extremely helpful as you begin to encourage staff to undertake the creation of a program that will meet your school's needs.

4. *Assess reality*. Principals have enormous influence in shaping the culture of their schools. An important way to do so is to ask people their perceptions of and to offer evidence that the school's behavior is consistent with its mission. Asking questions of school members about their degree of satisfaction with the school's social and emotional climate provides principals with a viewpoint other than their own. It also helps them determine who might be a contributor to the guiding coalition that will be involved in the change process. This type of reflective practice also enables principals to gauge the level of training, development, and program modifications that will be needed to assist the guiding coalition in its initial work.

5. *Build external support*. The need to keep district or central office administrators apprised of your plans is essential to implementing a successful social and emotional learning program. Create and share a timeline with them in order to be certain that your activities are in concert with budget schedules and program revision plans. In schools that have improvement teams or site councils, it is prudent to incorporate your ideas into the planning and development of the school's strategic plan. Keeping in mind that the obvious is not always obvious is a good idea. Communicate regularly and openly with key groups.

CONCLUSION

There are a host of factors to consider as principals plan to make social and emotional learning an integral part of a school's programs. It is clear, however, that there exists a moral imperative to do so. The skills of social and emotional literacy are no less important than academic ones. They are also no less difficult to instill in young learners. But the goal of providing a comprehensive education that prepares our students to successfully solve the pressing problems of our complex society is the charge of each school in America.

In his last major contribution to education, the late Ernest Boyer wrote a remarkable book, *The Basic School: A Community for Learning* (1995). He delved into great detail on how to construct schools that make a difference in the lives of children. I resonate to his words, "It is our deepest hope that not a single child, let alone a whole generation of children, should pass through the schoolhouse door unprepared for the world that lies before them" (p.12). You are urged to make that difference.

REFERENCES

Boyer, E. L. (1995). *The basic school: A community for learning.* Princeton, NJ: Carnegie Foundation for the Advancement of Teaching.

Cohen, J. (Ed.). (1999). *Educating minds and hearts: Social emotional learning and the passage into adolescence.* New York: Teachers College Press.

Covey, S. R. (1992). *Seven habits of highly effective people: Powerful lessons in personal change.* New York: Simon & Schuster.

Deal, T. E., & Peterson, K. D. (1994). *The leadership paradox: Balancing logic and artistry in school.* San Francisco: Jossey-Bass.

Elias, M. J. (1998). *Social and emotional learning: "The missing piece" in our system of education and socialization of children and youth.* Rutgers, NJ: New Jersey Association for Supervision and Curriculum Development.

Elias, M. J., Zins, J. E., Weissberg, R. P., Frey, K. S., Greenberg, M. T., Haynes, N. M., Kessler, R., Schwab-Stone, M. E., & Shriver, T. P. (1997). *Promoting social and emotional learning: Guidelines for educators.* Alexandria, VA: Association for Supervision and Curriculum Development.

Goleman, D. (1995). *Emotional intelligence.* New York: Bantam Books.

Kotter, J. P. (1996). *Leading change.* Boston: Harvard Business School Press.

Kozol, J. (1995). *Amazing grace: The lives of children and the conscience of a nation.* New York: Crown Books.

National Center for Children in Poverty. (July 1999). *Young children in poverty fact sheet.* New York: Columbia University.

Peters, T. J., & Waterman, R. H., Jr. (1982). *In search of excellence: Lessons from America's best companies.* New York: Harper & Row.

Saranson, S. B. (1996). *Revisiting the culture of the school and the problem of change.* New York: Teachers College Press.

Sergiovanni, T. J. (1992). *Moral leadership: Getting to the heart of school improvement.* San Francisco: Jossey-Bass.

Smith, W., & Andrews, R. (1989). *Instructional leadership: How principals make a difference.* Alexandria, VA: Association for Supervision and Curriculum Development.

Chapter 12

SOCIAL AND EMOTIONAL LITERACY FOR ALL IN THE TWENTY-FIRST CENTURY: A CHALLENGE AND A NECESSITY

Jonathan Cohen, Ph.D.

Teachers College, Columbia University and
The Center for Social and Emotional Education

Historically, literacy referred to our ability to read and write. In recent years the usage of the term literacy has expanded to include a number of additional forms of "reading" and expression. An expanded conceptualization of literacy has been endorsed by the National Literacy Act which defines literacy as "an individual's ability to read, write, and speak in English, compute and solve problems at levels of proficiency necessary to function on the job and in society, to achieve one's goals, and develop one's knowledge and potential." Solving problems, functioning on the job and in society, achieving our goals and developing knowledge and our potential necessarily rests on another form of literacy: social and emotional literacy. In fact, social and emotional literacy provides the foundation for learning, healthy development, and effective citizenry in a democratic society.

What is the essence of literacy? I would suggest that there are three core components to any form of literacy, be it linguistic, mathematical, or social-emotional: (1) being able to decode information in a given domain, (2) being able to use this information to solve real problems, and (3) being able to learn and/or create in any number of helpful ways. [Social] and emotional literacy refers to our ability to decode others a[nd] and to use this information to solve real social-emotional problems and to be a creative learner in any number of helpful ways.

In the history of human life, it has never been more important than it is at present that we become a socially and emotionally literate population. For the first time in our brief evolutionary history, conflict can—and does—result in massive destruction of life and of the environment. Although inadequate social and emotional abilities have resulted in interpersonal and international violence since the beginning of time, for the first time it can now result in worldwide annihilation. Our ability—or inability—to read others and ourselves and then to use this information to cooperate and solve problems in nonviolent and creative ways will determine our children's future. Our definition of literacy must expand to include not only reading and mathematics, science and technology, but also social and emotional competence. For our species to thrive in the new century, we must, through deliberate education, create a socially and emotionally literate society on a large scale—worldwide. The programs and perspectives described in this volume and others (Cohen, 1999; Elias et al., 1997) represent examples that educators and parents can use to put this work into practice.

In spite of the availability of effective social-emotional learning (SEL) programs, there are disturbing indications that our schools are not preparing our children to be socially and emotionally literate. A recent survey of the nation's employers reveals that over half of their employees lack the motivation to keep learning and improving on the job. Almost half are not able to work cooperatively with fellow employees, and only 19% of those applying for entry-level jobs are judged to have enough self-discipline in their work habits (Harris Education Research Council, 1991). Employers want entry-level workers who are socially and emotionally literate. For example, a national survey reveals that technical skills are now less important than social emotional capacities: to be able to learn on the job; to recognize what others need; to communicate in clear and responsive ways; to feel good about oneself; and to have the ability to be a flexible, collaborative, and creative social problem solver are qualities that employers want from their workers (Carnevale, Gainer, & Meltzer, 1989). Similar findings have emerged in studies of what corporations seek from MBAs beginning work: communication skills, interpersonal skills, and initiative (Dowd & Liedtka, 1994).

Social and emotional literacy provides the foundation for healthy relationships. "How do I feel?" "How do I feel about you and us?" "When there is a problem (as there always are in the course of human life), how can I learn from this and solve the problem in ways that let us grow together?" "What do we want to learn, to do together, to create?" "How can we collaborate?" How people understand and manage these questions determines what can and will happen in relationships over time. Our relative ability to be a social emotional reader, problem solver, and learner colors and shapes what kind of person, learner, worker, friend, mate and citizen we will be. What is more important than developing this foundational mode of literacy?

AN OPERATIONAL DEFINITION OF SOCIAL AND EMOTIONAL LITERACY: CREATING BENCHMARKS

I believe that parents, educators, and society have an extraordinary opportunity and responsibility to do all we can to promote social and emotional literacy. However, it is not clear what it means to be socially and emotionally literate at a given age.

Meaningful reforms in education depend on a long-term vision of the knowledge and skills that today's students will need as adults in the twenty-first century. I suggest that we need to operationally define what it means to be socially and emotionally literate at given grade levels for two reasons. First, benchmarks create helpful guidelines or norms that aid teachers, parents, and students to understand what is expected of them. Second, defining social and emotional literacy underscores that we consider this mode of literacy to be as important as linguistic or scientific literacy.

Many schools already have a set of behavioral guidelines that may overlap with benchmarks for social and emotional literacy. However, too often these guidelines emphasize what students should *not* do as opposed to what we expect students to be able to do socially and emotionally. In addition, these guidelines are typically considered a nonacademic matter. This is quite curious and unfortunate. Almost all schools include the notion of "achieving excellence," "preparing students for the future," and "learning to learn" as core facets of their mission. We need to be able to discover and recognize how we feel, what problem-solving strategies work for us, what our (healthy) passions are, and what helps our capacity to learn so that we can actualize these fundamental and profound educational goals. We need to foster social and emotional literacy and recognize that this set of abilities is an integral facet of academic as well as nonacademic discovery, learning, and problem solving. Finally, behavioral guidelines refer (by definition) to behavior alone. Social and emotional literacy is a broader notion referring to skills and sets of understandings, which in turn will affect and even determine behavior. If we want to go beyond behavioral guidelines to operationally define social and emotional literacy, there are two processes that we can set in motion, locally and nationally.

Local Initiatives

There is a great deal that we and our fellow educators, parents, and perhaps even children can do to define social and emotional literacy. Whatever national guidelines exist, it is ultimately most important that each community collectively and collaboratively define educational goals, standards, and assessment procedures. In local communities, parents and educators can reflect upon and collaboratively define what it means to be socially and emotionally literate.

In fact, we all have ideas about what our children can and should be able to do with regard to recognizing how they are feeling and then using this information to solve problems and to learn. For example, what do we expect third or eighth graders to be able to do when they are confronted with an interpersonal conflict involving a friend? Or, with a teacher? What do we expect an 8- or 18-year-old to understand and manage in terms of forming friendships; cooperating; being a leader/follower; communicating?

These are complicated questions that do not have simple answers. One may say, "Well, it depends on the child and the situation." And, it does! However, these are questions that every parent and every teacher answers: clearly or not; logically or not; alone or with others; consciously or in unrecognized ways. We all have expectations about how well our children can and should be able to read themselves as well as books at a given age. We have similar expectations, articulated or not, that determine when we are pleased or upset, cross or confused, about how our children act and feel.

When local communities define what it means for children of various ages to be socially and emotionally literate, there are many positive effects. First, it underscores that this mode of literacy is as important as linguistic and mathematical literacy. Second, we are creating positive goals that include skills and understandings rather than a list of behaviors. Perhaps most importantly, this process sets in motion a collaborative and reflective process about what matters most to parents and teachers and, ultimately, to our children as well: what does it mean to be a truly educated person? What kinds of social and emotional skills and related sets of understanding matter most to us in our given community?

In the following section are a series of steps and questions that some communities have found helpful in collectively defining what social and emotional literacy means to them. These steps and questions can be an essential process in the effective, long-term implementation of SEL efforts that have been described in this volume (Chapter 1 and Chapter 11) and elsewhere (Elias et al., 1997).

1. *Have your entire school or district define what social emotional literacy means.* This kind of community discussion is an intervention in and of itself: It enhances understanding and consciousness. Be it formally in faculty or PTA meetings or informally in the faculty room or around the dining table, this is a rich, even profound question: what does it mean to be literate and then, to be socially and emotionally literate?

2. *After your district reaches a consensual definition of social and emotional literacy, consider the specific competencies that support the definition.* There are many social and emotional skills and sets of understandings that we can focus on. Here is a list of overlapping skills and understandings that many SEL programmatic efforts emphasize:

- Active listening
- Recognizing how we—and others—feel
- Being able to name emotional states and talk about them
- Learning how to recognize and understand our relative strengths and weaknesses
- Adaptively managing our emotional reactions
- Solving problems flexibly and creatively
- Being able to articulate our goals and decision making
- Cooperating in pairs and small groups
- Empathizing
- Recognizing conflicts and learning to solve them in creative and non-violent ways
- Being able to say "no"
- Being able to ask for help
- Communicating directly and clearly
- Recognizing and appreciating differences and diversity
- Being a leader/follower and working effectively in groups
- Helping others

Typically, enhancing these kinds of skills and understandings contributes to children becoming more self-motivating and self-confident.

Which of the skills and understandings listed above are most important to your community? There are additional sets of social and emotional understandings that are not always closely linked to a particular skill or set of skills. Depending on the community and the age of the children, some of the following social-emotional understandings may be important to your community:

- Emotions affect and even determine behavior and self-esteem.
- Emotional life can be conscious ("I know how I feel!") as well as unrecognized (we can be affected by feelings we are not even aware

of which can result in, for example, how we do on tests, physical symptoms, who we initially like or don't, forgetting, and more).

- When we become scared and/or hurt, we often get angry to protect ourselves.
- Helping others often feels good.
- Feeling confused and "not knowing" is often uncomfortable but is also a foundation for true learning.
- It is important to gradually learn when it is okay to go with our feelings and when to stop ourselves.

SEL efforts vary with regard to how much they emphasize or explicitly focus on these kinds of understandings.

Some communities or districts may decide that they want to initially focus on one general set of skills and understandings. For example, some districts that have been plagued by verbal and/or physical violence may decide to initially focus on understanding more about the nature of conflict or the bully-victim-bystander cycle and specific social emotional skills and community practices that address this. Other communities may decide to focus more broadly.

3. *Discuss and determine which skills and competencies are developmentally appropriate for early childhood, middle childhood, and adolescence.* This is a difficult but important step. What do we really expect of our children socially and emotionally? Again, we all—knowingly and unknowingly—have answers to these questions. Often, we don't think about these questions until our children challenge us: "Why can't I do that? Why do I have to do this?" How we address these questions—before or after our children ask us—shapes family life. When we address these questions as a larger group, it shapes the life of our community in helpful ways.

Again, it is useful to remember that we will never have simple answers to these questions. In fact, we don't have simple answers in regard to our academic expectations at different grade levels. Social-emotional norms will probably be even less precise. Social and emotional development is certainly more multifaceted and hence more complex than the development of reading abilities. However, we can begin to articulate what we—as parents, teachers, and then as a community—believe are rough benchmarks in this area.

4. *Devise developmentally sequenced learning experiences that will help students develop into socially and emotionally literate learners as they progress through the K–12 school process.* Educators and parents can use the programs presented in this volume and elsewhere in order to consider

which programmatic efforts would further their social and emotional goals. Optimally, this process is always an educator-parent collaboration. This kind of planning sets the stage for educators, parents, and students to pilot the learning experiences at different grade levels. We can and need to be social-emotional-academic discoverers and problem solvers. What is working and what is not working? How can we shift our educational and parent-teacher plans to promote social and emotional literacy even more effectively? These are powerful questions that have changed the culture of schools and the lives of thousands of children around the world.

National Initiatives

On a national level, I suggest that we need to create a panel of developmentally informed social scientists, educators, and mental health professionals to operationally define social and emotional literacy. What facets of social and emotional functioning matter most to insure healthy, responsible, and knowledgeable development? There are many social scientists who have spent their professional lives studying social emotional development. These social scientists in collaboration with others can help us create social and emotional benchmarks and operationally define them and, further, help us use this information to solve problems, create, and learn. To the extent that a group of national experts can reach a consensus about these issues, the findings will be useful in many ways.

Currently, state and federal educational standards include goals related to social and emotional development and functioning. However, they are extraordinarily vague about what this actually means. The operational definition of these issues will create a platform to consider national and state benchmarks and standards that will help students of all backgrounds, abilities, and interests to achieve social and emotional literacy. These definitions can also be used by local communities as a springboard for people to agree and disagree with and build upon. There is another important reason to work on a national level. Defining social and emotional literacy will allow us to begin to clarify the economic costs of social emotional illiteracy. When we can document the extraordinary cost of this mode of illiteracy, it will enhance policy makers' and other leaders' ability and inclination to focus on this pressing problem. Given that empirical research has already documented that social and emotional competencies is associated with physical health, healthy marriages, violence reduction, adaptive peer relations, and productivity in the workplace, it is extremely likely that social emotional illiteracy is associated with a range of behaviors (e.g., physical illness, violence, poor productivity) that are economically costly to society. However, empirical study is needed to confirm and clarify this probability.

There is a danger in operationally defining this mode of literacy at a national level. Some people will then try to create a short paper and pencil measure to "test" these abilities. There can never be such a simple test. Not only is social emotional functioning too multifaceted and complex, but also there is a great deal of normal variation. In other words, there is a very complex set of abilities to consider and there is a significant range of social emotional ability for children of a given age—normal variation. In spite of the fact that standards can be, and often are, misused, we all have standards for our children: social-emotional and otherwise. Locally and nationally, parents, teachers, and other experts can help each other to become clear about what it means to be literate in this truly fundamental domain of social and emotional functioning.

CONCLUSION

Social and emotional learning efforts are designed to promote social and emotional literacy. I suggest that social and emotional literacy, like other modes of literacy, rests on three processes: being able to "read" the data, and then using this information to solve real problems, and to be creative in helpful ways. It is clear that our ability to read ourselves and others and to use this information to be flexible problem solvers and creative learners colors, shapes, and often determines the quality of our relationships, our work, and what kind of citizens we are.

Social and emotional literacy is a necessary and achievable goal for virtually all students. As this volume attests, there are a growing number of SEL efforts that clearly and dramatically promote social and emotional competencies, reduce violence, and often increase academic achievement.

We all have ideas about what we expect from our children socially and emotionally. However, we do not commonly define what it means in our community to be socially and emotionally literate. On both a local and a national level, we can work together to clarify what it means for children of given ages to be socially and emotionally literate. The clearer we are about what these fundamental social and emotional abilities mean, the more able we will be, as teachers and parents, to further this learning within our classrooms and homes, within the minds and hearts of our children and ourselves.

Acknowledgment. I am grateful to George Igel for his thoughtful and helpful critique of the ideas presented here.

REFERENCES

Carnevale, A. P., Gainer, L. J., & Meltzer, A. S. (1989). *Workplace basics: The skills employers want.* Washington, DC: U.S. Department of Labor Employment and Training Administration.

Cohen, J. (Ed.) (1999). *Educating minds and hearts: Social emotional learning and the passage into adolescence.* New York: Teachers College Press.

Dowd, K. O., & Liedtka, J. (1994). What Corporations Seek in MBA Hires: A Survey. *The Magazine of the Graduate Management Admission Council,* Winter.

Elias, M., Zins, J. E., Weissberg, R. P., Frey, K. S., Greenberg, M. T., Haynes, N. M., Kessler, R., Schwab-Stone, M. E., & Shriver, T. P. (1997). *Promoting social and emotional learning: Guidelines for educators.* Alexandria, VA: Association for Supervision and Curriculum Development.

Harris Education Research Council (1991). An assessment of American education. Unpublished study. New York: Harris.

About the Contributors

Ronald J. Areglado, Ed.D. is Principal of Potowomut School, Warwick, Rhode Island. He is former Associate Executive Director of Programs for the National Association of Elementary School Principals, Alexandria, Virginia. He is also the author of several books and articles on leadership and consults widely on issues affecting organizational behavior. Presently, Dr. Areglado is a member of CASEL and other national advisory boards.
E-mail: rid25482@ride.ri.net

Ruth Charney, M.S., M.Ed., is a cofounder of Northeast Foundation for Children (NEFC) and author of *Teaching Children to Care: Management in the Responsive Classroom* and *Habits of Goodness: Case Studies in the Social Curriculum.* She currently teaches seventh and eighth graders at Greenfield Center School, NEFC's laboratory school.
Contact Information:
Northeast Foundation for Children
71 Montague City Rd.
Greenfield, MA 01301
Phone: (800) 360-6332   Fax: (413) 772-2097   E-mail: info@responsive classroom.org   Web site: www.responsiveclassroom.org

Jonathan Cohen, Ph.D. is the cofounder and Director of the Center for Social and Emotional Education, New York City. A former teacher, he has worked in and with schools for over 25 years as program developer, school psychologist, psychoeducational diagnostician, staff development leader, and consultant. He is also Adjunct Associate Professor in Psychology and Education at Teachers College, Columbia University, and a practicing clinical psychologist and psychoanalyst. He is the editor of *Educating Minds and Hearts: Social Emotional Learning and the Passage into Adolescence.*
Contact Information:
Center for Social and Emotional Education
1841 Broadway
New York, NY 10023
Phone: (212) 707-8799   E-mail: SEL@csee.net   Web site: www.csee.net

Stefan Dasho, Ph.D., an educational sociologist, is Deputy Director of Professional Development at Developmental Studies Center, Oakland, California. He designs and conducts staff development for teachers and administrators in the Child Development Project.
Contact Information:
Developmental Studies Center
2000 Embarcadero, Suite 305
Oakland, CA 94606
Phone: (510) 533-0313   Fax: (510) 464-3670   E-mail: stefan_dasho@ devstu.org

Barbara K. Eisold, Ph.D. has a background in special education and school psychology, as well as psychoanalysis. At present she is a psychologist-psychoanalyst in private practice in New York City, where she also runs a mental health clinic for an "I Have A Dream" Foundation project. She has adjunct supervisory positions in New York University Medical College, New York University School of Applied Psychology, and Yeshiva University.

Peter Fonagy, Ph.D., F.B.A. is Director of the Child and Family Center and Clinical Protocols and Outcomes Center, at the Menninger Clinic, Topeka, Kansas. He is also the Freud Memorial Professor of Psychoanalysis at University College of London and Director of Research, at the Anna Freud Centre, both in London, England.

Joy E. Fopiano, Ed.D., N.C.S.P. is Assistant Professor in the Counseling and School Psychology Department at Southern Connecticut State University. She is a nationally certified school psychologist, a licensed educational psychologist, a certified elementary school teacher, and a certified elementary school principal. She conducts training for school personnel on critical child and adolescent issues such as resilience, mental health, and problem solving. She has established a program to address the psychological and educational needs of homeless children, youth, and their families.

Martin L. Gies, M.Ed. is Principal of Ross Elementary School, Topeka, Kansas.

Ann-Linn Glaser, B.S. is an educational consultant who specializes in early education and public policy issues, and a national trainer in the *I Can Problem Solve* (ICPS) and *Raising A Thinking Child* and *Raising A Thinking Preteen* programs for schools and families. In addition to ICPS, she does various training for children, teachers, and parents.

Mark T. Greenberg, Ph.D. holds the Bennett Endowed Chair in Prevention Research at the College of Health and Human Development, Pennsylvania

State University. He is Director of the Prevention Research Center for the Promotion of Human Development. Since 1981 Dr. Greenberg has been examining the effectiveness of school-based curricula (the PATHS Curriculum), and since 1990 he has served as an investigator in FAST Track, a comprehensive program that aims to prevent violence and delinquency in families. Dr. Greenberg is the author of more than a hundred journal articles and book chapters on child development and understanding aggression, violence, and externalizing disorders.
E-mail: mxg47@psu.edu

Norris M. Haynes, Ph.D. is Professor in the Counseling and School Psychology Department at Southern Connecticut State University and Director of the Center for School Action Research. He is also Associate Clinical Professor at the Yale Child Study Center and the Yale Psychology Department. He also served as Director of Research and Evaluation for the Comer School Development Program. He is a member of the leadership team of the Collaborative for the Advancement of Social Emotional Learning (CASEL). He has authored and coauthored many articles, books, and book chapters. His research interests include the influence of school climate factors on the mental health and school performance of students.

Debora Hess, M.S. is School Counselor at Randolph Elementary School, Topeka, Kansas.

Roxann Kriete is Director of Publishing for Northeast Foundation for Children and author of *The Morning Meeting Book*. She has also taught Grades 5 through 8 at Greenfield Center School as well as high school English.
Contact Information:
Northeast Foundation for Children
71 Montague City Rd.
Greenfield, MA 01301
Phone: (800) 360-6332   Fax: (413) 772-2097   E-mail: info@responsive classroom.org   Web site: www.responsiveclassroom.org

Carol A. Kusché, Ph.D. is a psychoanalyst and clinical psychologist in private practice in Seattle, Washington, where she treats children, adolescents, and adults. She is a faculty member at the Seattle Psychoanalytic Society and Institute and the Northwest Center for Psychoanalysis and Clinical Associate Professor in the Department of Psychology at the University of Washington. Dr. Kusché was a coprincipal investigator on the PATHS Project and coauthor of *The PATHS Curriculum* with Mark T. Greenberg. She is an author of numerous papers and book chapters on violence prevention, social emotional learning, cognition, cortical organization, and emotional development.

E-mail: ckusche@attglobal.net
For further information about PATHS, please contact the publisher:
Developmental Research and Programs (DRP)
130 Nickerson St., Suite 107
Seattle, WA 98109
Phone: (800) 736-2630   Fax: (206) 286-1462   Web site: www.drp.org

Catherine Lewis, Ph.D., a developmental psychologist, served as formative research director for the Developmental Studies Center. Currently she is a senior research psychologist in the Education Department of Mills College in Oakland, California. She has conducted both ethnographic and intervention research in a variety of institutional settings. Her book *Educating Hearts and Minds: Reflections on Japanese Preschool and Early Elementary Education* was named an outstanding academic book of 1995 by the American Library Association's *Choice*.
Contact Information:
Women's Leadership Institute
Mills College
5000 MacArthur Blvd.
Oakland, CA 94613
Phone: (510) 430-2019/3129   Fax: (510) 430-3233   E-mail: c_lewis@post.harvard.edu

Deborah Mugno, M.S. is Education Director at the Lucy Daniels Center for Early Childhood in Cary, North Carolina, and is currently working on her doctorate in Special Education at the Johns Hopkins University. She has been both a teacher and an administrator in the field of education and has been active in educational research.
E-mail: mugnod@aol.com

Donald Rosenblitt, M.D. is the founding and continuing Clinical Director at the Lucy Daniels Center for Early Childhood in Cary, North Carolina. His postmedical training includes child psychiatry and training in adult and child psychoanalysis. He has written and presented nationally about therapeutic preschools and the development of social and emotional competencies in young children.
E-mail: rosenblitt@compuserve.com

Frank C. Sacco, Ph.D. is President of Community Services Institute in Agawam, Massachusetts, and is also a member of the adjunct faculty at the American International College in Springfield.

Pamela Seigle, M.S. is the founder and Executive Director of Reach Out to Schools: Social Competency Program, a social emotional learning program

based at the Stone Center at the Wellesley Centers for Women, Wellesley College. She is coauthor of the Program's *Open Circle Curriculum* and is a former classroom teacher, school psychologist, and staff developer.
Contact Information:
Reach Out to Schools: Social Competency Program
The Stone Center, Wellesley College
106 Central St.
Wellesley, MA 02481
Phone: (781) 282-2861   Web site: www.wellesley.edu/OpenCircle

Myrna B. Shure, Ph.D. is professor of psychology at MCP Hahnemann University in Philadelphia. She is the author of award-winning prevention programs for schools, *I Can Problem Solve* (ICPS), and for families, *Raising A Thinking Child, Raising A Thinking Child Workbook*, and *Raising A Thinking Preteen*.
Contact Information:
MCP Hahnemann University
245 N Fifteenth St., MS 626
Philadelphia, PA 19102
Phone: (215) 762-7205   Fax: (215) 762-8625   E-mail: mshure@drexel.edu

Stuart W. Twemlow, M.D. is Director of the Erikson Institute for Research and Education, Austen Riggs Center, Stockbridge, Massachusetts; Codirector, Peaceful Schools Project at the Child and Family Center at the Menninger Clinic in Topeka, Kansas; and Clinical Professor of Psychiatry at the University of Kansas School of Medicine, in Wichita.

Marilyn Watson, Ph.D. is Program Director at the Developmental Studies Center, Oakland, California. Before coming to the Center, she was a preschool teacher and Director of the Children's School at Mills College, Oakland, California. She is the author of numerous articles on child development and is coauthor, with Joan Dalton, of *Among Friends*, which describes teachers' experience implementing the Child Development Project.
Contact Information:
Developmental Studies Center
2000 Embarcadero, Suite 305
Oakland, CA 94606
Phone: (510) 533-0313   Fax: (510) 464-3670   E-mail: marilyn_watson@devstu.org

INDEX